KU-661-394

Not Enough Time

Henrietta Knight was born in 1946 and has lived her entire life in the beautiful village of West Lockinge in Oxfordshire. The daughter of an army major, she was brought up around horses and with a deep love of the countryside. After graduating from Oxford with a degree in education, she taught history and biology at St Mary's School in Wantage. She is the author of two bestselling books, *Best Mate, Chasing Gold* and *Best Mate, Triple Gold*.

WITHDRAWN
FROM
STOCK

HENRIETTA KNIGHT

Not Enough Time

HEAD
of ZEUS

First published in the UK in 2015 by Head of Zeus, Ltd

This paperback edition first published in the UK in 2016
by Head of Zeus, Ltd

Copyright © Henrietta Knight, 2015

The moral right of Henrietta Knight to be identified as the author
of this work has been asserted in accordance with the Copyright,
Designs and Patents Act of 1988.

All rights reserved. No part of this publication may be reproduced,
stored in a retrieval system, or transmitted in any form or by any
means, electronic, mechanical, photocopying, recording, or otherwise,
without the prior permission of both the copyright owner and the
above publisher of this book.

9 7 5 3 1 2 4 6 8

A catalogue record for this book is available from the British Library.

Paperback ISBN: 9781784971359
Ebook ISBN: 9781784971328

Typeset by Ben Cracknell Studios

Printed at Clays Ltd, St Ives Plc

Head of Zeus Ltd
Clerkenwell House
45-47 Clerkenwell Green
London EC1R 0HT

WWW.HEADOFZEUS.COM

I am dedicating this book to Carol Titmuss who helped me throughout my weeks of writing by doing endless typing. She gave me a great deal of encouragement and seemed to enjoy reading the chapters as they took shape. Her spelling is superb.

Contents

Prologue

The worst day of my life was Sunday, 5 January 2014. Early in the morning, just after I had given him a little drink of water, my beloved husband, Terry Biddlecombe, lay back on his soft pillow and closed his eyes for the last time. I was alone with him in the farmhouse at West Lockinge in Oxfordshire, where we had lived together for twenty years. During that time we had been inseparable. We adored each other. He was my best friend and my *raison d'être*.

The previous August I had converted the drawing room into a bedroom, and it was there that I nursed Terry for the final months of his life. He had become desperately ill and, according to the medical profession, had been slowly dying for a number of weeks. We never talked about death and I never believed that I would lose him because, despite his illness, he remained optimistic for the future. His mind was always alert and he dreamed about the days when he would be better and able to stand up and walk again. All the same, he was a surprisingly good patient and resigned to being unable to turn over in bed – thankfully, the hospital bed on which he slept could be altered to give him different positions. He appreciated all the help we gave him. He could not feed himself properly, due to the arthritis in his left hand, but he could still hold a glass of whisky with his right one and he kept smiling. He often asked me to give him a kiss, and in return he would stroke my face.

There was no one around when the end came. The house was quiet and peaceful: no telephone, no voices, no dogs... not even the cockerel crowing outside. It was just the two of us in the bedroom together. Throughout the night before he died, Terry was exceptionally lucid. As usual, I lay down on my little bed beside him and pushed it up close to him. We held hands and we talked quietly through many of the endless hours of darkness. His breathing was wheezy at times, but he was cheerful despite this recent discomfort. A determined person, he was always ready to fight any new adversity – no wonder he had been a champion steeplechase jockey. As dawn broke, however, he slept peacefully despite his breathing problems. When he woke again, it was all the more heartbreaking to see him struggle to swallow the pills that I gave him. He was noticeably weaker, but still talking and ready for the new day. Those last breaths came quickly and unexpectedly. It was devastating to see him lose his fight for life.

Terry's death hit me hard, yet at the time I was in shock and felt nothing but numbness. I would never see that special smile again, but at least his pain had gone and he was at peace. There would be no more suffering.

Nowadays, in the mornings, when I walk through the drawing room to venture out into the garden, the early sun shines brightly through the big window and I stop to look back at the place where Terry died. I can still see him lying there, in the corner of the room, his head beneath the picture of my father, which hangs on the wall. I loved them both, but between Terry and me there was a special chemistry that is impossible to define. I have wonderful memories and numerous photographs, but the tears still roll down my face whenever I think about him. He is never far away from me and everything I do reminds me of him. I dream about him at night and I dream about him by day, but I try to be strong. My life goes on and I owe it to my friends to have positive thoughts. Terry did not like people who dwelt on the past, but my days with him will never be forgotten.

They were special.

They are the reason I have written this book.

CHAPTER ONE

Early Memories

In the autumn of 1993, I was forty-seven years old, unmarried and living on my own at West Lockinge Farm. I had been training racehorses with a professional licence for four years. I was not looking to share my life with anyone. Yes, challenges lay ahead of me, but I was confident that I could tackle them on my own, with support from my parents and countless wonderful friends. My weeks were extremely busy and I was enjoying my chosen career. I had always wanted to train, even from my early childhood days, when I designed and built model stables in the nursery. I used to have imaginary racehorses even then, and my toy ponies were put to work every morning. I hated dolls.

In the early 1990s my constant companions were three white Labrador dogs. I was devoted to them. On the farm I was surrounded by animals, not only horses and ponies but also geese, ducks and bantams, together with a few pedigree Simmental cattle belonging to my mother: cows, calves and a steady old bull. I was never lonely; my adored parents lived in the same village and I often spent time with them. I was resigned to being a spinster, but it didn't bother me. At that stage of my life, the idea of a husband did not enter my calculations. I had never wanted children of my own. I like them, but I had seen enough of them during my time as a schoolteacher and could never visualise myself pushing a pram.

Despite being a social person, I have always enjoyed independence. Many years ago I spent some good times with men, especially during my travels in Ireland, and I met some special people, a number of whom became great friends. Yet, I never had a proper boyfriend and I never fell in love with anybody. I used to think that having a man living in the house could easily get on my nerves and annoy me. A man might not agree with what I was doing with the horses. He might be a nuisance and take up too much of my time, as well as giving me extra work. No man had ever appealed to me as a likely husband nor had ever asked me to marry him. Perhaps I frightened men off, as I was always ambitious and always making plans for my future. I was not looking to change my lifestyle and I never wanted to leave Lockinge, the village where I had spent so many magical days as a child. It has always been my home and I am deeply attached to the place. It is a huge part of me.

My parents were married for many years and were devoted to each other, but they were often apart due to different commitments. My father, Guy, spent a large part of his early life in the army, was awarded a Military Cross for bravery in the Second World War and finished his career as a major in the Coldstream Guards. He began farming at West Lockinge in 1947. He liked horses

6

and could ride – albeit in a style of his own – but he was more interested in agriculture, cricket and shooting, as well as fulfilling his full social diary. It was as if he were making up time for those lost military years.

Dad rode a number of point-to-point winners (Mum trained the horses) and he enjoyed hunting. For a long time, he was secretary to the Old Berkshire Hunt. He was a strict father, but always fair. He was also extremely good-looking, had an excellent figure and a brilliant, dry sense of humour, yet he had a notable temper, and because I was the eldest daughter and did not leave home, there were plenty of times when I got on the wrong side of him. He could say some cruel and hurtful words to my mother and me. Maybe that is why I distrusted men and, as I grew up, did not want to share my life with one. Yet I was extremely fond of him and I knew that he loved me. Even though I clearly exasperated him at times, he was always proud of my achievements.

When my sister, Celia (known as 'Ce'), and I were growing up, Dad spent a considerable amount of time in London. For many years he was treasurer of the National Farmers Union (NFU) and its offices were in Knightsbridge. I always remember Mum saying how peaceful it was when he was away and how she could get on with her own life so much better when she was alone. Like me, she adored Lockinge; the little Oxfordshire village nestling at the foot of the Berkshire Downs. It was a haven of peace. Mum's family, the Loyds, had lived there since 1920, when Mum's father inherited the estate from a distant cousin, Lady Wantage. In more recent years, Lockinge has provided settings for films, notably Thomas Hardy's *Jude the Obscure*.

My mother, Hester, was brought up in the village and although she never went to school, was superbly educated. She shared a governess with her friends and they had daily lessons in a little hut at the top of a hill overlooking Lockinge House, where she lived, and the beautiful lake in the park. Mum was passionate about country life and a very intelligent person. She read hundreds of books, and had a natural flair for writing, producing two children's books: *Escape to the Downs* and *The Donkey Derby*. She also kept amazing daily diaries but never let us read them while she was alive (I now have them in safekeeping, and they are real treasures). Mum spent a great deal of time working with charitable organisations, and for many years was chairman of the British Red Cross in Berkshire, as well as being chairman of the Magistrates Bench in Wantage.

I always looked up to Mum. I adored her and we shared many similar interests. She was a unique person, and had an extraordinary way with humans and animals. She could read people a mile off and was a great judge of character. She was also universally popular and did so much to help others less fortunate than herself. Her gift with animals meant that she could catch even the most difficult horse or pony in an open field when nobody else could get near it.

From an early age, Ce and I were brought up surrounded by ponies, horses and dogs. We also had our rabbits and guinea pigs. Neither of us went to boarding school and we both had idyllic childhoods. Mum's determination and single-mindedness to pursue the aspects of life she most treasured moulded my future lifestyle. I often tried to model myself on her, but it wasn't easy. Like my father, she was strict with her children and she frightened me at times. Despite my admiration for her I found it hard to hug Mum, and now that she has gone I wish that I had been more affectionate and demonstrative.

I grew up in awe of both my parents. They had excellent values and high standards and I am grateful for all that they did for me. The warmth and friendliness of the home we all shared will never be forgotten. It was my stepping stone for the future.

CHAPTER TWO

My Background

When Terry and I began seeing each other on a regular basis, there were plenty of raised eyebrows. Many people thought that our relationship would never last, because of our different backgrounds. 'Oh yes, Terry Biddlecombe,' they would say, 'he's already had two wives and two failed marriages, plus countless girlfriends. He's hardly likely to stay with Hen for long. They are complete opposites.' Yet, in reality, our upbringings were remarkably similar. Our early childhood and schooldays may not have been on a par, but there were plenty of common threads. We both loved the countryside and riding our ponies, and we were really no different to many other children brought up on farms. As we grew up, we both became fascinated by horses and horse racing. When Terry turned into a superstar jockey, I was one of his greatest fans. I would read all the racing pages in the daily newspapers. Steeplechasing was my passion.

As children, my sister, Ce, and I had ponies from an early age. I suppose we were spoilt, but we did enjoy our lives to the full and rewarded our parents by being hugely enthusiastic in all our activities. We were also competitive and loved variety. All our pets had to have a purpose in life. We even sent our poor rabbits to special shows in London, packing them off from Didcot station to Paddington on a Friday afternoon, for a 'fur and feather' contest at the weekend. Looking back on those days now, I feel extremely sorry for the rabbits. Mine was called Fatty: a white, pink-eyed, Netherland Dwarf. Ce's was Mopsy: a beautifully marked black-and-white Dutch rabbit, who was often a champion. On Sunday evenings, Mum would drive us back to the station and we would collect them from the stationmaster's office. We would peer inside the lids of the travelling boxes to see if they had won any of the highly prized coloured cards or challenge certificates. Goodness knows what would happen to rabbits or guinea pigs today if they were sent off on a train to London. I doubt they would ever be seen again.

When Ce and I were teenagers, Mum bred Shetland ponies and built up a highly regarded stud. By 1970, there were over sixty ponies on the farm, comprising brood mares, their offspring and three stallions – Ce and I learned the facts of life at an early age. We also helped out as much as possible through those character-building years, and we were kept extremely busy. Nevertheless, along with the fun there were plenty of heartaches. Good days taught us to appreciate how lucky we were, but disasters rapidly brought us down to earth – and there were plenty of tears. With animals, accidents can occur at any time. Shetland ponies are not the easiest of breeders and we lost many unborn foals. We were delighted when Mum changed her allegiance to Connemara ponies in the 1980s. They seemed to have foals more easily.

My love for horses and fascination with training racehorses developed further during my childhood years, when Reg Hobbs came to live in our village. He had been a most successful trainer, and Battleship, a little 15-hand stallion ridden by his son, Bruce, had won the 1938 Grand National. Reg was a fine horseman and had a tremendous understanding with horses. He was quiet and patient, but very firm. I remember being struck by the way he used his voice and sang to his charges. I used to watch him for hours, spellbound, as he lunged, long-reined and backed the many youngsters.

After his retirement from racing, Reg advised my uncle, Christopher 'Larch' Loyd, to convert a disused double tennis court into a loose-jumping school, well sited in the former gardens of Lockinge House. We still use it today for the racehorses, and there is no finer place to teach a horse to jump.

Reg would stand in the middle and quietly encourage the horses to show off their paces and develop their jumping techniques. Sometimes he wanted the horses to be ridden, and it was on these occasions I gained valuable experience. He would leg me up onto the three- and four-year-olds and I would canter around, over the poles, in a complete dream. I loved my lessons. Reg later helped my mother train her point-to-point horses and was always on call to offer his advice. I often rode along the Downs with him, listening to him reminisce about his training days, but one thing always surprised me. He would happily canter up the middle of a tarmac road – something utterly frowned on by the Pony Club. But Reg maintained that it was safer to canter on a smooth, flat surface than on a softer, rough one. And it must be said that he never seemed to do any damage to his horses.

One spring in the late 1950s, during our rides after school, Ce and I decided to train our own donkey for the Donkey Derby, which was due to take place that summer in the neighbouring village of East Hendred. Sheba was huge, black and very stubborn; she was also extremely unpredictable, but we sweetened her up and, during her training sessions, used a Shetland pony called Florian to give her a lead. We cantered our charges bareback across the fields and up through the cleared pathways in the nearby woods. I usually carried a long stick broken off from an elder bush. I always left the leaves on the end. If I hit Sheba, she would stop completely, but if I shook the leaves, I could coax her forward. It was so much fun, and our excitement knew no bounds when she won the race, along with a huge silver cup. I felt as though I had already made it as a trainer.

In the early 1960s, my mother was given a good old chaser named Rowland Ward. He had been retired from racing proper and needed a good home. Luckily for me, she didn't particularly enjoy riding him because he frequently whipped round and, from time to time, dropped her on the floor, so she allowed me to exercise him in the winter months. I adored the horse, and even got him fit enough to win the Old Berkshire Hunt Members' Race at Lockinge in 1964. This was my first training success (apart from the Donkey Derby) and I still proudly show off the engraved winner's tankard. That victory gave me another taste of things to come.

After successfully passing my school exams, I bought my first event horse, Borderline, in 1964. He was a big bay thoroughbred, and he cost me £500. He drained my Post Office savings, but I was immensely proud of him. He was only five years old, but we learned together and did quite well, winning several events. He was a very fast horse, and one spring I entered him for a couple of point-to-points. He was placed every time he ran, and later went into training with renowned National Hunt trainer Tim Forster.

In 1965, my parents sent me off to London and loosed me into the world of debutantes. They wanted me to broaden my horizons and wean myself away from Lockinge. That kind of party season does not happen any more, but in the sixties and seventies it was thought to be the best way to bring up 'young ladies'. The hope was that, through numerous cocktail parties and dances, they would meet Prince Charming, get engaged, be married and live happily ever after – all pretty dubious to my way of thinking. Hundreds of girls enjoyed the parties, but they seemed to have little ambition; getting married and having children were their priorities. As I look down the list of those of us who attended Queen Charlotte's Ball in

May, 1965, I see a lot of familiar household names, including that of my good friend Camilla Shand, now the Duchess of Cornwall. We were all there, in long dresses and long white gloves. What a ridiculous performance and hugely expensive. I'm surprised that my father tolerated it, because he was always extremely careful with his money.

Basically, I hated the whole thing. I was quite backward socially and shy at crowded parties, so I continued to pine for the country and for my horses. I had always been blissfully happy at Pony Club camps and rallies. I worked hard to pass my Pony Club 'A' Test and then helped Ce to get hers, with honours, a few years later. My school days had been at Didcot Girls' Grammar School – a wonderful school where we were made to work hard. I wanted to have a career from an early age. I never liked the idea of a boarding school and leaving my animals for any length of time. I did go to a weekly boarding school when I was nine years old, but I was unbelievably homesick.

Parties and dances in London, as well as balls held in beautiful stately homes throughout the country never appealed to me, spectacular though a number of them were. Up until I was twenty-one, I never had any success with, or interest in, the opposite sex. I spent a lot of my time at dances sitting with my girlfriends, waiting for the breakfast to be served around 2 a.m. – and delicious it was too. The men known as 'debs' delights' never appealed to me. I was the original wallflower, but I suppose it did me some good, in that I had to discipline myself to do something I did not enjoy. I regarded my months in London, mostly spent in a dingy basement flat in Montagu Square, as a duty to Mum. I had been excused boarding school and now I had to go along with her wishes, even though I remember telling her she was wasting her money. I would have been far happier if my parents had bought me a new horse instead of lavishing their savings on yet another ballgown.

Fortunately, my spell in London did not last very long, and after the months of torture I enrolled in a four-year course at Westminster College in Oxford. This was a teacher training college, and it was here I obtained my Bachelor of Education degree. I was happy again – especially as I was able to commute from home. The London scene had not been for me. I do not like many towns or cities, except maybe those in Italy, such as Rome, Florence and Venice, which do not give me the same claustrophobic feeling. I also enjoyed Paris, where I was sent for six months after leaving school in order to improve my French.

But London? That was entirely different. I even have bad childhood memories of the place.

Before Ce and I were ten years old, we were regularly taken to a special dentist, Mr Endicott in Cavendish Square, close to Harley Street. We travelled up on the train from Didcot to Paddington and were then taken in a taxi to be tortured by this man who, I remember, had hairs on the back of his hand that tickled the roofs of our mouths. We were fitted with painful plates and wires to help realign our teeth and make them grow straight.

Other childhood days in London remain indelibly printed on

my mind for other reasons. We used to get dragged to the Adelphi Theatre every two years to perform in a special children's dancing matinée in aid of the NSPCC. From the ages of six and seven, Ce and I went weekly on Friday afternoons to Donnington Castle House, near Newbury, to have dancing lessons from Miss Violet Ballantyne. She was a very famous dancing teacher at that time: a perky, hearty individual who dressed herself in short, brightly coloured ballet-type dresses with frilly square collars and matching hairbands. Donnington was the home of the Parker Bowles family – Dad was Derek Parker Bowles's second cousin – and here we were drilled and regimented in all sorts of dances, while another powerful lady loudly played the grand piano in the corner of the ballroom. I was a poor dancer. I have never been very musical and I was usually feeling sick, as I was also a bad car-traveller. I remember that I always missed lunch on Friday and was given a 'quell' or some similar pill to counteract the effects of the bumpy car ride to Newbury.

On one occasion in the London matinée, I played the huntsman and my sister one of the hounds. My best friend, Mary Ann Parker Bowles (now Hanbury), was one of the followers. The costumes were excellent and we were plastered in red lipstick. The performances made good money for charity and I suppose it was fun when we got there, but I used to worry about the journey to London – more travelling in the car. There were no motorways in those days.

———

It pleased my parents when I took up teaching as a profession. At least it was something I could fall back on if all else failed. Ce trained as a nurse at Westminster Hospital in London and they were very proud of her. She had become less country-orientated than I and, despite the rigours of the medical world, she enjoyed London and came to know its streets like the back of her hand.

When I began teaching, I was given a job at St Mary's School in Wantage, where I stayed for nearly five years. Biology and history were my two main subjects. In later years, Terry often introduced me as 'the ex-human biology teacher, and barren mare who specialised in sex-education' – although nothing was further from the truth. Teaching locally suited me because I could always escape home at lunchtime to ride my horses; the school was barely two miles away.

I was blissfully happy and could continue training my event horses. I even rode at the Three Day Event at Badminton in 1973, finishing twelfth. In those days there was a phase called 'roads and tracks', which came before jumping the cross-country obstacles. On this part of the competition, the competitors rode a number of miles through woods and along the edges of fields, and there was a set time in which to complete the exercise. I remember walking round in the starting box with pupils from St Mary's cheering me on.

When I decided to end my career as a teacher and gave in my notice, I was surprised to be offered the post of headmistress. It would have been a huge challenge and I did attend some interviews, but in the end I turned down the offer as it would have been too restricting and there would have been no time for my horses.

My interest in three-day events continued well into the eighties. In 1980 I was asked to join the senior selection committee under the chairmanship of Chris Collins, former Champion Amateur National Hunt rider who had himself become involved in the eventing world and had successfully ridden around Badminton on several occasions. It was an honour to be asked to go onto his committee, and when Chris retired in 1984, I took over as chairman. During my time in office, we selected the horses and riders for the Seoul Olympics in 1988 and I travelled over to support them in person and make the final decisions. It was an unforgettable experience. The team won the silver medal. I spent ten days in a rented house with team vet Peter Scott Dunn and his wife, plus several other officials. In the evenings I was sent out to buy supper from the local fast-food stores. I remember being surprised by the looks I got as I innocently walked down the streets, but I later learned that our lodgings were right in the middle of Seoul's red-light district. I enjoyed many travels as chief selector, and my visits to Australia, Germany and Poland were especially interesting.

My work with the event riders fitted in well with the activities in my livery yard. Most of my horses were at grass during the summer months, and the point-to-point horses enjoyed their well-earned rests. I trained over 100 point-to-point winners in the eighties. They were memorable days and enormous fun. My runners were sponsored by Piper-Heidsieck Champagne, and apart from having the logo on the horsebox, we were regularly supplied with cases of champagne. It was not surprising that I made so many new friends when I took bottles of it to the point-to-points, where we had huge picnics for our supporters. Sadly, the sponsorship ended when I saddled my last point-to-point runner in 1989 – the same year that I started training racehorses with a licence – but I had definitely got a taste for champagne.

I was still drinking it when Terry entered my life in 1993.

CHAPTER THREE

Terry's Background

The main livelihood of the Biddlecombe family was farming, but there were always horses and ponies to be seen about the farm. When Terry and his brother, Tony – older by two-and-a-half years – were little boys, they attended Hartpury School, near Gloucester. Their father, Walter, took them to school with a pony and trap, or, if he was in a hurry, he simply lifted them up in front of him on his horse. They regularly fell off, but the bruises and grazes didn't bother them. The brothers hated school and loathed walking home, especially in the rain. They rode their ponies on many days of the week and their father, a talented rider himself and a great judge of a horse, gave them lessons. He was strict with his sons, but they always looked up to him. Terry told me that they were always told to speak out and tell the truth. As well as having huge respect for their father, they both adored their mother, Nancy, who looked after the whole family. I'm told she was a brilliant cook.

It was a close-knit community as well as a happy one, full of love and happiness. In the school holidays and at weekends there were countless gymkhanas and local shows. The Biddlecombe boys were extremely competitive and won many classes. They were excellent riders, and mounted games and showjumping competitions were their forte. In later years, both of them competed at the Horse of the Year Show.

Barry Hills, the successful flat-race trainer, was a good friend of the Biddlecombe family. 'It was about 1950 when I got to know Terry at shows around Hartpury,' he said. 'His father was the best gymkhana rider I ever saw and he did all the shoeing himself at the farm.'

On many occasions during his childhood days, Terry helped milk the cows in the family dairy – and in the 1950s, this was done by hand. There was no proper electricity and no mains water, and much of the work was carried out by the light of hurricane lamps. Today's farmers are spoilt by comparison. Dairy equipment is elaborate and ultra-modern, and if milking parlours were not run by electricity there would be serious problems. Few people nowadays can imagine how a farm could operate with water being brought to the dairies in buckets, yet Terry was well accustomed to these hardships. He was made to work hard, even though he didn't always enjoy it.

Terry and Tony were inseparable as children and remained the best of friends as their lives progressed. They both enjoyed racing, and in their twenties, as professional jockeys, they often rode in the same races. Their sister, Sue, who was born seven years after Terry and supported her brothers in their racing careers, was an excellent rider herself as a child, but later she had a bad fall and injured her back. Afterwards she handled their fan mail, answered telephone calls and dealt with the newspaper cuttings that outlined her brothers' racing successes.

As a child, Terry enjoyed everyday life with the horses and ponies at Lower House Farm, Upleadon, but Tony told me that he did very little in the yard and never liked preparing the ponies for shows. 'He never mucked out a stable anywhere in his whole life and always said, "It's not my job – my place is on top of a horse."' Tony remembers when their father had two acres of potatoes planted in the fields and got his boys to pick them and bag them up in big brown sacks. On one occasion when Terry was about fourteen, he went missing early in the morning and everybody got worried. A few hours later they found him, curled up asleep in a potato bag after a good night out. Even then he had an eye for a pretty girl.

After Hartpury School, Tony and Terry moved to King's School in Gloucester, where their father had been educated. During those schooldays they would speed home in the afternoons and ride their ponies in order to get plenty of practice in before the summer gymkhanas. Terry was not academically minded, and although he enjoyed football, athletics and cricket, he could not wait to leave school. Indeed, both brothers left school at the age of sixteen.

Terry had his first ride on a racecourse in 1957. By the spring of 1960, he had won a number of races as an amateur jockey, and it soon became clear that he was exceptionally talented. Racing soon became his way of life. Jeff King, a top professional jockey during Terry's riding days, remembers a particular occasion when Terry was still an amateur. Jeff was riding for Bob Turnell – a highly respected trainer – and the pair of them gave Terry a lift home from Ludlow races. When they got close to his parents' farm, Bob said, 'Where do I go now?'

A shy Terry said, 'It's fine. Drop me anywhere and I'll walk home the last few miles across the fields.'

He was duly let out of the car onto a grass verge and set off across country with a heavy bag on his shoulders. Bob was impressed and said to Jeff, 'That boy will go places.'

How right he was.

Terry joined the professional jockey ranks in the autumn of 1960, a season that marked the beginning of his extraordinary rollercoaster of a life. During those years, Jeff and Terry continued to get along famously and had many good times together. Jeff says he remembers the times when Terry rode at the races after an evening out in London. 'He would sit on his bench in the weighing room and examine his private parts to see that they were still intact.'

Terry was unusually tall for a jockey and heavy-boned too. When he was riding, his weight was always a problem, but he constantly drove himself to shed many pounds in Turkish baths all over the country, only relieving the boredom by mixing a few sips of water with countless bottles of champagne, Babycham or brandy. He later told me that the alcohol helped him to lose extra pounds because it made him sweat more. He maintained that if he had not rigidly stuck to his routine in the Turkish baths he would not have been able to carry on riding, but the punishment he gave his body had a serious effect on his health in later life. To lose twelve pounds in twenty-four hours was not uncommon, although he proudly told me that he lost almost a stone one hot summer's night in Scotland, when he slept with a certain lady in a bed made up with nylon sheets.

Indeed, girls of all ages queued up to meet Terry and he became famous for his film-star good looks. Yet, while it is true that he loved members of the opposite sex, he also adored his public and never forgot to acknowledge them, right up until the end. He rewarded his followers with some great wins in the saddle, while his wicked sense of humour, his burning of the candle at both ends and his sheer brilliance as a jockey singled him out as unique. Brough Scott, one of his many good friends and a fellow jockey, wrote in the *Racing Post*:

He was the Prince Hal of his time and the last of the true cavaliers. He was big, bold, blond and beautifully athletic in and out of the saddle. He took life as well as fences at the gallop. We used to call him 'The Blond Bomber'. At his peak, he was irresistible with his flair and fearlessness; he wanted to take on fences, drink, girls, food, cars and anything else available. We ordinary mortals looked on in awe as he strode through life as if he owned it.

Throughout his racing career, Terry lived dangerously and fearlessly. He demonstrated his highly competitive streak and was a brilliant jockey. Yet despite his exceptional talent, Terry suffered many hardships, and had more than his fair share of misfortunes. He had innumerable crunching falls and spent many weeks in hospital beds. yet his courage and determination never diminished.

In the 1960s, Terry was at the top of the tree in his profession as a steeplechase jockey. During that decade he won three jockey championships, but at the same time struggled even harder to control his weight and suffered enormously from the after-effects of his many falls. His injuries were countless and he admitted that, at times, he was at a low ebb. He was a lot more complex than people ever realised. In fact, in the early 1970s, his zest for race-riding noticeably diminished. He had married Bridget Tyrwhitt Drake in 1968, but domestic pressures built up and, although their two daughters were born in 1972 and 1974, times were not particularly easy and he was often unhappy.

To his friends and admirers, he appeared outwardly to be the same Terry Biddlecombe, but inwardly he was mixed up and unsettled. There was considerable pressure on him to retire, but he dreaded the future. In 1973, he applied for a permit to train some racehorses from his yard at Corse Lawn, near Gloucester, but it was turned down on the grounds that his stables and premises were unsuitable. This was a blow to his pride and he was bitterly disappointed.

Terry's last ride as a jockey was at the Cheltenham Festival in 1974. After this, his first marriage disintegrated further and finally came to an end in 1976, when Bridget returned to her family home in Hampshire and took their two children with her. Once again Terry was left on his own. Fortunately, he had his family close by and plenty of friends. He was kept busy with his livery horses and there were some good parties. In addition, Gary Newbon from ATV Midlands gave Terry a once-a-week racing spot on his television sports programme. Yet Terry remained unsettled. His second application for a permit to train had been rejected again in 1975. When he gave up race riding, it had created a sense of bereavement. His occupation had gone. He was no longer in the public eye and his purpose in life had been taken away from him. It was possibly while on the rebound from race-riding that, in 1977, he met and fell in love with Ann Hodgkins. They married in 1981, and she was to give him three more children, including two sons.

Although Terry's life had changed drastically, nobody fully understood why he decided to uproot himself and move to Australia in 1988. True, he had been offered a job connected with the racecourse in Perth, but by the time he arrived, that had fallen through. It broke Terry's parents' hearts when he left England, and it broke Tony's heart too. The brothers had never previously been separated and Terry had always lived close to home. His new life in Australia was a big contrast. However, he still managed to gather up a number of horses and cattle on the land he had acquired and later told me that he enjoyed his freedom and the complete change of scenery. Life moved at a slower pace and he made plenty of new friends: good people who supported and appreciated him.

Nevertheless, it was during his years in Australia that his alcohol consumption finally spiralled out of control and he stopped seeing eye to eye with Ann. At the beginning of the nineties she returned to England with the children and left him to fend for himself – which was disastrous. He was completely at the mercy of the bottle. Terry did return to England when his father died in December 1991, and again in July 1992, to be with his mother in her final weeks, but he was noticeably unhappy and sinking even deeper into the evil depths of drink.

Eventually, at the end of 1992, Terry flew back to England for good, having divorced Ann that spring, but by all accounts, he was in a very poor state of health and living on alcohol. His liver was in pieces. Tony and his wonderful wife, Sandra, together with Terry's first wife, Bridget – who was still extremely fond of him – did a wonderful job to get him back onto an even keel. Without their care and attention he would most probably never have bounced back. He had lost all his confidence and no longer believed in himself. He needed to re-establish himself as one of racing's greats. He unashamedly admitted to me that he had lost his self-esteem and did not know where to go next.

After spending a number of months drying out and accepting counselling at Farm Place, a rehabilitation centre near Dorking, in Surrey, Terry returned to his old home at Upleadon, in Gloucestershire, under the watchful eye of his brother and sister-in-law. At that point, Terry Court, director of the auctioneering firm Russell, Baldwin and Bright (now Brightwells), stepped into the fray to rescue his lost friend from the abyss. He found Terry a job as an agent within the business and gave him a company car. Once again, Terry had a purpose in life.

It was because of Terry Court's kindness that Terry Biddlecombe and I happened to meet up at the Malvern Horse Sales in September 1993.

The wheel had gone full circle. Terry had been to hell and back, but was once again full of enthusiasm for a new life, and he was ready to start the wheel rolling for the second time.

CHAPTER FOUR

Chance Meeting

The third of September, 1993, was a memorable day for me, because it proved to be the turning point in my life. It marked the occasion when I re-met Terry Biddlecombe, the three-time champion steeplechase jockey of the sixties and seventies. He had always been my childhood heart-throb. In those days he was not only highly successful, but dashing and startlingly good-looking. Terry was five years older than me, but I had often walked down to the last fence at race meetings to watch him at close quarters. I used to marvel at his riding style and his film-star appearance.

It was around eight o'clock on that bright autumn morning that I set out for the Russell, Baldwin and Bright sales at Malvern. I was due to judge the young thoroughbred horses in the pre-sales show. Julian Pritchard, my then assistant trainer and later a leading point-to-point rider, drove me to the Three Counties Showground. I always enjoy judging and I was honoured to have been asked to assess the sales entrants with two such well-known racing personalities as Jack Doyle and Toby Balding. When we reached our destination, we parked close to the ring. 'There's Uncle Terry,' said Julian, pointing to a man wearing the auctioneer firm's official tie. 'Fancy seeing him here.'

Julian's 'Uncle Terry' – in reality his second cousin – was none other than Terry Biddlecombe, the man who became my future husband, greatest lover and best-ever friend. Of course at this point, I had no way of foreseeing the future. All I knew was that it felt weird to see Terry again. I had not set eyes on him for eight years and I did not even know that he was back in the country. I thought he was still living in Australia.

Life is strange, however, and I believe in fate. Looking back, I cannot help feeling that our meeting was meant to be. Terry had been instructed by the sales company to look after me that morning – and he certainly made a good job of his assignment. At the end of the judging and during lunch with the officials, I allowed myself to be charmed by him. It wasn't difficult. We found plenty to talk about and I was enthralled by some of his past racing stories. At the sales, he was cheeky and witty with the people around him. His jokes (both clean and otherwise) made everyone laugh and he seemed to be ultra-happy now that he was out and about once more, with a purpose in life and surrounded by his friends. I remember thinking to myself, 'Fancy discovering my old heart-throb propping up the white railings under a tree at the Malvern showground.'

I had first met Terry in 1985, when he was working for Central Television. He had become a regular on *ATV Today* and the

Central News Sports programme on Friday nights. His boss was sports presenter Gary Newbon, who described Terry in the *Racing Post*, 6 January 2014 issue, as, '... a good-looking bloke, a bit like Jack Nicklaus. The girls loved him. He was a great guy and a great character and lived life to the full.' It was certainly true that Terry was much-loved in the Birmingham area and his presence on Central's sport programmes produced good ratings. On those Friday nights he would talk about racing. 'Terry's Tips' were always eagerly awaited.

In the summer of 1985, Terry had visited West Lockinge Farm with a film crew from Central Television. He had been asked to interview, 'a girl in Oxfordshire who ran a livery yard and broke in horses for Tim Forster and Fred Winter', two top-class National Hunt trainers who had superb horses. Yet, in the excitement of the legend of the sixties visiting West Lockinge Farm, I must have lost any common sense that I possessed.

It was a hot day, and I wanted to impress my childhood hero, so I decided that, for the filming session, I would wear a skimpy blue cotton dress and high-heeled shoes instead of my usual jeans and jodhpur boots. I must have looked more like a trainee nurse than the working boss of a livery yard.

Terry was not taken by my appearance and even less so by my handling of the horses in my care. Indeed, I had wound up my staff to such a degree that when a saddle was placed on one of the unbroken three-year-olds in the outside arena, the girl in charge barely had time to do up the buckles of the girth before the horse exploded in a series of rodeo leaps, which snapped the girth in two and sent the saddle into orbit.

I watched this performance from outside the perimeter fence, leaning over the rails from the adjacent flower bed. Terry stood beside me. It was a hot day, the roses were prickly and I was extremely embarrassed, but I will always remember Terry's hand on my bottom and the slap he gave me, as if to say, 'It doesn't really matter anyway.' Later he told me that he thought I was half-mad. He returned to Gloucestershire and I did not set eyes on him again until the Malvern meeting in 1993.

After the sales, I remember hoping I would see him again, but I had no idea where Terry was living or even how I could contact him. Since I have always been superstitious, I decided to leave everything to fate. I did not chase him up. I just waited.

What would be, would be.

A couple of weeks after our chance meeting, the telephone rang. My secretary, Christine Douglas Home, took the call. It was Terry, and he wanted to talk to me. My heart missed a few beats before I picked up the receiver. It was great to hear his voice again. He told me he would be racing at Cheltenham the following week and asked if maybe we could meet up. When I found Terry by the weighing room that day, I'm sure there were goose pimples on my skin. It was a strange feeling. My horses didn't cover themselves in glory in their races but it didn't seem to matter. I took Terry up to the Royal Box for some refreshment, courtesy of my brother-in-law, Sam Vestey, who was at that time chairman of the racecourse.

Coincidentally, my father had come racing with me that day. He was not a regular race-goer but had been invited to have lunch with Sam. I introduced Terry to Dad and was happy to see them talking to each other for quite some time. On the way home Dad told me that he had enjoyed meeting him. Sadly, however, it was the first and last time they ever met. Three weeks later my father died from a heart attack while out shooting with the Vesteys.

Dad's sudden death was a huge shock – I'd had dinner with him only the night before and he had been in tremendous form. From that day on, during the autumn, everything in my life became a blur. Looking back now, however, it was a wonderful way for my father to go. He lived for his shooting and he particularly enjoyed his days at Stowell Park with my sister and her family. He was 76 in 1993 and hated the thought of getting older. He always pretended to people that he was ten years younger and had even successfully changed the birthdate on his passport from 1917 to 1927.

I spent a lot of time with my mother in the weeks following Dad's death, and strangely one of the first people to telephone me was Terry. Many people are embarrassed by death and don't know what to say, but Terry was different. He told me how hard it had hit him when his own parents died. He was incredibly understanding and I remember him saying that he was thinking of me all the time. His words gave me a huge boost. Here was a person who really cared about me. His call was poignant.

Terry did not visit the stables at West Lockinge Farm until the end of November 1993, but when he did drive over to see the horses, he seemed to enjoy himself. This time he was complimentary about my charges and how I ran the yard. I trained the types of horses that he liked: big, strong, well-proportioned future steeplechasers with lovely outlooks. He did not stay long, but after a cup of tea in my kitchen, he announced that he would soon be back again to watch my charges on the gallops. How true these words turned out to be. I remember being sorry to see him leave, but at least I had not worn that ridiculous blue dress. I missed him as soon as he drove out of the yard. Although he was still working at the Russell, Baldwin and Bright offices in Hereford, we managed to talk on the telephone most days.

My first proper date with Terry was in December. I had runners at Hereford Racecourse and he suggested we could meet there; afterwards I could go back to his family farm at Upleadon. At that time, Terry was living in his late parents' old house, next door to his brother, Tony, who had taken on the farm. I remember the day well. We had several runners and a winner, ridden by Jamie Osborne, who partnered many of my horses that season. Indeed, he rode over 100 winners for me when I was training. After racing, Jamie offered to drive my car home to Lockinge so that Terry could chauffeur me to Lower House Farm.

The next twenty-four hours seemed like a dream – the kind from which you awake wondering, 'Did that really happen?' Terry drove an oldish second-hand Honda; apparently it was his company car. We chugged slowly back to the farm with me sitting nervously on the edge of the passenger seat. The seats were so low that later I teased Terry on many occasions and told him that he looked like Humpty Dumpty. He drove carefully along the little byroads he knew so well. It was a far cry from the swift Jaguars of his jockey days, but eventually we reached his home.

It was a dark, dreary evening and cold. As soon as we arrived, I was introduced to Tony and Sandra, then shown to my room for the night. What a shock. The lovely old farmhouse was uninhabited by anybody except Terry. Before that, it had been empty for a few years and there was hardly any furniture to be seen. The bedroom – which Terry expected me to share with him – was in a bad state of disrepair. There was no heating and it was extremely damp. Water and condensation dripped down the inside of the dirty old windows. What clothes Terry had were either strewn all over the floor, or had been left hanging on the two bedroom chairs. I pretended not to be shocked but it was difficult to hide my surprise at the lack of creature comforts. He told me that the bed had belonged to his parents. It was a large double bed with a horsehair mattress, which was probably as old as the house. At Terry's request, Sandra had supplied an under-sheet and a duvet, plus a few pillows. As we would be dining out I wanted to change out of my racing clothes, but shivered and shook as the wind whistled through the broken windowpanes and into the freezing-cold adjacent bathroom.

We had an excellent dinner at The Glasshouse Restaurant near Newent, run by a very good friend of Terry's called Steve Pugh. As a reformed alcoholic, my escort was not drinking, but I definitely needed something to get me through the next twelve hours and Terry bought me a lovely bottle of Chablis. I only drank two glasses but, characteristically, he had the remainder of the bottle corked up for me to carry out. He never wasted anything – yet it was not exactly a romantic gesture.

That night with Terry was unforgettable, more for the discomforts than anything else. I have always hated camping but this was even worse. I had never slept with Terry before, nor indeed taken my clothes off in front of him, but I was instructed to do both. I seldom shirk an issue and my feelings for him were strong, so I did as I was told. I remember thinking to myself that if I got through the night I would be able to tackle anything.

I had taken a long, warm Viyella nightdress with me, but Terry soon whipped that off. The room was still bitterly cold and I was glad to get under the duvet. At least Terry provided some extra warmth, even if the bristles of the horse-hair mattress were almost unbearable. I had heard about Terry's success with women in his racing heydays yet really did not expect my own first night with him to be so uncomfortable.

Fortunately, I still found him irresistible at eight o'clock the next morning. He was always a very passionate lover and lived for sex. In later years he used to say to me, 'Any place, any time.' Although he didn't always get his way, we always had sex on the nights before the Cheltenham Gold Cup, because he maintained it brought us luck and he knew that I was superstitious.

That first morning after, however, I woke to find that the hair on my head was soaking wet from the condensation on the bedroom walls. Terry thought this was very funny. There were icicles on the windows and water dripping off the ceiling. My back was almost raw from where I had been scratched by the protruding bristles on the mattress. It was too cold to venture out of bed to get dressed so I nervously dressed under the duvet. Even my clothes were damp. There was no breakfast, no proper kitchen and just a kettle for a cup of coffee. After this extraordinary experience, I was grateful that Terry drove me back to West Lockinge Farm. It would probably have been better if I'd had my own car, but we did eventually get back to the farm in the old Honda. It was a quiet journey. I was still shell-shocked but despite everything, I knew that I had fallen in love with him. There would be no turning back.

It seemed that there was some strange kind of chemistry between Terry and me and it lasted for the next twenty years. Once he moved into West Lockinge Farmhouse, a few months later, we seldom spent any days or nights apart. It was a treasured relationship and Terry often told me that we were made for each other. He often stressed that we should never be parted. I found him to be a special person, full of devilment, not afraid of anything. Of course

41

there were plenty of occasions when I wished the ground would swallow me up. His remarks to people were often outrageous, but many loved him all the same.

In his younger days Terry wasn't possessive about his girlfriends and, apparently, often shared them with his mates, but as he grew older, he became extremely jealous. He hardly ever let me out of his sight and I was never allowed to go to Ireland on my own to visit my own old friends. 'If somebody lays a hand on you, I'll kneecap him.' he would say. Strangely, having travelled a lot on my own in earlier years, I never wanted to go away without him.

The twenty years that we spent together were magical. We had so much fun and laughter, and he completely changed my outlook on life.

CHAPTER FIVE

Terry Moves In

It took a while for me to adjust when Terry moved in at West Lockinge Farm. This was hardly surprising, since I had lived in the farmhouse on my own for over fifteen years. Terry was still working for Russell, Baldwin and Bright when, at the beginning of 1994, he decided to spend his nights with me, yet he continued to drive to work in the Hereford offices on most days of the week. It was a good ninety-minute journey and the old blue Honda covered many miles. Terry would leave early each morning while I was feeding the horses. He always looked extremely smart in his dark suit and tie or blazer and grey trousers. I would watch him go down the drive and wave to him. I remember longing for his return in the evenings.

Although we were very much in love, there was little contact between us during the day. He was hopeless with mobile phones – as indeed were many people at that time. Terry, however, never improved his skills with these valuable communication aids for as long as I knew him. To send a text message, or even to receive one, was beyond him. He used to say to me, 'We managed perfectly well without them when I was riding and we didn't have jockey agents, either.' Although, at a later stage, his truck on the farm was fitted with a car phone, he frequently got into a muddle with it, as he only knew how to press two knobs. On one occasion the mobile phone he had at home had 360 unread messages recorded on it.

During those early months when Terry started living with me, I was extremely busy with the racehorses in my care. I had about sixty horses in training. On most days I was on the road, saddling runners at different racecourses and chatting to my owners, who had no idea that their trainer had suddenly acquired a live-in-lover who knew more about racing than she did. At that time my horses were performing well and stable morale was high, but as more and more horses arrived at the farm, it was clear that I needed extra help.

Julian Pritchard was still my assistant and he was a great asset, but I needed another pair of hands and more advice about placing the horses and race-riding tactics. In early January 1994, I remember telephoning Terry while I was walking the course at Nottingham Racecourse. Mick Fitzgerald was due to ride Easthorpe in a hurdle race that afternoon and the horse needed good ground to show his best form. It had rained and the turf had cut up badly, especially on the bends. Terry told me exactly how Easthorpe should be ridden and he duly won the race – leading throughout and hugging the inside rails where no other horses had been.

Later in the spring of 1994, Terry came home one night from work and told me he had a surprise for me. He had decided to give up his job with Terry Court and turn his attention to helping me full-time. The daily travelling to the offices in Hereford had become unbearably monotonous. The Honda was painfully slow and the gearbox was old and well worn. Terry had wanted to be part of my set-up for several months and I was thrilled with the news. At last, he could settle down and relax with a new challenge.

When Terry started living full-time at West Lockinge Farm, my training timetable altered. He was hands-on twenty-four hours a day. We often stayed awake and talked long into the nights, discussing the horses as well as the many problems Terry had encountered in the earlier years of his life. I was gradually getting to know and understand him better and better. April 1994 marked the beginning of our successful partnership and we both took on a new lease of life. In previous years, I had constantly worried about my training methods and had often wondered whether I was on the right lines. Now there were the two of us and I could share everything with Terry. His wisdom with horses and racing knowledge were invaluable.

We had an extraordinary understanding from the very beginning, even though we argued constantly over minor issues, because Terry loved to be different. We were both strong characters and had our own views. However, these disagreements were mostly harmless and of a friendly nature. People found them amusing and laughed at our differences of opinion. We never had any fierce rows, even though both of us were stubborn and decidedly set in our ways. Once or twice, Terry threatened to leave me over some stupid little issue, but I used to laugh at him and that annoyed him more than anything. He never had an answer when I asked him where he would go if he left the farm.

On one occasion, he strongly disapproved of the sandwiches I made up for the staff when they went racing. Ever since my point-to-pointing days, I had always enjoyed making picnics, but Terry now told me that this was a waste of money. He was right. On another occasion, however, he frightened me. During my early training years, when I was on my own, I had kept up my strength and held my nerve by consuming a bottle of white wine every day. Of course, by the time Terry came to Lockinge, he had dried out and was teetotal. But I was still enjoying the wine. Now he put his foot down and said, 'It's either the bottle or me.' I suppose it had been rather selfish of me to continually drink in his presence and so I took the decision to give up. In fact, I refrained from drinking anything alcoholic for many years. Terry's tirades may have been harmless, but I respected his views. I hated upsetting him. I never wanted to sever our extraordinary bond.

It had certainly been a celebration day for me when Terry had agreed to assist me in my training operation, but to begin with, it was not always easy to integrate him with the staff. I employed around sixteen people at that time and there was a good atmosphere, but Terry was outrageously outspoken on the yard.

My employees gradually accepted him, but it took a while for them to understand his 'special language'. His swear words and his own personal vocabulary needed to be heard to be believed, yet he never consciously meant to hurt people; the cursings and swearings were just part of him. I have always been broad-minded and consider myself unshockable, but there were days when even I was left speechless. If Terry liked a member of staff or a jockey, that person was invariably referred to as a 'cunt'. For him, it was a form of endearment and he used this word with great frequency. Everybody got bollockings and I remember lecturing him – in schoolmistress fashion – to go easy on those around him.

On one occasion, in the autumn of 1994, he totally overstepped the mark. The morning had gone well and the horses looked great when I set off for Didcot station en route to London to see my dentist, Alan Ross, in Sloane Street. I was to have a tooth taken out. I left Terry in charge of the yard and told him to supervise evening stables. I travelled back on the train at around 6 p.m., with a throbbing mouth and a handful of painkillers, only to be met at home by my beloved, who proudly told me that, in my absence, he had sacked everybody. He had decided that they were cutting corners and leaving work earlier than usual.

'There's been a mutiny in the yard,' he said. 'When I told some of the staff to sharpen up and stop taking shortcuts, they answered me back, so I told them to fuck off.'

Of course, I was extremely angry and I did not speak to Terry for the rest of that night. Over the years, I had built up a really good core of loyal workers and we got on extremely well. My staff were my friends and respected me – even though they might not always have agreed with me. On the morning after Terry's tirade everything was total pandemonium. I remember saying to him, 'You just cannot talk to people like that. Treat the staff like you'd like to be treated yourself. Have consideration for them. After all, they are only working for us because they enjoy it and love the horses. If you upset them, of course they will leave us.'

Fortunately, once I had repaired the rift, most of the lads and lasses returned to work and they gradually came to realise that Terry's bark was far worse than his bite. There continued to be plenty of banter but they started to accept him and he had many heart-to-heart talks with them, especially at the end of a morning. I was touched by the number of ex-employees who came to his funeral and memorial service. They had learned to treat him as an equal and confided in him. In return he constantly gave them advice. They said exactly what they liked to his face and put up with the string of four-letter words he invariably unleashed in response. Those still on the yard today continue to miss him. He was a proper friend to them.

Several of these longstanding members of staff now tell me that you had to know Terry to understand him. Apparently he often frightened the young lads, who could not believe he had been a three-time champion jockey. He would say what he wanted to them, but seldom remembered their names. He was a very good judge of character, however, and although his language was strong, he never offended those around him once they accepted his ways. He was always fair and happy to talk to them about their problems.

At one point, we had a lovely girl working for us called Katie Clark. She was skinny and Terry christened her 'Twiggy'. While with us, Katie was diagnosed with Hodgkin's lymphoma – a form of cancer – and she had to undergo serious hospital treatments. Her bravery was astonishing. She says she will always remember Terry saying to her, 'Keep smiling, Twig,' because this is something he always did. Katie says that his smile could light up any room. It is great that she is well again now. In 2008 we nominated her for The Godolphin Stud and Stable Staff Awards and she won the category for 'Special Merit/Hero'.

Interviewing new staff, however, was frequently a nightmare for me. Terry always wanted to be present but there were times when I cringed at the questions he asked.

One of my former employees, Victoria Patten, told me, 'I will never forget the first time that I met Terry. I had come to West Lockinge for an interview. I was sitting in your conservatory with you, when he strode in, wearing very short shorts, wellies and his green Husky waistcoat. He proceeded to stick both his hands down your shirt while asking me why I wanted the job. I think he was trying to see whether I was shockable – fortunately I managed to give him suitable answers and it was the start of some extremely happy years. The saddest thing is that I don't think that they make people like Terry any more. I wish they did! He was truly one in a million and I will never forget him.'

How fortunate that Terry did not conduct the whole interview that day! I used to dread it when he wanted to be in charge. He had the same questions for all potential new staff: how old are you? Do you drink? Are you on drugs, and do you like sex? I used to tell him that he must not be so personal but he always laughed and said, 'I'll say what I want.' He certainly did. And he usually got away with it, although he probably infringed many rules.

The layout in the farmhouse changed when Terry moved in. I knew he was untidy, so I started off by giving him his own bedroom/dressing room and bathroom. I thought he'd like his own space. He didn't have many clothes but we gradually added to his wardrobe.

He loathed shopping and it was extremely difficult to get him to try on clothes or shoes in a shop. There were many times when I got out the tape measure and then sent his measurements off with mail-orders. It was a challenge, yet apparently when he was riding and in the public eye, he took great pride in his appearance. He loved dressing up in those days. He told me that jockeys should always look smart and wear ties. Indeed, in the 1970s, Terry had even done some modelling, in particular for DAKS, and he had much enjoyed his time on the catwalk among what he called 'the flashy birds'. Apparently he once forgot the format, went the wrong way and collided with all the female models head on. I can well picture the occasion. He must have been in his element.

At Lockinge, my own bedroom had to undergo massive changes when Terry arrived. He only slept in his dressing room for a few nights before he became lonely and moved in with me – a bit like a puppy you leave to sleep in the kitchen, but when it starts barking, you take pity on it and bring it upstairs to shut it up. My comfortable old bed was no longer comfortable with the two of us in it and the springs soon gave out, so it was replaced by a new king-sized bed, which served us well for twenty years.

It is a very peaceful room and looks out onto the garden. It is spacious and airy with the window always kept open, even in the winter. Nevertheless, some strange things did happen during the years that Terry shared it with me. Firstly, there were often disturbances on the other side of the house, in the farmyard, involving the ducks and the bantams. We were constantly invaded by foxes, which would kill at random and pluck sitting poultry off their nests. It used to upset Terry hugely, because our feathered friends were part of the furniture on our Old MacDonald's farm. We both loved them.

On most nights Terry would get up to have a pee. He only had one kidney and lived on diuretics. His own bathroom overlooked the brightly lit duck pond and on several occasions in the middle of the night he noticed foxes prowling around the pond perimeter. The geese and ducks swam around in the middle but there was always a lot of noise and commotion. He decided that the only way to solve the problem was to shoot the foxes, so he kept his twelve-bore shotgun beside the bed, ready to dispose of the invaders. I got used to Terry having his gun in the bedroom but it was rather unnerving to begin with. I well remember that on one summer's night, a fox was spied and a naked Terry – he never wore any clothes at night except in the coldest months of the winter – crept downstairs. He shot the intruder stone dead, but as I looked out of the bathroom window, I wondered what on earth the police would say if they had seen a naked man prowling around the farm at 3 a.m. with a shotgun.

Terry removed several foxes over the years at West Lockinge Farm, yet the Old Berkshire Hunt still visited us each spring. We supported the hunt but although the hounds penetrated the woods adjoining the farm and did find further foxes there, they seldom killed any. On one occasion, Terry had great delight in showing one of his prize quarries to John Francome and a Channel 4 film crew. They had come to film our superstar horse, Best Mate. Terry laid out his fox on the steps beside the feed room, for all to see. He was very pleased with himself – but it was not a pretty sight. The horses shied at it and the dogs kept sniffing it.

A few years later, when I had the honour to train for the Queen, both Terry and I spent a most enjoyable morning at Windsor Castle. We were invited to have morning coffee with Her Majesty after seeing the horses in the mews. Terry Pendry, who was in charge of the Queen's horses at Windsor, took us to the castle. My Terry remarked to the Queen that a couple of her dogs looked like foxes – and to my horror, proceeded to tell her about his nude night-time antics with his gun. I was most embarrassed, but she is a lovely person and has a great sense of humour. She seemed amused, even though somewhat surprised.

Our nights were usually uneventful. Terry was a good sleeper. Once he had finished watching yet another western on the television – I frequently told him that he was wasting his time, because the goodies always win and the baddies lose – only his snoring could be heard. However, on one hot summer's evening as I lay dozing, I heard a strange scratching noise. What on earth could it be? A rat in the attic, or birds, or mice? It was too loud for mice and what would birds be doing in total darkness? I've always had a horror of rats and immediately woke Terry. We both lay there listening. It was a peculiar scuffling noise and I shuddered, lest it *was* a rat. After what seemed like an age, Terry calmly said, 'It's a hedgehog. It's just run across the floor.'

I thought he'd lost his marbles and told him not to be so stupid, but he insisted that in the light of the window he'd seen a hedgehog, so I turned on the bedside lamp and behold: behind the armchair, there were further rustlings. I gingerly pulled the chair forward and was confronted by a confused Mrs Tiggywinkle. I'm not the bravest in this sort of situation and I got no help from the other side of the bed. All Terry said was, 'Pick it up and take it into the garden.'

It's all very well, in the middle of the night, to pick up a prickly animal in one's bedroom and I was shaking. I put on a pair of gloves from the chest of drawers, and grabbed a towel from the bathroom. I covered the surprised animal with this and whisked it off down the stairs and onto the lawn. Terry told me that I was being ridiculously over-reactive, but I kept thinking about fleas – hedgehogs are supposed to be alive with them. I prayed they had not hopped into our bed. I scratched for days afterwards, mainly through shock and the fear that fleas had got under the duvet. How on earth the hedgehog managed to get upstairs remains a mystery. The only way it could have made it to our bedroom would have been by climbing the staircase. It must have entered the house via the open French windows. It gave me a real fright, although Terry remained calm and unconcerned.

Two months later, we had a visit from a second hedgehog. This time, it was scuffling in the newspapers beside my bed. It got the same treatment as hedgehog number one. Since then no hedgehogs have been sighted in the garden or around the farm. It's sad, as they are lovely animals and getting close to extinction in some parts of the country.

If ever the tack room alarm went off in the middle of the night – which it did about three times during my years with Terry – who was it who had to go downstairs, put on Wellingtons, a dressing gown and brandish a torch? Me, of course. Terry never moved, but just ordered me to go outside to investigate. I didn't even have his shotgun to take with me. His laziness on these occasions really annoyed me, but his excuse was that he didn't understand the alarm system. Too bad if there had been a burglar lurking. I told Terry that his behaviour was typical of men. He should be protecting me, not ordering me outside into a potential danger zone.

I was forever telling him that men cannot survive without women – in fact, Terry couldn't even change a light bulb or replace the fuse in a plug. He always left these tasks to me, and if the television blacked out, he was totally lost. Sometimes, I'd be at the races and he'd ring me to say that he couldn't change channels. Which knob should he press? How could I possibly help him from fifty or a hundred miles away?

While Terry was settling himself in at his new home and adapting to a different lifestyle, it pleased me enormously that he had such an excellent rapport with my mother. She had been living alone at Lockinge Manor since my father's death in the autumn of 1993. It must have been a huge surprise for her when Terry and I joined up, but she never showed it and from day one she accepted him. She seemed proud to have him in the village. In return, Terry loved her; he called her a 'proper lady'. He did countless jobs for Mum, especially with her Connemara ponies – he always seemed to be mending fences and sheds, or dragging hay bales around to her fields in the winter months.

On many occasions, we had supper at the manor in Mum's lovely kitchen. She was a brilliant cook and taught me all that I now know (I love cooking; it is one of my favourite hobbies). A well-prepared dinner was most welcome, especially after a long and tiring day at the races.

Terry and Mum also shared many jokes and enjoyed a banter, usually about the ponies and the fences they had broken. Mum had a great sense of humour. Once she complained that she could not drive her car into a certain field to feed her ponies, because a strange man always parked in the gateway. Terry immediately said that the man was probably having a wank. Mum was highly amused by this and that particular parking place, just off the side road to Wantage, has been called 'Wanker's Gateway' ever since.

In December 1996, we celebrated my fiftieth birthday with a most enjoyable lunch at The Savoy Hotel in London. It was hosted by my sister and brother-in-law. Mum came with us. Several close friends were invited, including Hector and Pam Brown, with whom we later shared a holiday in Ireland, and who kept several good racehorses in the yard. Hector remembers Terry's kindly reactions when one of the guests – my nephew William – felt decidedly off-colour. 'Quick as a flash,' he recalls, 'Terry whisked the young man off to his room. He returned ten minutes later to tell us that, unfortunately, the sufferer had not quite made it, so he had stuffed his head into a potted plant en route and now everything in the garden was rosy.'

Terry would get away with anything.

He adored animals and the countryside. He had, of course, a great gift with horses. He was firm, but surprisingly gentle. My dogs loved him too. To begin with I had Labradors, but later on I switched over to golden retrievers because Terry preferred this breed. He had owned a wonderful dog in the 1980s called Digby, who went with him to Australia, but he was forced to leave Digby there when he returned to the UK, on account of his age. He always wanted another retriever with the same bloodlines and the two dogs that later entered our lives at Lockinge – Elsa and Tiger – were Digby's relations. They proved wonderful companions to both of us and were highly intelligent.

On most mornings Terry fed the wild ducks and ducklings up the lane, or took bowls of corn to throw out of his car window for the pheasants and partridges in the fields. When sitting in his truck, close to the gallops, and waiting for horses to appear, he watched the daily habits of the wild birds around him, marvelling at the red kites gliding in the thermals and the buzzards swooping down on their prey: field mice, baby rabbits or rotting carcasses. He continued to hate foxes because they killed our chickens and ducks in the yard. If he saw a fox ambling across the fields he would tell me exactly which way it had gone. He was fascinated by the large numbers of hares that lived on the farm. They are beautiful animals and seem to pair up for life, and it always upset Terry if he found a dead hare, because more often than not its mate would be sitting beside it. He would never shoot a hare. Yet he often shot the rabbits, which did untold damage to my schooling fences by burrowing into them and digging holes in the turf on the take-offs and landings.

Terry never missed anything during his mornings beside the gallops. He would return to the farmhouse at lunchtime and relay endless new observations. Not only would he tell me, in great detail, how the horses had gone or how the riders had ridden, but he also described the wildlife. He watched all the David Attenborough programmes on the television.

On one occasion, when we attended a special dinner in London's Natural History Museum, courtesy of philanthropist Charles Cadogan, he was fascinated by our tour of the special exhibits in the vaults.

Terry analysed the everyday lives of animals in the same way that he studied people. He told me that, when he was racing, he enjoyed getting into the minds of the horses he rode. This was unusual, since most jockeys tend to treat their horses as numbers on a board. Terry, however, maintained that every horse is different and needs understanding. He never labelled a horse as being ungenuine, but believed that if one of the horses he rode ran an inexplicably bad race, then something was hurting it. He was seldom wrong – especially, in later life, when he watched our horses. For example, if a horse held its head high in the closing stages of a race, he suspected it was struggling for oxygen and suffering from a breathing defect. When horses repeatedly jumped badly, or hung to the right or left, he suspected back or tooth pain. Terry believed that no horse is born bad, but that human beings are often responsible for their behavioural changes in later life.

———

During Terry's first year at West Lockinge, my whole life changed. He was a tremendous help to me with the training of the racehorses. He had such a wide knowledge of how horses should look and perform, and we developed an excellent working relationship, dividing our daily duties. From the day I began training in 1989, I had always given the horses their breakfast feeds at an early hour. It is a good time to observe them; it is peaceful and there are no staff around. It is the perfect opportunity to examine horses' legs and assess their general well-being. I always felt for any heat in the legs and feet – a sign that something was not right. I would see whether or not my charges had eaten up their feeds from the previous evening, and if there was still food in the manger I knew that something was wrong. Either the horse had been given too much to eat, or else he was off-colour. However, horses can leave their feeds purely due to the stress of travelling or racing, so I monitored the leavers carefully and took their temperatures.

Terry greatly enjoyed helping me with the early morning feeding regime. We would get up around 5.15 a.m. and be in the yard at 5.45 a.m. – sometimes earlier. He never missed a day. Once the five alarm clocks in the bedroom had rung, he made sure I got out of bed. I was always the last to get up, as I could get dressed very quickly. Terry was noticeably slower and took ages to sort out his clothes, but he was always the first to throw off the bedclothes. I hated getting up in the mornings, and still do, but I never missed a day.

The breakfast feeding was fun, informative and entertaining. At one point we had over eighty horses in training and we divided the yard into two halves. Terry fed the geese and ducks around the pond before we started pushing our trolleys. At night there was always a light shining across the yard, which meant we could see where we were going in those early mornings, yet Terry frequently got on the wrong side of Nobby, the Chinese gander, who would creep up behind him and viciously peck him on his leg or bottom. This bird was – and still is – a great character. He makes a lot of noise and quickly senses danger. He is the gander that gets all the ducks onto the pond when a fox appears and is the yard mascot. Geese can live a long time, and our last farmyard gander, Grandad, died when he was thirty-five years old.

We had a number of disturbances during our breakfast rounds. The top barn usually housed about a dozen bantam cockerels, which roosted on the lovely old beams above the horses' stables. When we turned on the lights, they thought it was daytime and the crowing began. At times in the mornings, neither Terry nor I could hear ourselves speak. There was plenty of swearing.

On one occasion, in midwinter, when it was bitterly cold and frosty, I well remember feeding my horses at the end of the barn and letting out a scream. There was a man huddled up in the corner of the stable – presumably a tramp. He was lying in the shavings and never moved when I opened the door. I yelled to Terry to come and help me and eventually the intruder stood up, shook himself and apologised. Terry fired questions at him and gave him plenty of abuse. The swear words were red-hot. The intruder told us that he had been lost in the night and could see lights at the farm. He had climbed in through the tiny window for shelter and warmth. When I found him, my heart missed a beat. It was extremely scary and I am not one of the bravest. However, the man seemed harmless and proceeded to leave the buildings and walk back to Wantage. We informed the police, but they were not at all interested – just another waif and stray. Surprisingly, the horse in that stable was unperturbed and continued to eat his breakfast as though nothing had happened.

As well as overseeing the morning feeding, Terry proved invaluable when it came to watching horses on the gallops. He drove his truck to a suitable vantage point, observed everybody, then reported back to me – by this time he had managed to master his car phone and mine was the only number he had to dial. He could see whether the horses needed more work and whether or not certain lads, lasses or jockeys got on with the horses they rode. He was quick to correct the riders and give them advice. He would put down his truck window, lean out in his scruffy old green Husky jacket and shout to them. He rarely got out of his vehicle unless there was a loose horse to be caught and somebody to be legged back into the saddle. While sitting and waiting for horses to appear on the gallops he tuned into Radio 5 and listened to all the news and topics of interest. I was always surprised by how much information he gleaned.

Terry drove three different trucks during his years at West Lockinge Farm. The first and third were Daihatsus – they had plenty of batterings, but he didn't seem to care when they were scratched and dented. The interiors were always dirty and untidy. Dust from the open windows covered all sorts of rubbish: buckets, head collars, ropes, farmyard tools and so on. If I ever asked our weekly car cleaner, Malcolm, to tidy up one of Terry's trucks, there was plenty of opposition. Terry would curse and swear for days afterwards, especially if the radio programme had been changed or the numerous old copies of the *Daily Sport* that had been stuffed into the pockets inside the doors had been thrown away. He used to enjoy browsing through what I called this pornographic newspaper while he waited in the fields to see more horses on the gallops. 'Surely you've seen enough naked human bodies to keep you going for the rest of your life!' I'd say to him. But he said that he never got bored of seeing new models and that everybody was different. Such are men.

The second truck Terry used on the gallops was a Land Rover Freelander, but he hated it and said it had far too many knobs inside. The truth was it was too sophisticated for him. A lot of the buttons were computerised and electronic. We had bought the car because of its superior performance and I hoped it would serve two purposes – work at home and journeys to the races. But that was wishful thinking. Terry only kept it for three months and, on one occasion, he got it well and truly stuck in a muddy gateway. The farm tractor had to pull him out. He only liked his battered Dahaitsus. They passed their MOTs each year and were fully licensed, but nobody ever volunteered to sit in the driver's seat. I remember one day when Timmy Murphy, one of the top steeplechase jockeys, borrowed Terry's truck after his own car had broken down. He drove it along the main road but brought it back almost at once, saying that it was dangerous. I think it frightened him because the steering and the brakes were tuned into Terry's way of driving. For Timmy it must have been like riding a rough, mannerless horse and he had no patience with it.

Having been through so many hardships as a jockey, Terry was extremely helpful and patient with the many jockeys who came to West Lockinge Farm during the days of our joint training venture. Some were aspiring young riders, others were well-established jockeys. He was always ready to give advice and constructive criticism. They respected him and listened to his comments, even if they might not have agreed wholeheartedly with what he said, or were surprised by his bluntness and the constant flow of swear words.

Terry spotted the talents of Jim Culloty when watching racing on the television at the kitchen table. He saw him ride one day at Fontwell in the early nineties and said at once, 'That jockey has got what it takes to go further.' At that time, Jim was only an amateur but he joined our yard in 1995. Personally, I had my doubts when Jim first arrived. He could barely tack up his horses correctly and often rode down the road with his girths so loose that the saddles slipped backwards dramatically and he had to bring his mount back to the yard to re-saddle it. I was always correcting Jim and, on many occasions, I was on the verge of losing my temper with him. He had endless bollockings, yet never seemed to improve.

Thankfully, however, he listened to Terry on the riding front. Not only was he given a huge amount of help on the gallops and on the schooling ground, where jumping is of prime importance, but he was well tutored by his mentor at the races. Jim won 227 races for us from West Lockinge Farm, including three Cheltenham Gold Cups on Best Mate, but he could never have achieved this without Terry's help and belief in him. He must have taken in some of our advice, because he is now a successful trainer himself and has already saddled a Cheltenham Gold Cup winner.

In my early training days, Jason Titley rode over sixty-five winners for West Lockinge Farm. He and Terry got on well, but they had plenty of arguments. Jason was amazingly good-natured and used to take Terry's abuse with a smile. He remembers many of the days when he worked horses for us on David Gandolfo's neighbouring gallop. Terry habitually stood close to the end of the gallop and often shouted out to Jason afterwards, 'You went too fast, you big Irish cunt! What are you doing? Trying to get feelers?' In other words, he was trying to feel how fast the horses could go.

On another occasion, when Jason came to ride out on a Monday morning with Roger Marley, he was in poor shape. They had both been to the jockeys' celebrations – The Lesters – the previous night and were noticeably the worse for wear. In fact, they had found it imperative to stop en route for one of them to be sick in a ditch before they got to the farm.

Terry came into the farmhouse and said to me, 'You'd better change the list, Hen. Those fuckers are not fit to ride out.' Then he went up to the two boys and said, 'You're in such a bad way, you'd better come into the kitchen and have a brandy.'

Another of my employees, Clare Allen, was always a good rider and Terry was, from day one, impressed by her style and her way with horses. Although she tended to be extremely vague and laid-back, she was allowed to school several horses at West Lockinge Farm, which she did well. When Clare left Lockinge, she spent a summer in France with well-known French trainer Guillaume Macaire, then went on to be point-to-point Ladies' Champion in 2007.

Claire Hart was another of Terry's pupils, and his tuition is still bearing fruit, because she rides plenty of Hunter Chase winners. She is a great person and she adored Terry. Finally, in our early training days, Paddy Young came over to us from Northern Ireland. He proved to be an exceptional horseman and educated many of our younger horses. He later moved to America, where he was Champion U.S. Jump Jockey on three occasions.

It was much later on that Aidan Coleman became one of Terry's protégés. He did not join the yard until 2006, having been a leading rider on the pony-racing circuit in Ireland. He always looked good on a horse and was very stylish, but had done little jumping and hadn't even ridden in point-to-points. It was my job to teach him and I gave him plenty of horses to ride in the loose jumping school. Fortunately, he picked up the techniques quickly and is now riding numerous winners. Terry watched him closely when he joined trainer Venetia Williams' yard and was proud of him. They kept in touch with each other, and to this day Aidan maintains that Terry was a great help to him when he started in England.

'I always rode short because I was tall, and Terry constantly told me to put down my leathers,' he says. 'On one occasion I was riding upsides two professional jockeys and I decided to put my stirrups up two holes. Yet, sharp as a razor, Terry noticed and gave me a piece of his mind. I always consider that Terry was a real jockeys' man and he understood everything from a jockey's point of view. He was sympathetic because he knew it all. The stories he used to tell me got me ready for the real world and his tips about what to say to owners and the general public added up. He told me always to dress smartly and to walk tall on a racecourse – never drag your toes. The first impressions are extremely important to owners and they need to have confidence in the jockeys who are riding their horses.'

Matty Batchelor was one of Terry's favourites because of his brilliant attitude to life and wonderful sense of humour. He always called Terry, 'Mr B' and was one of the ushers at his funeral. The first thing Matty did after riding out was to put on a cookery apron. He would then fry up a huge breakfast for everybody – bacon, sausages, eggs, mushrooms, the lot. He was excellent in the kitchen and a few years later won a Channel 4 celebrity chef cookery contest, *Come Dine With Me*. Many of the jockeys enjoyed breakfast time at West Lockinge Farm.

As a rule, I was in charge of the schooling, which comprised jumping the racehorses in a special field over practice hurdles and steeplechase fences. Terry sometimes found time to watch the horses on his way back from the gallops, but he usually opted out of the main sessions in the schooling field because he tended to get annoyed by the way in which some of the jockeys rode their horses. They often went too fast. He maintained that horses learn a lot more when they are jumped quietly and slowly, as it gives them time to think and work out their techniques.

Terry loved the loose school. Fred Rimell, for whom he had ridden in the sixties and seventies, had one at Kinnersley in Worcestershire, and Terry agreed that these enclosed jumping arenas are invaluable when teaching horses to jump. They learn to measure the obstacles and put themselves right on the take-offs without the impediment of riders on their backs. If they misjudge it, they pay the penalty by hitting the solid poles.

Jim Old, who later became a successful trainer, was with Fred Rimell from 1967–9. During that time he worked as a stable lad and Terry was riding at his peak. Jim got to know him well and remembers many of their times together. 'It was never plain sailing,' he says, 'and there were plenty of disagreements between Terry and his boss.'

This I quite believe – nobody could ever tell Terry what to do. He always had to have the last word and was, in his own mind, never wrong. I often said to him, 'Thank God I was never your teacher at school; you would have been impossible to teach!'

On one occasion Jim accompanied Terry to the schooling ground at Kinnersley. Terry was riding a horse that had lost its nerve in a race and Jim was riding the schoolmaster. Fred Rimell followed them to the field, then got out of his truck brandishing a big whip, known to horsemen as a long tom. He said to Terry that his mount needed a good sorting out because it was too cautious at the obstacles. Terry totally disagreed and said that all he wanted to do was regain its confidence under quiet, sympathetic handling. They jumped a line of small steeplechase fences and all went well. Then they pulled up and began to walk back to the beginning in order to repeat the exercise but the boss man was standing beside the track brandishing his whip and ready to pounce.

Terry said to Jim, 'When we get level with the guv'nor, trot past him as fast as you can so that he can't hit my horse.' As they went past Fred, he lurched forward to have a crack with the whip and fell flat on his face onto a sea of mud. He fell so awkwardly that he was unable to get back onto his feet quickly. Terry and Jim had rejumped the fences and were on their way home by the time he had recovered. Fred was furious and realised that Terry had tricked him. Terry never did like using a stick on horses unless it was really necessary – and in this case, it certainly was not.

Terry hardly ever rode a horse in the days when I knew him, although he often longed to sort one out himself or to jump it over the steeplechase fences. However, he did volunteer to ride out once with one of my owners: Sir Anthony Scott. I trained a rather scatty, home-bred mare for him called Too Sharp, who won a number of races but was exceptionally lively and easily wound up. Nevertheless, Sir Anthony loved riding her and came over to the yard at weekends to hack her out. On one particular morning Terry decided to go with him on a horse of Chris Brasher's called Storm North, which was a very sensible and relaxed individual.

They set off up to the Downs, but the mare was alarmed by the sight of some pigs in a field on the other side of the main road to Wantage. She immediately started playing up: whipping round and snorting. Sir Anthony was apparently dumped on the grass beside the point-to-point course and Too Sharp broke lose. Terry became the outrider on Storm North, captured her, and led her back. However, in his attempts to leg-up the fallen jockey, he managed to let go of his own horse. Both horses then took off at the gallop and set their sights for home. Miraculously, they were caught close to the Lockinge Estate grain dryer by an extremely helpful farmhand, but they had stepped on their reins and both bridles were broken. Sheepishly, Terry and Sir Anthony were forced to lead them home with bits of leather tied up with baler twine. Apparently I was seething with anger when they came back into the yard – probably more through shock than genuine outrage. Both horses could have been badly hurt and fallen over on the road, but fortunately they were unscathed and Too Sharp won another race three weeks later.

After his dressing down, Terry was annoyed and refused to go out riding ever again with any of my owners. The only times he rode horses after the aforementioned fiasco were with me. We habitually went for rides on Christmas Day, choosing two sensible conveyances and quietly pottering around the farm and the villages. We missed all the church services and visited another of my brilliant owners, Charles Cadogan, to wish him a happy Christmas.

Those mornings were magic; they were romantic and fun. It was an honour to ride out with Terry. Never in my wildest childhood dreams would I have imagined myself riding side by side with my hero.

CHAPTER SIX

Wedding Bells

When Terry and I had lived together for over a year at West Lockinge Farm and he had become accepted by my owners, my staff and neighbourhood friends, we decided that an engagement would not be out of the question. We were already sharing our lives. Terry was proving to be an enormous help to me with the training and we continued to adore each other. We hated being apart – fortunately we seldom were – but even a day seemed a long time. I cannot remember which of us decided that we should get married, but I do remember that there was no special romantic proposal from Terry, who had twice 'been there and done that'. We just agreed that we wanted to be together for the rest of our lives. How lucky that I had met and fallen in love with somebody who had the same interests as myself.

Mum fully supported our decision and was responsible for putting our names in the engagements sections of *The Times* and the *Daily Telegraph* on 25 March 1995. She always wanted things to be done properly, even though it was probably not the marriage she had originally envisaged for her eldest daughter. Also, I'm not sure how pleased my father would have been if he had seen me on the brink of marriage to an impecunious former National Hunt jockey who had lost most of his hard-earned savings through two unsuccessful earlier marriages and divorces.

I well remember Dad telling me that I was crazy when I started training racehorses. He said it was throwing good money after bad, although he did become hugely supportive and proud when I began turning out winners. He used to follow my career closely. There is no doubt that he mellowed with age, and at least my sister had married Sam Vestey, of whom he greatly approved. Perhaps he would have accepted Terry after all, although his unbelievable tidiness would not have complemented Terry's extremely untidy existence. If Dad had ever seen the inside of Terry's truck he would have exploded with shock and horror. When we were children, everything was kept immaculately tidy in and around Lockinge Manor. We weren't allowed to leave any of our possessions scattered about the house, and if Dad picked them up, he would place them on the staircase so that we would take them up to our bedrooms on our way up.

Once our engagement was announced in March 1995, we were inundated with wonderful letters and cards. Terry and I were extremely touched; even now, I still have those lovely 'well done' messages filed in a drawer in my office. After Terry's death, I read them again. Although they made me cry, I will treasure them for the rest of my life. We tentatively pencilled in July as the best month for our wedding because there would not be too many horses in work and the weather is usually good at that time of year. Mum announced that she wanted to give us a reception in her house afterwards. It took a while to draw up a list of possible guests, but in the end, over 200 invitations were sent out for Sunday, 30 July.

Then disaster struck: I could not find Terry's divorce certificate. We would have to cancel our booking at the local register office and the well-laid plans for us to tie the knot would have to be put on hold. In retrospect, I suppose I should have paid more attention and read the small print more carefully. I learned later never to take anything for granted with Terry. It turned out he did not even have an up-to-date passport, driving licence or shotgun certificate. How could I ever have expected him to possess a valid divorce certificate? I couldn't even find his birth certificate. Paperwork was alien to him and he totally disregarded it. As far as he was concerned, it had no importance in his everyday life.

Initially, it was a shock when I realised that Terry and I could not be legally joined. For the first time in my life, I longed to be married, and for Terry to be my husband. I loved him with all my heart and we both wanted to rubber-stamp our union, but now it was impossible.

It was with some trepidation that I told Mum, but she reacted superbly and insisted that she wanted to hold the party, come what may. Terry said, in his usual matter-of-fact way, 'Don't worry, darling. Fuck it: we'll celebrate first and get married later.' As it happened, nobody even mentioned the register office on that memorable day. Everybody assumed that I was now Terry's third wife. I had already decided to continue training racehorses under my maiden name, so I didn't even need to be called Mrs Biddlecombe. Terry and I were already inseparable and we continued to lead our lives as if we were married. In later years, I did track down the missing document but we did not visit the register office until 2011.

There was a lot of excitement before Mum's party in 1995. I had spent many weeks thinking about it and I wanted to look my best on the big day. I ate very little during May and June, which meant that my weight was good and, of course, neither of us was drinking any alcohol. My special aunt – Catherine Clanwilliam, Mum's sister – announced that she would like to give me my wedding outfit and I spent a considerable amount of time choosing it. I ended up with a cream silk dress and jacket – virginal white wouldn't have been appropriate and I preferred cream anyway. Terry wore a smart pin-striped dark-grey suit, and a blue silk tie emblazoned with small ducks. He looked wonderful. He kissed and cuddled me throughout the day and, as usual, I found him utterly irresistible. Never in my wildest dreams had I envisaged attending my own wedding reception. It was a wonderful day – possibly the happiest of my whole life.

My mother organised the celebrations superbly, leaving no stone unturned. She had always been brilliant at arranging parties.

Not only was there delicious food, but plenty of champagne on hand to loosen peoples' tongues. Our guests seemed extremely happy. Sam Vestey, made a short welcoming speech and referred to Terry as his new brother-in-law. My sister was, as usual, hugely supportive and in top form. Looking back, I can hardly believe that she had a life-threatening stroke barely four months later. As we cut the enormous wedding cake, I thought how great it was to see Terry enjoying himself amid so many of his old friends, a number of whom had not set eyes on him for many years. I could see that, once again, he was experiencing a feeling of pride and happiness. His confidence had returned.

The autumn following our celebration party was exciting and we had a lot to look forward to, but on 30 November 1995, while I was at Leicester Racecourse, everything changed. It was a cold, dreary day. I had saddled four runners but none of them had covered themselves in glory; all had completed their races but there were no winners. Then the telephone rang. It was my secretary, Christine. My sister, Ce, had collapsed at her home and been taken to hospital, unconscious.

My heart almost stopped. Ce and I have always been extremely close, right from our childhood days, and she had been an immense support to Terry and me at our reception that summer. I longed to be with her, but I was stuck many miles away from Lockinge on a grey day in the shires. It was a tense journey home and there was no further news when I rang the office again. Mum had driven to the hospital in Cheltenham, but, like Terry, she never used a mobile telephone and I couldn't talk to her.

When I eventually reached the farmhouse, I remember wandering around in a daze. Terry was both supportive and sympathetic. He tried to keep me calm, but everybody was anxious. We waited and waited for news. Eventually, I spoke to Mum. Ce had suffered an aneurysm, a haemorrhage in her brain, and would have to be transported in another ambulance to Frenchay Hospital near Bristol for an emergency operation that night by a top neurological surgeon. She was only given a fifty-fifty chance of surviving the anaesthetic.

There was nothing that Terry or I could do. My brother-in-law, Sam, and Mum travelled to the hospital and said they would ring us when there was news. Terry and I went upstairs to bed, but neither of us could sleep. Indeed, I cried my eyes out. I felt tense and strained. We just lay side by side and held hands. Terry constantly tried to reassure me. The telephone was beside the bed – we waited and waited. Finally, at 3 a.m., it rang and I picked up the receiver, shaking with fear and anticipation – the news was slightly better. Ce had survived the surgery, but was still in a coma. Over the next few months, she just lay there in Frenchay Hospital, with tubes and machines attached to her. At first she was in the intensive care unit but later was moved into a side ward.

We visited her daily. She looked beautiful but hardly stirred. We will never know whether she subconsciously recognised us when we visited her, because there was never a flicker on her face. It was extremely depressing – heart-breaking, in fact. We were told that it was unlikely she would ever be able to talk or walk again.

During the months of anxiety with Ce, Terry was the most wonderful support. Together we drove down the M4 to see her every single day and talk to her, even though she couldn't respond. Terry would take her hand and stroke her arms. I don't know how I could have coped without him. At home, I still had my stables full of racehorses and most of them were ready to run. We continued to feed them early in the mornings, but I hardly ever went racing in December.

We relied on a great team at home and, in particular, Jane Brackenbury, my assistant, who took over a lot of the responsibility. She did most of the travelling to the racecourses. Fortunately, I was still able to study the racing calendar and form books, as well as talk to owners on the telephone, while Terry drove me down the motorway. I did all the entries from the car and we had six winners and eight placed horses in the weeks running up to Christmas. The only day I do remember going racing was 13 December. We had a double on that day at Exeter. Both horses were ridden by Ger Ryan and one of them, Bishops Island, was owned by Sam Vestey. I remember saying to the press that the win was for my sister and for her speedy recovery. It was an emotional day and I found it hard to fight back the tears.

———

After a difficult Christmas in 1995 and further visits to Frenchay Hospital, Ce miraculously started to show a little improvement. She began moving her arms, and on several occasions, tried to pull the tubes out of her nose. In January, she was moved to Gloucester Royal Hospital, which was closer to her home. I took a number of photographs of her during her months in both hospitals. She has always been a fighter and she defied all the doctors to make an amazing recovery, even though she was, and still is, slightly handicapped on her left side. Her mind and speech gradually returned, and nowadays, I find that Ce's memory of our childhood days is far better than mine.

She has achieved a great deal since her stroke. For many years she successfully ran the stud at Stowell Park, where she and Sam bred many good thoroughbred flat racehorses. Sam was a tower of strength throughout her illness, as indeed, was Alison Roberts, the housekeeper/nanny, who was with Ce when the stroke occurred. It was Alison who immediately called an ambulance, and without her swift actions, it is unlikely that my darling sister would be with us today. Alison saved her life.

Mum, too, was superb during the crisis with Ce and kept icy-cool. We often took her with us in the car when we paid our visits to Frenchay. She was deeply shocked, but she never panicked. It was even more difficult for her, since she had lived on her own after Dad's death in 1993 and had nobody to talk to during the long evenings. Ce and I could never have wished for a better mother, but her life did change dramatically after Ce's illness and she began to show a lot more anxiety. Both Terry and I watched her carefully and involved her as much as possible in our own daily lives, which she really seemed to appreciate.

Once we had openly set up home together, it became obvious that Terry's three youngest children – James, Robert and Lucy – would greatly benefit from their father having a solid base in the countryside. They loved coming to Lockinge to visit us at weekends and in the school holidays. Terry often drove to Gloucester to collect them from their grandparents' house. There was always plenty to occupy them on the farm and Terry kept them busy. Shooting played a big part for the boys and Terry managed to buy a clay pigeon trap so that James and Robert could practise with the guns he bought them. There was plenty of rabbit shooting too – especially after dark by the light of the car's headlights. Our rabbit population was never significantly reduced, but there were some fun days. The dogs adored these outings and used to get thoroughly overexcited in the back of the car.

During the days at Lockinge, James practised his driving skills on our two tractors and helped me on the farm. He and Terry spent hours together doing the topping and the harrowing of the fields, and this laid the foundation for the contracting work James later undertook on farms around Gloucester. James has many happy memories of those days with his father, but one in particular stands out. 'It was the Lambourn Charity Open Day in the 1990s,' he recalls. 'Dad was taking part in the camel racing and he took myself, Robert and Lucy with him. Hen had to stay at home as she had owners in the yard. The number cloths were constantly changed on the camels but after the first heat, Dad worked out which was the best camel, and said to us, "That's my camel – make sure you watch it. Don't let it out of your sight; I want it for the finals." He got his way and duly won the biggest camel race of the day, but it was the first time that any of us had seen him so competitive. There was determination in his eyes and it made me realise what he must have been like in his racing days.'

Whenever there was snow at Lockinge, Terry towed the children behind the car on toboggans – in particular on an old model known as, 'The Flexible Flyer', which they could steer with their feet. It was great sport – accompanied by plenty of swear words when he stopped the car too quickly. They also used to sledge down the slopes by the farm on old tin trays. Terry really enjoyed the fun, and James vividly remembers those days of being pulled across the fields and up the lanes before rolling down the snowy slopes.

Not only did James enjoy driving the tractors, he helped with repairs to the farm buildings and was brilliant with fencing jobs. Terry made him work hard, but he seemed to enjoy it. From the age of sixteen, James's other interest was motorbikes, but these terrified Terry. He was devastated when James had a bad accident in 2012 and broke his thigh. In earlier years, James also played rugby but once he had damaged a leg on the pitch, this put paid to a potentially good career.

Robert was less interested in machines but was hyperactive and a bit of a daredevil. He loved shooting and fishing. As a child he used to fish for trout on many local rivers and lakes. He was also keen to ride horses, having ridden a pony when he was very young, but he had never done any jumping. I used to give him lessons on a retired event horse, the wonderful Sir Wattie. Robert seemed to have natural balance and saw good strides. Later, in the 1990s, when Charles Cadogan was looking for a home for Rectory Garden, one of his old steeplechasers, I asked him if we could have the horse as a schoolmaster for Robert. He had been trained by Tim Forster and had won some good staying chases under rules. Rectory was a great character and Robert won nine point-to-points on him.

After his point-to-point days, Robert went on a course at the British Racing School in Newmarket, then spent six months working for trainer Nicky Henderson. After that, I gave him a job in my yard for six months before he moved over to his godfather, Nigel Twiston-Davies. Robert won thirty-seven races under National Hunt Rules, firstly as an amateur, and then as a conditional (professional) jockey. He had several wins for our stable too, in particular on Fragrant Rose, a charming mare owned and bred by David Jenks.

Much to Terry's disappointment, however, Robert hung up his boots at an early age and began another career: he embarked on a master saddler's course. He now owns his own business, The Biddlecombe Saddle Company. Robert would have struggled to make it as a fully fledged professional jockey because he had several bad falls and injuries to his wrists. He also lacked his father's drive and dedication. There have been many changes in the racing world since Terry's riding days and Robert saw that he would not be able to make a proper career as a jockey. Nevertheless, he was always a very fit boy and loved running. After giving up race-riding he trained hard for triathlons and, as an amateur, ended up seventh in the Triathlon European Championships in Ireland and fourteenth in the Triathlon World Championships in Budapest. Robert is also an excellent artist and I have two lovely pictures by him in the house. One depicts my favourite gander, thirty-three-year-old Grandad, and the other is a sketch of a duck in the yard.

Terry and his sons did plenty of driving around the fields on the farm, mostly in Terry's old Honda – the very same car in which he had driven me to his parents' house in 1993. This splendid vehicle endured plenty of hardship but always sailed through its MOTs. It was in this car too that Terry accompanied Robert to his first driving test in Newbury. He did have a few lessons from a professional driving instructor, but Terry reckoned that he could do the job just as well. He was never one for spending money unnecessarily. On the morning of the driving test, Terry asked me for a bottle of Tippex. Then he painted the letters 'L' and 'R' on either side of the steering wheel. Robert would now be sure to know which way to go when the examiner asked him to turn left or right. Not surprisingly, he failed his test and it was pronounced void due to unfair outside assistance. Robert has many memories of his father, but above all, he says he misses Terry's sense of humour and infectious laugh. 'He used to come up with joke after joke,' he says. 'Life with him was so much fun.'

Lucy Biddlecombe, Terry's youngest daughter, always loved my dogs. When she was at West Lockinge and aged seven or eight, she would drag my three white Labradors – Alice, Daisy and Caro – into the outside arena, where she put up jumps for them. She spent hours leading them over the poles and thoroughly enjoyed herself – though I doubt whether the enjoyment was mutual. When Lucy was ten, she began having some lessons at a local riding school and Terry decided that she should have a pony of her own. She was a nervous rider to begin with, but we came across a wonderful 12-hand black pony called Meg, and Lucy spent many years of fun with this super little animal. Meg was not the easiest of ponies to ride; she had a mind of her own, a very straight shoulder and a short neck. Sometimes Lucy's friends came to Lockinge to have a ride on her, but they nearly always fell off when Meg put on the brakes. At the time of writing, in 2015, Meg is still alive, aged thirty, and looks great.

Later on, Terry and I found Lucy two horses, which she kept at home with her mother, Ann. It gave Terry enormous pleasure to watch her jump at the Three Counties Show and, on her travels with Ann, she won numerous first prizes at shows around Gloucester. However, like Robert, she never had the killer instinct nor the desire to pursue her career as a showjumper and she now prefers to buy and educate young horses, as well as working at Tweenhills Farm & Stud. One of Lucy's greatest memories was standing beside her father during the runnings of Best Mate's three Cheltenham Gold Cups. Terry used to cling to her and tell her that she was his lucky mascot.

Terry hugely enjoyed seeing James, Robert and Lucy during their childhood days and sharing his life with them. He adored them and he talked to them every week. Sadly, he saw less of his two eldest daughters, Laura and Libba. By the time Terry moved to Lockinge, they were both already established with their successful lives and careers in London.

Nevertheless, he was extremely proud of their achievements, and from time to time they, too, visited us at the farm. Yet it does seem that Terry's relationship with his two elder girls was rather a sad one. They never properly got to know him when they were young – which often happens when parents separate. Later in their lives, Terry went to both of their weddings and thoroughly approved of their husbands, Stephen Vakil and Mike Morrison, although he was bitterly disappointed that he was not allowed to give Libba away at her 2007 wedding in East Meon Church. He believed firmly that fathers should lead their daughters up the aisle, but in Libba's case, the rest of the family obviously thought differently and she was accompanied by her mother. He cried on the way home, it had greatly upset him.

It was a happy occasion in 2013 when Laura married Stephen in The Bingham Hotel in Richmond upon Thames, in Surrey. Despite not being in good health, Terry thoroughly enjoyed himself and there are some lovely photographs. After Terry died, both Libba and Laura wrote to me about him. Although life had been hard for them when they were children, they still loved their father, and I found their letters very moving.

Libba wrote: 'My earliest memory is of Dad trying to make my sister, Laura and me, lunch. We were at his house in Corse Lawn. It was a tuna, sweetcorn and mayo sandwich. I was about five years old. I'd give anything to be have been a fly on the wall, watching him so lovingly trying to feed his two young girls – solo parenting. He had no idea what to do, but if there was any panic, it didn't show. It was the most delicious sandwich I'd ever tasted and I thought he was the coolest Dad ever. And if I'd been that fly, I would have told him.

'Whenever I introduced Dad to a friend, his usual ice-breaking comments had us all falling around, giggling in astonishment. My husband, Mike, remembers the banter well. He also remembers phoning Dad to ask permission for my hand in marriage. After a minute of small talk, Mike nervously announced the real reason for this call. Dad immediately exclaimed, "You should have come to see me, you fucking cunt!" We have recounted this tale many times and most people react with shock and horror, tinged with amusement. I hope Dad's reaction to Mike's proposal was his way of saying that he cared about me. Either way, his shocking outbursts provoked much laughter.

'Mum and Dad divorced when I was two years old, so we never really lived together. I grew up wanting us to be closer, but things got in the way. I often craved his attention, approval and affection, but only saw him a few times a year. My sister, Laura, and I were complete strangers, in awe of him, looking up to him, hero-worshipping him. I was too young to have seen him ride, but I could feel the magic. Seeing how people behaved around him, it was extraordinary. It made us feel all puffed up. "That's our dad!" we'd say. By default, I probably worshipped him too, but not in a "normal-daughter" way. For many complicated reasons we considered that he was incapable, in those days, of being a father.

'Even when he hit rock-bottom in his addiction, his fans or anyone who recognised him only had lovely things to say about him. I feel that I am the only one who can tell you bad things about him. If any other people had a bad story about him, they didn't want to tell it, because he was the "legendary Terry Biddlecombe".

'That didn't stop me trying to make a father of him. I tried to spend time with him and still vied for his attention, but there wasn't a natural stream of conversation and we had many awkward moments and silences. Laura, naturally chatty, could handle these situations, but when it was my turn to speak, I'd rack my brains, thinking of things to say and end up asking the same old questions about horses. We didn't know how to react around each other. We should have been close, but the truth was we didn't know each other. Despite the awkwardness, I deeply loved my dad, and although it was only ever demonstrated in a tuna-and-sweetcorn sandwich, and a tearful farewell at Perth Airport in Australia. I think he loved me too.

'His battle with booze was a tragic test of his strength. His journey to recovery was not only fully supported by my Uncle Tony and Aunty Sandra, but also by my mother, Bridget. It confused the fellow "recoverees" at Farm Place that his ex-wife of many years should be supporting him, but my mum and dad loved each other once, and it was natural that she wanted to help him. Very weirdly, it was the only time I felt part of a normal family: just the four of us. We were all being open and honest about our dad. At times it felt like being on the family holiday we never had. I'm proud of the way he confronted his addiction and tried to change. Helping him through his therapy at Farm Place was certainly an education for a rebellious teenager. It made me rethink my "I can drink eleven pints of lager in one night" mantra. Seeing Dad's recovery was inspirational, but heart-breaking for me. I longed for him to be well again. The outside world was scary for him, but I saw him face his difficulties with courage and determination.

'On his road to recovery it was wonderful to see my complicated and courageous dad nesting down on the farm with Hen. He completely adored her and she made the latter years of his life very happy ones. Almost two years after his death, I still haven't been brave enough to go and see his empty chair at Lockinge. But very soon, between juggling two young children and building a new house, I will grow some of those Biddlecombe balls and go and have a cuppa with Hen.'

Laura also has conflicting memories of Terry. 'For much of my life, and as his eldest child, Dad was a stranger to me and my sister,

Libba. We were brought up single-handedly by my mother, Bridget – Dad's first wife – with occasional visits to Dad at "handovers" from Mum to my wonderful grandmother, Nancy, in a pub halfway between Hampshire and Gloucestershire.

'Dad was a superb-class jockey and at the top of his game, with adoring fans, but incapable – for whatever reason – of demonstrating his love to his two eldest children. Despite a lifetime of effort on my part, I regret not having known him better.

'My first memory of Dad was of sitting on top of his shoulders while he mowed the lawn at The Woodlands at Corse Lawn. My second memory of him, to my mother's horror, was of him feeding me neat mustard when I was about two. Thankfully I love it today and can eat it by the spoonful.

'My happiest memory of Dad was when he asked me to join him at the men's final of Wimbledon; I don't think Hen could attend that year. We sat next to each other at a lunch… and, despite me not knowing anyone at the table, we had great fun and I was proud to say I was Terry's daughter. It was a rare occasion to have him to myself and we chatted and laughed for most of the day. It was magic. That memory will stay with me for ever. I couldn't even tell you who won the final; I was just happy to be spending quality time with Dad.

'Now that he has gone, I can breathe easier and I can stop trying to win his affection. From the few memories I have and countless stories I hear from other people, I can now see him for his brilliance from a distance, and it is no longer painful. I think

Hen, aged three, on her mother's point to point horse, 'Mr Pippin'.

Hen and Ce appear in *The Tatler* with their guinea-pigs in 1957.

Terry, aged 11, show jumping at a local gymkhana.

Terry on his favourite horse, Coral Diver, at Cheltenham, 1972.
Photograph © Bernard Parkin

Tony and Terry at the wedding of their sister, Sue, to Bob Davies in
1970. Photograph © Bernard Parkin

Hen and her
mother at a dance
given by Uncle
Christopher Loyd
at Lockinge in
1965.

Hen's parents,
sister and nephew
William, at a
Cirencester Polo
Match in 1987.

Hen and Terry on the day of their engagement, 1995.

Hen and Terry at their reception at Lockinge Manor in 1995.

Dave Dick and Terry shooting at Stowell Park, 1995.

Terry's photograph of Hen in the Poppy field at Lockinge, 1995.

...m and Celia Vestey with Karshi after he won the Stayers' Hurdle ... 1997. Hen's first Cheltenham Festival Success. Below, Terry ...ngratulating Karshi after the race.

Hen and Terry at Royal
Ascot Races, 1996.

Hen with Queen
Elizabeth, the Queen
Mother, at Hester
Knight's funeral,
November 2001.
Photograph © Bernard
Parkin

of him with his best chum, my wonderful godfather Josh Gifford, getting up to no good. They had lots of fun and laughter and that's how I will remember them both.

'It meant a lot to me when he and Hen came to my wedding in London in 2013. It was another magical day. Despite our unconventional relationship and his absence from my childhood, he was my dad.'

Although Terry had apparently enjoyed many parties in his younger days, he became extremely choosy as he got older. He did not enjoy late nights. When we were training the racehorses and getting up at 5 a.m., we were usually tired out by the evening. We always asked our owners to ring us well before 9 p.m. because after that hour we never answered the telephone until the next morning. Yet there were times when we had to attend special functions connected to our business, and there were times, too, when we went to select lunches or dinner parties. Nevertheless, eating at home in the kitchen or having an early dinner in a local pub were always preferable. If Terry did not want to go out, he made it very clear, especially if it meant meeting up with people he did not want to see or did not know. He told me to refuse many invitations. It was almost as if he were turning into a hermit.

During my years as a trainer, we always gave a Christmas party for our staff and invited a few select jockeys and friends. The parties were held either at the Loyd Lindsay Rooms in Ardington, or at Lains Barn, a converted farm building approximately a mile away. The parties seemed to revolve around Terry and several members of my staff enjoyed organizing strippagrams for him. Terry always reacted superbly and played to his audience, even though his heart must have sunk on several occasions.

On one of these evenings, there was a big fat lump of a girl dressed up in riding clothes. She wore huge baggy jodhpurs, an ill-fitting tight tweed jacket and long, black rubber boots. Terry visibly winced when she sat herself down on his knee and demanded a cuddle – in vain, despite twirling a riding whip and pretending to ride a chair like a horse. At most of the parties, the hired girls were good-looking and had decent figures, and Terry enjoyed covering them in baby oil and shaving foam, while the onlookers wolf-whistled and cheered him on. He entered whole-heartedly into the spirit of the parties and our staff always looked forward to the Christmas festivities.

At home, however, Terry liked his own routine. He was a useless cook and could barely boil an egg, but he was particular about what I gave him to eat. He had some strange tastes; his favourite foods were caviar, jellied eels, oysters and steak tartare. I dislike all these, but fortunately my sister always gave him a pot of caviar at Christmas and he could get pots of jellied eels at the races, especially Plumpton, Newbury and Fontwell, where he was very friendly with Barry Cope, the wonderful man who ran the fish bars, but who sadly died a few years ago. Barry and Terry went back a long way and they always had good chats and reminisced. Terry usually ordered oysters if we were eating out at a fish restaurant. He adored them and if there were six on the menu then he would order twelve – horrible, slimy-looking things. – but they were like nectar to him. He claimed they had aphrodisiacal qualities, though I was never convinced. After a good dinner, Terry usually fell asleep very quickly. As for steak tartare, which I always told Terry looked like a plate of raw dog's meat – he used to get chefs to send the ingredients to our table where they would be specially mixed to order in front of him. To my surprise, I found Terry's own recipe for steak tartare in one of the cookery books on my kitchen shelf. The book is *Seasonal Country Kitchen* by Nikki Rowan-Kedge and Angela Rawson, and they recommend using best-quality fillet steak, which Terry advised should be accompanied by three large glasses of port: 'Vintage or non-vintage, depending on who's paying.' I never saw Terry drink port during the twenty years we were together, but presumably it was a favourite tipple in his younger days.

Despite not being able to cook in the proper sense of the word, Terry did consider himself to be the master of what he called, 'Biddlecombe Mushroom Soup'. It was utterly undrinkable by anybody but himself. Every autumn we had an abundance of wild mushrooms in our fields and Terry picked baskets of them. He didn't mind what age the mushrooms were; some of the older ones were almost black and crawling with maggots. He put a saucepan of water on the stove and added the chopped-up mushrooms, stalks and all, then added milk, pepper, salt, a lump of butter and several spoonfuls of cornflour. The whole lot would be left to simmer for at least an hour and all the maggots and creepy crawlies would rise to the top of the grey-coloured liquid. Once strained, the mixture was then left to set, and it became almost gelatinous – but that didn't bother Terry. He often ate it cold, from a cereal bowl. Unsurprisingly, this recipe does not feature in any of my cookery books, nor have I ever seen this soup-making method recommended on any of the cookery programmes that Terry constantly watched on television. If he had appeared on *Celebrity MasterChef*, I think he would have been thrown out. Fortunately, the wild mushroom season is a short one.

Terry was, on the whole, a very good eater and made up for the many years of dieting during his jockey days. He would poke about in the larder at lunchtime and give himself a plateful of cold meats, cheese and tomatoes, together with pickled onions and piccalilli, but at nights I did the cooking and he ate virtually everything I put in front of him. This was very rewarding, although I did have to be careful what I gave him, in case the food brought on one of his frequent attacks of gout. Herrings, sardines, liver, mackerel, kidneys, asparagus or spinach containing high levels of purine all gave him extreme pain in his joints. Our good friend and neighbour, Chris Brasher, who started the London Marathon and won a gold medal in the 3,000-metre Steeplechase at the 1956 Sydney Olympics, also suffered badly from gout. He and Terry used to compare notes, but neither of them completely avoided unsuitable foods. When Chris and his wife, Shirley, took us out for dinner, both men used to badly suffer the next day.

CHAPTER SEVEN

Training for Success

When it became common knowledge that Terry and I were training horses as a double act, we were flattered when many racing enthusiasts started queuing up to become owners in our yard. We had a considerable number of orders to buy new horses and it was an exciting time for both of us. However, it entailed plenty of extra work – as in most cases we were searching for future stars.

We preferred Irish-bred horses on account of their durability and toughness. It is well known that the Emerald Isle produces outstanding horses, not only for racing but also for showjumping, hunting and eventing. The milder climate in Ireland, together with an abundance of rich grass, has always produced individuals with stronger bones – probably helped by the many essential minerals naturally occurring in the soil. In the National Hunt world, many successful horses have also been bred in Europe, particularly in France and Germany, but there is something about Ireland that gives it the nod over those countries. Horses are bred in Ireland in vast numbers and buyers are spoilt for choice.

In the summers, with our racehorses resting in the paddocks, Terry and I always had more time on our hands, and we often travelled to Irish horse sales. In particular, we enjoyed our visits to the Tattersalls Derby Sale at Fairyhouse every June. This two-day sale always has upwards of 400 horses catalogued, all unraced and usually unbroken. These horses are what is known as National Hunt stores: in other words, mostly three- and four-year-olds, specifically bred for jump racing. They are reared and stored until they are ready to race. Many of the horses we inspected had pedigrees going back to horses Terry rode successfully in the sixties and seventies. We saw some stunning animals.

We loved these sales. It is always fascinating to see so many lovely horses in the same place at the same time. However the days can often be extremely tiring; there is endless walking around on concrete to assess the entrants and one has to concentrate at all times. Nevertheless they provide a great opportunity to meet up with breeders, vendors, fellow trainers and other horse racing enthusiasts. We learnt plenty from attending auctions. Over the years we had a number of excellent journeys to Ireland and managed to purchase some good-looking, sensibly priced individuals that won decent races for us at West Lockinge Farm.

Unbroken horses, however, do have their drawbacks and, of course, it takes longer to get them ready for a racecourse. Many are excessively overweight because the vendors have crammed them with extra food so that they look more impressive to buyers. This is not good for their development. Too much fat is difficult to get rid of and means that the horses cannot be hurried. The other drawback of National Hunt horse sales is that one cannot see the horses jump.

Terry and I always liked to assess jumping ability, since good jumpers have obvious advantages both in hurdle races and steeplechases. Jumping is the name of the game. Most horses can be taught to jump, but the ones with natural talent from an early age often prove to be the best. At non-thoroughbred sales where young sport horses are presented there are always facilities for loose jumping, which is a bonus to vendors and buyers alike. Despite enjoying our visits to Fairyhouse and also to the sales at Goffs in Kill, close to the town of Naas in Co. Kildare, Terry and I gradually found that we preferred buying horses either out of point-to-points, or else from certain individuals at their own establishments. Under these conditions we could view horses contesting races, or else watch them being ridden on home gallops or loose jumping. For this reason, our annual visits to horse sales gradually petered out as we acquired more contacts in Ireland's country areas.

Our excursions to the Irish point-to-points were always memorable. We were usually guided by a very good friend of ours, Michael Moore. The Moore family is well-connected in the horse world and under the banner of Ballincurrig Stud produces many young horses for clients at the major sales in Ireland. In the 1990s, Terry introduced Michael to Terry Court of Brightwells, and for many years Michael had an extremely prominent role within the sales company. He recruited some of the top point-to-point horses from the Emerald Isle and from Northern Ireland for the Cheltenham sales.

On point-to-point days we often flew to Cork on a Sunday morning. It fitted in well with racing in the UK because there were seldom many race meetings at home on Sundays. We usually stayed in a lovely hotel in Co. Cork called Ballymaloe House, near Ballycotton Bay. The Ballymaloe Cookery School is well known throughout the world and the Allen family has made it one of the most sought-after places to learn about cooking at the top level. Darina and Rachel Allen, who often make appearances on television and have written numerous cookery books, have been called the food ambassadors of Ireland. Darina is an amazing person, and her mother-in-law, Myrtle Allen, who started it all with her husband, Ivan, is a special lady. Terry admired her hugely and was always on his best behaviour in her presence. He enjoyed talking to her.

Whenever we travelled to the Irish point-to-points, Michael did plenty of homework beforehand and scrutinised the pedigrees of the four- and five-year-olds entered in the maiden races. He knew exactly who trained the horses and how they had been prepared. He also introduced us to many interesting people. At the point-to-points, Terry and I first looked at all the horses in the paddock, then watched them carefully in their races.

Terry had an amazing talent for spotting potential stars. It was at Carrigtwohill point-to-point in 1998 that he picked out Lord Noelie as a raw five-year-old. The horse did not jump particularly well, nor did it win, but Terry considered him exceptionally promising because of the way he galloped and stayed on at the end of the race. The next day we visited the stables belonging to his owner, Louis Archdeacon. Noelie was not an impressive horse to look at; indeed, he appeared extremely lean and hungry, but I agreed with Terry there was something one had to like. He had good forelegs, a lovely head and he was a straight, light mover. This horse went on to win the Sun Alliance Chase at the Cheltenham Festival in 2000, having been bought by a most enthusiastic syndicate, Executive Racing. He gave us some memorable days on the racecourses in England.

Michael Moore has many memories of Terry and always tells a certain story about him. 'Hen and Terry had flown over for a local point-to-point one Sunday morning. I received my normal phone call from Hen to say that they had landed at the airport and were setting off in their hired car. I remember being worried that the journey seemed to be taking them so long. I was waiting at the entrance to the horsebox park for them to arrive. Finally, they both turned up with broad smiles on their faces. Terry had found himself in a major spot of bother when a call of nature meant that he urgently needed a gent's lavatory. They had been travelling down a country road with only very few houses in sight when, rounding a corner, they came across a solitary pub.

'However, it was only ten o'clock on a Sunday morning. The pub was closed and the owners in bed. This tested Terry's patience to the limit. He knocked on the door and the windows, then rang the bell. Eventually, a frail old lady appeared at the door. On being asked, without preamble, where the "shithouse" was situated, she nearly fell down in shock. Luckily Terry's charm won the day. From then on all the directions that I gave to Hen for the point-to-points in the Cork area focused around "Terry's shithouse" – it went down in my family's folklore. Every time I think of Terry, I always have a smile. It was a privilege to have known him.'

We both loved the Irish point-to-points. I used to worry about losing Terry in the crowds because he never had a mobile phone, but luckily he was easy to spot in his emerald green Puffa jacket. It carried the Channel 4 logo, and had been given to him by Jim McGrath. Terry was usually at some strategic spot watching the horses race, or having a small wager with the bookies. He loved getting a good price on a horse he fancied. He went round with his pocket full of euros, but he never dared risk more than ten euros per race. He took an amazing amount of exercise on those days, often climbing fences to watch the horses race past him. Sometimes he hurt himself by jumping over ditches or over gates and could barely walk afterwards. I well remember a day at Kildorrery point-to-point, close to Fermoy, in Co. Cork, when his back gave out completely and he was doubled up in pain. Michael Moore and I had one hell of a job getting him back to my hired fourtrack vehicle. It was even worse the next day when I borrowed a wheelchair at Cork Airport. He gave orders to everybody and behaved like a naughty child.

On another occasion, at a point-to-point in Co. Waterford, the boot of a car shut on Terry's head. We had been enjoying one of Mrs Moore's famous picnics – smoked salmon sandwiches and chocolate éclairs – when suddenly the tailgate of the car collapsed. Terry was in considerable pain afterwards and reckoned that he had put his neck out. At that time, we were staying with Enda Bolger for the night and he suggested that his neighbour, Fran Stone, should come and look at Terry's injuries. As Fran remembers, 'I got an emergency call from Enda, who used to call me "The Medicine Woman", to go down asap that evening to manipulate Terry into place. He was disappointed that I didn't need him to undress. However, his flirting words were stopped abruptly when I crunched the first disc back into place. Several choice expletives followed, interspaced with soft pleas not to hurt him. Enda and company, myself included, were doubled up with laughter, as the whole operation was conducted on the sitting room carpet – the best floor show Terry ever gave! Thankfully, he was cured and was able to enjoy the rest of that particular Irish stay. He even enquired whether I could return the following day to give him a massage.'

It was in late February 1999 that Terry and I had our most memorable visit to a point-to-point. It was the West Waterford point-to-point at Lismore and it was there that we spotted our future stable star, Best Mate, for the first time. The point-to-point is staged in a most attractive part of Ireland, in the grounds of Lismore Castle, on the banks of the Blackwater River, which is famous for salmon fishing in the spring and summer. It was a typical Irish winter's day: wet, grey and dreary. The car parks were virtually unusable and hundreds of cars were parked down side roads and avenues to avoid the mud. The opening race was all-important, because it was for maiden four-year olds – horses that had never won before. Despite the atrocious conditions, sixteen of them had been declared.

The unsuspecting youngsters, already saddled up, were led across a muddy grass field from the horsebox park to a roped-off area beside the secretary's tent. This was the parade ring, and especially keen spectators gathered round in the pouring rain to look at the horses. Terry and I stood at the entrance to this pen and watched every horse go by, trying to assess them as possible future stars, but it wasn't easy under those dreadful conditions.

As the horses walked round and round, one of them stood out: a 16.3-hand bay gelding called Best Mate. He seemed unperturbed by the rain and marched through the mud with his head held high. Terry spotted him at once. He loved his alert manner and the athletic way in which he moved. Best Mate came from the Tom Costello yard in Co. Clare. We had heard a lot about these Costello horses, but had never ventured to Tom's establishment. What we did know, however, was that he had already been responsible for five Cheltenham Gold Cup winners and that another famous horse, Florida Pearl, had made a winning debut in the four-year old maiden race at Lismore in 1996. This point-to-point track was notorious for producing good horses and so was Tom Costello.

As the horses made their way to the start we watched them canter across the heavy ground to a line of trees alongside the estate wall. Here they walked in a big circle before being lined up for the off. Many of the runners looked green and unsure of themselves. Several were barely four years old. Terry was impressed by the fact that Best Mate made his way sensibly to the start. He looked well-balanced and held himself correctly with an arched neck and his head close to the ground.

Terry watched him carefully from the moment the tapes went up until he was pulled up three fences from home, despite still being full of running. The horse had jumped superbly and Terry liked everything that he saw. We did not buy Best Mate that day because he was not for sale – his owners wanted him to win a race before putting him on the market – but I put him in my notebook and we waited until he raced again a few weeks later. On that occasion, he won a four-year old maiden race at Tuam in Co. Galway, but it was only a two-horse affair and the other runner was a mare. It would have been disappointing if he had been beaten.

We did not see our future champion in that second race, but fortunately we were at another point-to-point in Ireland the same weekend, which meant that we could drive to Tom Costello's yard on the Monday morning. The narrow and winding approach to his house, Fenloe, runs beside the shores of a strikingly beautiful lake and nature reserve, where various species of wildlife are always to be seen. The entrance to Fenloe overlooks the lake, and as we drove through the gateway and up the short drive, we were immediately impressed by the extreme tidiness of it all. The tarmac roadway was edged by well-kept grass verges. The fields, surrounded by stone walls or wooden railings, were immaculate. Several groups of part-Charolais beef cattle – all in perfect condition – grazed contentedly as we passed by. There were superb views across these fields to the woods and hills beyond. Magnificent old trees completed a scene that was idyllic in every way. As we were to learn later, attention to detail was one of the hallmarks of Tom's establishment.

The man himself was waiting on the steps of his house as we drove up to the front door. He was intently watching our arrival. Terry parked the car facing away from the house. He always did this wherever we went so that we could make a quick exit if we did not like the horses we had come to see. As it turned out, Terry could have parked the car anywhere that Monday morning. We saw two horses in the stable yard. Both of them had won their point-to-points. One, of course, was Best Mate, but we also looked at another potential superstar, called Be My Manager. We loved them both and after spending a considerable amount of time discussing their special qualities, we put our names down for the pair. The only fly in the ointment was that we had to find owners within the next forty-eight hours. People had constantly been ringing Tom up, trying to buy them and he did not particularly want to sell both horses to the same trainer. Be My Manager was the best horse on paper and was listed at the top of the Irish point-to-point form book, Formcard. Best Mate was not even mentioned in the top ten. But we couldn't leave him behind.

It is never easy to find the right owners at the right time, but these two four-year-olds at Tom Costello's looked exceptional. We longed to have both of them in our yard. By Tuesday morning we had talked to one of our most loyal and straightforward owners, Charles Cadogan, and although the price was high, he agreed to buy Be My Manager. We were delighted with the news. But we had to ask Tom to wait another forty-eight hours in order to persuade a second owner to take a look at Best Mate. At this point, fate came to the rescue, because we decided to tell Jim Lewis about Best Mate. I had trained Jim's first winner at Wincanton in 1989; the horse was called Pearl Prospect. I knew Jim liked French-bred horses; in fact, he had just sent us a new horse from France called Edredon Bleu. By a lucky coincidence, Best Mate's pedigree was French, not Irish.

I remember sending a fax message to Jim (there were no emails in those days) and I wrote, 'Dear Jim, Terry and I have just seen the horse of our dreams. He is in Ireland but he is French-bred.' Amazingly, Jim agreed, at once, to travel to Ireland to see the horse. On 29 March 1999, we met Jim and his wife, Valerie, at Heathrow Airport and the four of us flew together to Shannon. Tom Costello met us at the airport and within half an hour we were once more walking up to the front door at Fenloe. We did not

103

spend long in the house and neither Terry nor I dared to breathe as we followed Tom up his garden path to the yard. Jim and Valerie caught their first glimpse of their future star as Best Mate walked out of his stable, across the cobbles and onto the smooth tarmac. He stood to attention in the sunshine, looking superb, before being led through sliding doors into a huge indoor school.

Along the sides of this rectangular building were two jumps. One of these comprised timber poles balanced on large oil barrels, and the other one was a big plastic steeplechase fence – it was over four feet high. I remember that we all stood in the middle of the enclosure as Best Mate was let loose. He cantered round and round the outside, bucking and squealing on the soft, sandy surface, before jumping the two obstacles correctly every time. He never made the slightest mistake and looked a supreme athlete. Jim was impressed.

Later, when we returned to the house, Tom took his prospective buyer into a small room. Ten minutes later, they emerged with smiles on their faces: they had shaken hands and agreed on a price. Jim told us later that we could have the horse to train. What a day. The fairy story had begun.

After our introduction to the Costello family in 1999 and the buying of Best Mate, we continued to forge excellent links with Tom and his five sons. On many occasions during the next ten years, we flew over to Shannon Airport and looked at other horses they were offering for sale. We had some memorable visits. Racing Demon, Calgary Bay and Somersby confirmed the Costello skills in producing National Hunt horses to race at the top level. The Costello boys have now produced eight Cheltenham Gold Cup winners, including The Thinker, Cool Ground, Imperial Call and Midnight Court. They have a tried-and-tested system, buying their horses as foals or yearlings before teaching them to jump as two-year-olds. Terry and I had huge respect for Tom Senior, who, sadly, died in 2009, and we continued to do business with the family in the ensuing years. Tom Junior and brothers John, Dermot, Adrian and Tony have sent some top horses over to West Lockinge Farm. When I stopped training in 2012, many of my former owners wanted to go on buying horses from the family.

The beauty of the Costello horses was that they had been well broken and were unspoilt. Also, there was very little walking for Terry and it was an easy journey to Shannon. We were usually collected from the airport, which is only fifteen minutes from the Costello home town of Newmarket on Fergus. There was one occasion, however, when we were supposed to be travelling over to Co. Clare with a very good owner, Ann Humphries, but we never arrived at our destination. After boarding the plane at Heathrow and sitting down in his seat by the window, Terry blacked out. I thought he had died, because I could not get a glimmer of movement from him. He slumped over towards me and my own heart almost stopped beating. Paramedics were called. Take-off had to be delayed. Fortunately, we had no baggage in the hold.

Terry was carried out of the aeroplane on a stretcher to a waiting ambulance on the tarmac. He had regained consciousness but was extremely confused. Ann and I followed him down the steps. It was frightening.

We were sent back through the terminal to collect our vehicles from the car parks and eventually joined Terry in the hospital at Hillingdon, by which time he was giving out to everybody and was extremely perky. We stayed at the hospital all day and Terry had numerous tests. Eventually he was diagnosed as having low blood pressure and dehydration. Poor Ann; she had travelled a long way from Upton-on-Severn and we never did get to see any horses in Ireland. I drove Terry home in the evening and put him to bed. I insisted that he kept quiet, but he appeared normal the next morning.

Ann's travels with us seemed doomed. A few years earlier she had accompanied us to the Tattersalls Derby Sale at Fairyhouse, but on that occasion Terry had collapsed in agony on the floor of the hotel with gallstones. After that, he had his gall bladder removed. How glad I was that, the year before, we had been lucky enough to find Ann a good mare in Co. Tipperary called Hati Roy who was owned by Elizabeth Kennedy and had won a point-to-point in Wexford. She later won several good races in England, including a chase at Cheltenham in October 2000, which fulfilled one of Ann's greatest ambitions.

———

Terry and I also enjoyed viewing point-to-point horses at Wilson Dennison's home in Northern Ireland and managed to select some useful recruits from his beautiful estate at Loughanmore in Co. Antrim, where we could see them jumping. Wilson became a great friend of ours; assisted by the successful trainer Ian Ferguson, he buys some lovely young horses from the major sales. Over the years Wilson has been responsible for many high-class winners on either side of the Irish Sea, including Bindaree, who won the Grand National in 2002. Coincidentally, he bought Bindaree from Tom Costello as a yearling.

Terry had a wonderful eye for a horse. He was a natural judge and I learned plenty from watching him look at prospective purchases. He always insisted that horses should have strong hindquarters and be athletic individuals. He liked to watch them move from their shoulders as well as from behind. He maintained that if horses were tight behind their elbows, they would not bring their forelegs forward with a good jumping technique. Movement is all-important, and a poor jumper will not win big races.

While we were training, most of our horses came to us from Ireland, with the exception of Edredon Bleu, Foly Pleasant and Impek, all of which were sent over to us from France. We did visit a few yards over there and enjoyed our French trips, but we were less successful with our own purchases from that country. This was mostly because we were way down the list of renowned bloodstock agent Anthony Bromley – and because we did not have enough money to spend. Anthony has done exceptionally well with the

French horses he has found for trainers and our visits with him to Auteuil and Enghein racecourses were always fascinating, even if many of the horses we wanted were well out of our price range.

Occasionally we bought English horses, either owner-bred individuals or ex-flat racers from the Tattersalls October Horses in Training sales. It was at those Newmarket sales in 1991 that I first linked up with Sir Martin Broughton, who at that time was head of British American Tobacco. He later became chairman of the British Horseracing Board as well as chairman of British Airways. I remember telling him that it was important to buy an individual with a big, bold eye, and no white showing around the edge. I'm not a fan of horses whose eyes show a lot of white, as they are quite often ungenuine – but of course, there are always exceptions to the rule.

That autumn we came home empty-handed from Newmarket, but Martin was still anxious to find a future steeplechaser. Three weeks later, a horse arrived at West Lockinge Farm from Mick Easterby's yard in Yorkshire with a 'For Sale' label on it. I liked it straight away and it had run well in a novice hurdle at Wetherby with Richard Dunwoody. It was not ridiculously expensive and I advised Martin to buy this horse. The only downside was that the horse had two white eyes. When the Broughton family arrived at the farm to view their possible purchase, I did feel somewhat embarrassed, especially after the lecture I had given to Martin at the sales on horses' eyes.

The horse in question was Easthorpe, and he turned out to be very lucky. He won fifteen steeplechases and over £100,000 in prize money in the Broughton colours – red with green sleeves and a green Cross of Lorraine. He became a yard favourite, and both Terry and I experienced a long, happy relationship with Martin and his wife, Jocelyn, as well as with Martin's twin brother, Stephen, and some lovely partners. All in all, I trained fifty-four winners for them from 318 runners, which represents a high win-to-run ratio and, despite some health problems with a few of their horses in later years, I never remember a cross word between any of us.

My phobia about white eyes was not without foundation, however, because although he won numerous races, Easthorpe was a crafty horse and never exerted himself unless he wore a pair of blinkers to make him concentrate. He would, on many occasions, show signs of a quirky temperament. Nowadays, the Broughton family have a number of top-class horses in training with Jonjo O'Neill and Paul Nicholls. Tarquin de Seuil won at the Cheltenham Festival in 2014 and Dodging Bullets won the Tingle Creek Chase at Sandown, plus the Queen Mother Champion Chase at Cheltenham in the 2014–15 season. I am proud to have been their first trainer and to have set them on the road to success.

From 1994 until the beginning of 2012, Terry and I managed to send out over 700 winners from West Locking Farm. But racing is a great leveller, and events did not always go right. We had plenty of disappointments, often linked with tragedies, but then we just had to get a grip on ourselves and keep positive. It was a big advantage for me to have Terry at my side. His advice was invaluable and his knowledge of racing priceless. We had daily discussions about the horses and the ways in which we were training them. They were all different. Certain individuals needed a lot of work, others did not. Some horses were hugely competitive at home, while others were laid-back and took longer to get motivated.

We found that the best horses on a racecourse were not necessarily the most exciting ones to watch work at home. In fact, Terry and I loved the relaxed, almost lazy individuals because they expended far less energy and did just enough on the gallops to keep fit. Races can easily be lost at home. Many horses sweat up and worry or try too hard in their work and overexert themselves when it is not necessary. Our star horses would have made many flat-race trainers tear their hair out. They would have despaired at the sight of them working on their gallops and at their inability to quicken and overtake their workmates.

We never did a great deal with our jumpers at the farm, we often travelled to away gallops for work; we liked to keep them fresh and enthusiastic. We tried hard to keep the condition on the horses we trained and maintain strong, muscular necks and backs with rounded hindquarters. I personally organised the feeding and I studied every horse as an individual. I always thought Fulke Walwyn was a master, with the training of his big, strong three-mile chasers. They always had fantastic back ends on them, and they almost looked like show horses. Terry said that Fred Rimell's horses were the same. One only needs to look at how many top steeplechasers these two trainers produced – Cheltenham Gold Cups and Grand Nationals aplenty – to see what superb trainers they were.

Our horses were rarely tested on the gallops, and when we worked them, they mostly went in pairs, head to head. We never allowed one horse to finish in front of its companion for fear of disappointing the slower one. Terry used to say that the horses should never come off the bridle and should enjoy what they were doing. The work riders were not allowed to use whips, even though they often carried them, in order to keep their horses straight, or to threaten the exceptionally lazy ones.

The horses cantered every day, but often in fields and beside the woods. They would exercise in groups or pairs but never in a string. We liked them to steadily climb the hills, in order to build up muscle. They only worked hard once or twice a week. They say that you cannot get a horse fitter than fit, and it is absolutely true. It is all too easy to send a horse over the top.

I remember one year, as Cheltenham approached, we took our would-be runners to Peter Cundell's gallops near Compton. They worked strongly for a mile and a half on the beautiful old downland turf, but blew hard afterwards. They had done too much, and when we raced them at the festival, they were flat. After that, we did all our serious work at least ten days before Cheltenham and other big meetings, then kept the horses fresh with short, sharp canters. I read Seb and Peter Coe's book, *Running for Fitness*, where I learned that the top athletes do not overstress themselves close to big races. They conserve energy.

We never used half-tree saddles because we thought they gave the jumpers sore backs, and every horse had its own bridle plus a suitable bit. Terry used to say that I worried too much about the bitting and all horses should go in plain snaffle bridles, but I disagreed with him. Horses' mouths come in different shapes and they need to be comfortable and happy in their work. I have a collection of over 200 different bits in my attic. I still buy new ones, especially at the big horse shows. Whenever I came back from a show with a new bit, Terry went mad. He hated me spending money on what he called unnecessary items, but buying new tack has always been one of my weaknesses. People often ask me for the loan of a special bit and I am more than happy to help them. When it came to racing, our horses mostly wore plain metal snaffles or rubber or plastic bits – it depended on the individual.

In the 1980s, whenever American three-day event world champion Bruce Davidson came to England, he kept his horses in Lockinge. He would get them fit on our gallops and up the surrounding hills. I used to think his horses looked fat, but in reality they were superbly fit and had strong, hard muscles for endurance purposes. They were clear in their wind and seldom blew hard, even after several hours of work. I admired these horses and often thought about his training methods. Perhaps watching Bruce training is what persuaded me that our racehorses should do flat work in the arena or indoor school between their work days. It helped to develop extra muscle along their backs and necklines.

At the races, Terry and I prided ourselves on how our horses looked in the paddock. People used to call them typical Henrietta Knight horses. The way we trained them and the way we fed them certainly paid dividends. They may have looked big and round but they were fit and hard. Our horses won many races first time out in a season and kept their condition right through until April or May.

A. P. McCoy did blame me once for not having Edredon Bleu one hundred per cent fit when he was beaten at Sandown six weeks before he won the Queen Mother Champion Chase in 2000, but it was Cheltenham we were training him for, and we wanted to keep a bit left in the tank.

We fed plenty of good oats and the best possible hay. The horses enjoyed many hours turned out in the paddocks, so that they were happy and relaxed. We never weighed them but we did take blood tests to check for any muscle-enzyme problems. We also had their backs regularly looked at. In later years, Simon Thomas, the ex-Welsh Rugby player, did a great job with his muscle massages.

Mervyn Richings was our farrier during all the years that I trained. I have always believed that correct shoeing is essential and that unless horses' feet are properly balanced they will be more susceptible to injury. After all, athletes have specific footwear for their sporting activities and their shoes are designed to help their muscles and ligaments work correctly when they run. If horses' feet get too long, there is more strain on the back tendons, and these structures are especially vulnerable in jumpers when they land steeply over a fence. I often look at other peoples' horses at the races when they walk around the paddock and am appalled by the degree of bad farriery and ill-shaped hooves. Mervyn's wife, Angela, reminds me that, 'Mervyn was farrier for Henrietta and her mother, Hester, for 50 years, and was usually in the yard most days. He was very much part of the West Lockinge team – a long service. He had followed Terry's career in earlier years before he came to Lockinge. Terry always pulled up in the yard in his vehicle, arm resting on the door to have a chat. He told Mervyn how the horses were working or running and talked about certain individuals with problem feet. As well he loved talking about shooting and fishing, as both he and Mervyn had the same interests. Of course, the conversation would usually end up with a crude joke but that was Terry!'

Mervyn remembers that on one occasion Terry asked him to cut a hole in the roof of an old VW Golf so that he could go rabbit shooting at night, saying Hen would be his driver. He said it was 'good fun!' Mervyn recalls that in later years, when Terry needed to use a stick, he presented him with one he had made using an antler and a crab-apple wood shank. Terry treasured this stick and I still closely guard it in the house. It became part of Terry and everybody admired it.

Certain horses and races stick in my mind from our early training days. In the early nineties we had some memorable wins with Lackendara: the pint-sized pony by Monksfield who was barely 15 hands, but had the heart of a lion. He thrilled us with his two-mile steeplechase wins round the grade-one tracks at Ascot and Kempton. He had a special partnership with Jamie Osborne and always raced at great speed. Watching him was nerve-racking but he was both quick and accurate. Lackendara was owned by an extremely enthusiastic syndicate headed by Malcolm Kimmins, whom Terry had known for many years. Terry rode Zellaman for him, trained by Fulke Walwyn, to win at Kempton in 1974. Afterwards he suffered a severe bout of stomach cramp due to excessive dieting. Malcolm always remembers that day.

Other owners included Anne and Richard Lavelle – trainer Emma's parents. I used to buy my white Labrador dogs from Anne; she is a noted breeder and has judged at Crufts. In his working days, Richard was a much sought-after Harley Street ENT specialist, but he would still lower himself to sort out Terry, who often went semi-deaf from too much time out shooting. On one occasion we visited the Lavelles' house near Ascot and Richard syringed Terry's ears into a large dog bowl – or it may have been a pudding basin – while I inspected a new litter of puppies in the stables. Terry adored Anne and teased her mercilessly. Fortunately, she gave back as good as she got.

Another special horse that we trained in our formative years was Edimbourg by Top Ville, which won nine races, having come to us as a sour flat horse, with just a handful of poor runs over hurdles. He had a very low handicap rating and we were able to take advantage of this, gradually working him up through the grades. He was a real character and had plenty of problems. It was a challenge first of all to keep the weight on him and secondly to keep him sweet. We hardly ever worked him at home. He needed humouring, not bullying. He had experienced plenty of tough times in his early years.

Edimbourg was owned by Iva Winton, an American lady who was married to Harold Winton, another loyal owner. Over the years, Harold had numerous horses with us, including shares in Stompin, Full of Oats, and Yes Man. (Another partner in Yes Man was Aziz, who owns the quality Indian restaurant of that name in Oxford.)

Harold was a great enthusiast but also a gambler. He invariably lost more money than he ever made. Terry had known him during his riding days and was surprised to meet him again one day at Hereford Races, when Edimbourg raced and won. Later, Harold sponsored several races at Exeter in the 1990s and on three occasions he asked the racecourse to put on the Henrietta Knight Birthday Handicap Hurdle in December. He loved his involvement and I always tried to find a horse to win this race. We had some excellent celebrations when our plans worked out, including one day at Exeter in 1994 when, after saddling three winners, I was presented with a huge surprise birthday cake.

Full of Oats was a good servant to the yard and won us five steeplechases, including a couple of big races at Warwick with Jim Culloty in 1995 and 1996. He was usually a good jumper and stayed extreme distances, even though he was painfully slow at home. He was a laid-back horse and, on occasion, had lapses in concentration. In the Grand National in 1997, he fell at the first fence. This was the year of the bomb scare, when the race was rerun on the Monday afterwards. Yet the horse redeemed himself in 1998 by finishing fourth in the Irish National. Terry had volunteered to fly over to saddle him at Fairyhouse, but I forgot that he never bothered with credit cards; when he arrived at the Avis desk to pick up his booked car, the firm would not allow him to take it. There were frantic telephone calls between the two of us while Terry remained at Dublin Airport, but not even his charm worked at the hire-car desk, as there were no girls to chat up. Eventually a good friend of ours drove to meet him and lent him extra money.

I'll never know how an experienced and well-travelled ex-champion jockey could get himself into such trouble whenever he ventured away on his own from West Lockinge Farm. As always, he had refused to take his mobile phone with him. I used to tell him that he was hopelessly disorganised, but nothing ever bothered him and he went on pretending that nothing untoward had happened. He always treated his misadventures as jokes and enjoyed talking about them afterwards.

Before the Cheltenham Festival each March, Andrew Coonan, the respected Irish racing solicitor, would come and stay with us. He rode as an amateur in the nineties and had been recommended to me by Valerie Cooper – wife of the famous bloodstock agent Tom – as a suitable jockey for my brother-in-law Sam Vestey's horse, which was running in the Kim Muir steeplechase for amateur riders. Andrew remembers the occasion all too clearly:

'The first of my very many visits to Hen and Terry at West Lockinge was in 1995. It was the Monday evening before the Cheltenham Festival and I had been asked to ride Bishop's Island in the Kim Muir Chase. In those days the race was run on the Tuesday.

'I jumped the horse over a couple of fences the next morning, with Terry and Yogi Breisner watching. This was an experience in itself! He was a horse with a history of poor jumping, but until he made a howler at the top of the hill, after which I pulled him up, he jumped surprisingly well at Cheltenham.

'I was expecting to go home that night but Hen very kindly asked me if I would like to stay an extra day – an offer I keenly accepted, since the Monday night had proved most convivial, with just the three of us sitting around the kitchen table eating steaks and me in awe of "The Bear", as I called Terry.

'Despite the pressures of the festival, the Tuesday evening turned out to be even more fun and, as it progressed, with again just the three of us, I became ever more loquacious. Hen was as gracious as ever, filling up my glass with red wine and reminding me that I'd done a wonderful job on her brother-in-law's horse, but I realised that I had told the story just one time too many, when The Bear looked at me and said, in that inimitable growling voice of his, "You're some cunt. You're the only fucker I have ever heard getting praised for giving a horse a cunt of a ride and pulling it up around Cheltenham. I am going to bed." I loved The Bear for that. He always said what others were thinking and often the consequences were shocking or hilarious – usually both.'

Encouraged by our good start as joint trainers, and excited by the many new horses we had managed to buy for our owners, Terry and I continued to look forward to our future training years. Racing in the nineties was only the beginning. We had our sights set on greater achievements. More Cheltenham Festival wins were our prime goals, especially after Karshi had won the Stayers' Hurdle in 1997. But it was Edredon Bleu and Best Mate that changed our lives out of all recognition, eventually turning even the most fanciful dreams into reality.

CHAPTER EIGHT

Holidays

After the wedding that never was, and our reception party in July 1995, Terry and I did not take any special holiday. We decided that a honeymoon would have been inappropriate but, over the years, we did enjoy many breaks abroad – mostly during the summer months when life at home was quieter and the horses that we trained were resting.

Days spent away with Terry were special experiences. We had adventures and laughs, coupled with many hours of unparalleled happiness. Away from home and without the continual disturbances of the training yard it was far easier to relax and chill out; the day-to-day stress factor was removed and we had far fewer differences of opinion. We could rest up and recharge our batteries in preparation for the busy winter racing months ahead.

Our first summers away were usually in Italy. It was, and still is, one of my favourite countries. We both appreciated its beauty, its food and its atmosphere. We never travelled to the same place twice but covered plenty of ground and stayed in some lovely hotels. Places that we visited included the Italian lakes, Positano, Portofino, Sorrento and Venice, plus Taormina in Sicily, where Terry was fascinated by the constant volcanic eruptions of Mount Etna.

Our holiday in Lake Como in 1997 was particularly enjoyable and memorable. We stayed for ten days in a beautiful hotel in Bellagio: the Grand Hotel Villa Serbelloni. It was there that Terry decided to take me out in a boat into the middle of Lake Como. He told me he had done plenty of rowing when he was younger, although I had my doubts. As the weather was extremely hot, Terry insisted on taking off all his clothes while we were in the boat. This wasn't particularly unusual – he often seized the opportunity to strip off when it was hot and sunny – but I was horrified when he steered our little boat close to a huge vessel brimming with tourists. I am sure many of the passengers were amazed by the sight. Apart from this incident, we didn't encounter much traffic on the lake and it was surprisingly calm and peaceful. Terry wanted me to take off all my clothes as well, but I was far too shy, although he did remove my bikini top. I certainly didn't want to have sex in an Italian rowing boat in the middle of a lake, which was another of his bright ideas. It was a huge relief to me when we finally arrived back at the hotel and he redressed before disembarking.

Venice provided us with another memorable holiday. Terry was fascinated by the city but not that keen on viewing the interiors of many churches. He looked inside a few of the most famous ones, but reckoned that when he had seen one, he had seen them all. However, he was struck by the beauty of St Mark's Basilica and the amazing statues of the four bronze horses. We took home a huge photographic print of these horses and it is now framed and hanging on the wall on the staircase at West Lockinge farm. He was also intrigued by the prisons close to the Bridge of Sighs and couldn't believe that prisoners had managed to stay alive in such dark, dingy and miserable little cells. They looked like torture chambers.

During one summer, a most generous owner, Val McCalla, treated Terry and me to a few days in Paris. I had spent four months there when I was sixteen, close to the Arc de Triomphe, in order to improve my French. During Terry's heyday, he had apparently enjoyed the company of a rich Parisian girlfriend, so neither of us were strangers to this amazing city. But when I suggested we make a visit to the Musée d'Orsay to look at the Impressionist paintings, there was a definite lack of enthusiasm. Surprisingly, however, Terry thoroughly enjoyed the tour of the gallery, and on our return to Lockinge decided that he would produce his own version of Claude Monet's famous poppy field – the *champs de coquelicots*.

It was a hot summer's day and we went for a drive in my old Subaru up the lane at the back of the farm. Terry was at the wheel. From the top of our gallops, he had spotted a cornfield, red with poppies, on the Lockinge Estate close to the point-to-point course. Terry decided to shock me. We drew level with the poppy field and he picked up my camera from the back seat of the car. Then he asked me to walk into the middle of the field and strip off from the waist upwards. Doubled up with laughter, he photographed me, semi-naked among the poppies. The resultant pictures were hilarious, and Terry kept saying, 'Who needs Monet when I can create my own version of his painting?' Sheepishly and with some embarrassment, I took the film to be developed at Boots in Wantage. On collection of the photographs, it was a relief to find that there were no adverse comments. I have kept the pictures well hidden in a special drawer ever since.

After a number of enjoyable holidays in Italy during the 1990s, we then switched to Ireland for our summer breaks, due to a deterioration in Terry's health. In the late nineties he had suffered a series of heart fibrillations and had been prescribed warfarin. He found that one of the side effects of this drug was that he could no longer enjoy the hot sun. His body overheated and he felt claustrophobic. It is never too hot in Ireland and many beautiful places there are totally unconnected with horses. Terry always enjoyed fishing and pottering around the countryside. He also fully appreciated the breathtaking scenery at our chosen destinations.

In the summer of 1990, after a tiring few days at the Tattersalls Derby Sale, we travelled at the end of June to Sheen Falls Hotel in Co. Kerry. It is a fantastic hotel, overlooking the Sheen Waterfalls in Kenmare. We much enjoyed our days there and dined out at a number of little restaurants in the town, but it was the fishing

Terry most enjoyed. Fortunately the hotel staff were extremely tolerant of his 'unusual methods'.

It was always tantalizing to look over the bridge on the road beside the hotel and see large numbers of salmon lying on the gravel bed beneath, but although these fish ventured down the river, they proved extremely difficult to lure onto fishing lines. Terry would stand on the riverbank with his rod and cast into the water. He attached purple and red dried prawns to his hooks but the fish wouldn't take a bite. On one occasion, in desperation he added sausages, chunks of bacon and pieces of bread, but still no joy.

I remember him hurling his line into the river and accidently letting it go. Everything became tangled in an overhanging tree branch, but Terry was unperturbed. He went back to our hotel room and brought out a window pole, which had a hook on the end and was used to close high windows. He poked around the tree and tried to dislodge his rod and the fish hook, but the pole got stuck on the branch as well. Everything, including the window pole, was now dangling over the water. I was so embarrassed that I pretended Terry was nothing to do with me when a knowledgeable and disapproving fellow fisherman walked by. So many times I would say to Terry, 'You can't do that.' to which he replied, 'I can do what I like and nobody will stop me.' This was his life's motto. On this occasion, a ghillie did eventually sort out the chaos. He even smiled and Terry gave him twenty euros. Nobody else would have got off so lightly, but Terry always managed to extricate himself from difficult situations. He just laughed and others laughed with him. Who else could regularly park their car in Wantage on a double-yellow line, then give the traffic warden a hug when she came along to report him? He never got a single fine.

We did not always have our holidays alone; occasionally we were joined by friends. When we stayed at Sheen Falls Hotel, two smashing owners, Hector and Pam Brown, drove to Co. Kerry to meet us.

Hector remembers the stay as just one long laugh from start to finish. 'An outing on the hotel croquet lawn revealed that Terry was a dab hand, not only at the game itself, but also at making the rules up as we went along,' he says. 'We should have suspected something, as just before the bully off, he said to me in a typical theatrical whisper, "Usual side stake, Hector?" There followed a series of double hits, a mysterious movement of hoops and free kicks "sans mallet", but remarkably Pam and I just about managed to lay up with the Biddlecombes. The final *coup de grâce* came from an unexpected quarter. At Sheen Falls the croquet lawn effectively doubles as a helipad, and just as I was about to play the stroke that would have put Terry's ball on its way to Dingle, the hall porter appeared, quickly followed by a helicopter bringing Ronan Keating and his new bride from Dublin on honeymoon. "Match abandoned!" shouts our self-appointed umpire. "Bets to be settled on the positions at the time of abandonment!" The T. W. B. cackle burst forth as I handed over the crinklies.

'We got a little bit of our own back in the clay-pigeon shooting the following day. Terry excelled at this sport and proceeded to show us how it was done in the early rounds. However, Hen stuck with him and things came to a head with the final traps, when the clays were thrown high and at an awkward angle. Terry shot first and missed one of his clays; Hen followed and hit both of hers. I cannot repeat what he said, but he was very gracious and produced the champagne later in the day.

'He hadn't really got over this setback when he drove us down the coast in the pouring rain the following day on a trip to some exotic gardens on an island just off shore. Clearly for T. W. B. this was the trip from hell, but his interest in everything animal came to our rescue when he spotted a colony of seals on some rocks and immediately perked up. In true Terry style, he persuaded the boatman to slow down and get as close to the seals as possible so that he could carry out a detailed inspection. After that, the day just went downhill and ended with us all getting soaked in the gardens. There are photographs to prove it.

'Our final challenge at Sheen Falls came on the nearby river, which we understood to be well stocked with salmon and trout. We found two places where the fish seemed to be active and perfected our casting such that we could plop the bait down almost on a sixpence. Terry was very excited by the prospect of catching fish and was casting his line in a most determined way. Unfortunately, by lunchtime not one of us had had so much as a bite and spirits were beginning to sink a little.

'However, the thirst for the fight was rekindled when we went in to lunch and en route were shown a large fish that another guest had supposedly caught that morning. Terry's grit and determination were instantly fired up again, and from then on he spent every free moment pursuing the elusive prey. In fact, the Biddlecombes stayed on for two more days to enable him to complete this "old man and the sea" saga. We never heard the final score, but often wondered who would plant the catch of the day in such a place that every frustrated angler returning from a fruitless outing would take the bait and go back for more of it. Couldn't have been Terry, but it is just the sort of thing that he would have revelled in doing, particularly if he got a reaction.'

From 2002 onwards, we began to visit Connemara for all of our holidays, and this proved to be the place that Terry and I enjoyed more than anywhere else. We became hooked on its magical powers, and our weeks spent in that quarter of Co. Galway, nestled close to the Atlantic Ocean, were unforgettable. It became our second home; there was nowhere else we wanted to go and we were hypnotised by the place. We fell in love with the countryside and we fell in love with its people. The beautiful, constantly changing scenery has to be seen to be believed. No two days are ever the same and the light changes wherever one looks. We went for many drives admiring the coastline, the mountains and the lakes. It was like being on another planet.

Terry particularly enjoyed our visits to Leenane, alongside Killary Harbour. It was here, in this tiny village, that the film *The Field* was made. It featured Sir John Hurt, who was a good friend of Terry's and with whom he had worked on the making of *Champions*, the story of Aldaniti and Bob Champion winning the Grand National. John Hurt's girlfriend had been killed while riding a horse, but John still wanted to do the film. Terry taught him so much about riding that he was personally able to appear on a horse in many parts of the film. Terry and John complemented each other famously. Bob Hall – Central Television's sports presenter in 1982 and freelance journalist – remembers going to Cheltenham during the making of the film.

'Terry continually reminded me that John should be treated with kid gloves, because he was in a delicate state having lost his soulmate, but on one day, after half an hour at the racecourse, Terry had had enough of waiting. He marched over to John's caravan and banged on the door. Moments later, John Hurt's face emerged at an open window. "Oi, John! Get your fucking arse out here! We're waiting to get this filming done." I doubled up with laughter: kid gloves, eh? But oh so typical – so Terry. Even John Hurt saw the funny side as it suddenly dawned on Terry what he had said and done.'

During our holidays in Connemara we met some amazing people – they mostly lived close to the town of Clifden, on the edge of the Atlantic, and it was there that we spent some of the happiest days of our years together. Ballynahinch Castle Hotel, which overlooks the famous Ballynahinch River and is surrounded by mountains and woodlands, ranks as my favourite place in the world. From day one, Terry and I were charmed by its beauty and tranquillity. We both got excited for days on end when we knew we were travelling over there for a holiday.

One of Terry's greatest mates in Connemara was Cyril Biggins, the ghillie who used to take him fishing on that beautiful Ballynahinch River, with its stunning and peaceful beats. As well as being an expert fisherman, Cyril is also a racing fan and is often to be seen at Cheltenham. He and Terry had plenty in common, though I often wonder how much serious fishing was done. Many a time I would find them watching races in the betting shops in Clifden. Terry never caught a salmon, despite having a lifelong ambition to do so. Apparently, he once had a large fish on his line, but he and Cyril lost it before it was landed on the bank.

I often left the pair of them chatting and fishing beside the river while I visited the numerous Connemara pony breeders in the area. At home in England, I have a small stud of these ponies inherited from my mother, and it was probably my desire to learn more about the breed and its unique history that made Terry and me travel to Galway to see these special animals in their native land. Also, our friends in Connemara own some beautiful ponies. They taught us a huge amount about conformation and pedigrees.

Four of them made a special journey to England in 2014 for

Terry's funeral – Ciaran and Gearoid Curran, Padraic Hynes and Henry O'Toole. I was immensely touched. Our pony friends could never believe Terry's stories of life in the fast lane when he was young.

Emer McNamara, who is one of the secretaries to the Connemara Pony Breeders' Society, always enjoyed racing. Together with her father, Joe, who stood many good Connemara stallions, they trained a number of horses for 'flapping' races (unlicensed meetings). Emer spent several weeks at Lockinge and we took her racing with us. Terry thought the world of her and she rode beautifully on the gallops. He used to tell her she was wasting her life in Connemara and that she should make a career in the racing world in England.

In 2014, Henry O'Toole, who is a noted breeder, told me: 'A photo of Terry, taken during one of his many visits to Ballynahinch still sits on our kitchen dresser. It is a reminder of the character that we came to respect and love over many years. We never knew the legendary "Blond Bomber" of the glory days, but over the time that we got to know him, his stories gave us a glimpse of the colourful life that he had led in his earlier years. It was Hen's passion for Connemara ponies that first brought them to our home one spring on a Sunday morning.... It was to be the first of many such visits, each of them full of fun and laughter, as well as serious horse and pony talk. That day, one of the children had broken the lavatory seat and there was consternation when our lady visitor asked to use the bathroom. Terry was not in the slightest bit concerned. "Don't worry," he said. "It will cool her arse."'

I still go back to Connemara, even now that Terry's gone. It is the only place in the world that I feel secure and totally at ease. There is no pressure, no hassle and the slow day-to-day pace of life over there is special. One never feels forced to do anything.

There is no stress, just one day at a time, but I miss sharing its magic with Terry dreadfully and there are plenty of poignant moments when I visit our old haunts. It makes me both happy and sad. I am often tearful, but I never want to lose my memories or my friendships with its wonderful people. To visit Connemara is like venturing into another land. A unique unspoilt corner of the planet. From the first time I ever went there I felt it had stolen my soul away.

CHAPTER NINE

A Crack Shot

Terry always enjoyed shooting. He met some wonderful people during his days out on shoots. Despite living in the heart of the Ledbury hunting country in Herefordshire, he always preferred to go off with his gun rather then tidy himself up and attend a nearby meet. When he went shooting, he could switch off from horses and racing. When out hunting however, members of the field flocked around him, questioning him about the races in which he had ridden in. 'Why didn't you win on my friend's horse at Chepstow?' 'Which horses do you think will win at Cheltenham in March?' The questions were endless. There was never any peace nor time to relax.

Apparently, it was Terry's grandfather, Bert Biddlecombe, who first took him out shooting. 'He had his old twelve-bore and I had my little .410 side by side,' Terry said. 'We'd go off pigeon shooting in the lower woods. I loved it. I could only have been seven or eight then. One morning during a walk around the fields, Grandad spotted a rabbit. He handed me his old egg hammer gun and asked me if I would like a shot. The kick it gave nearly sent me back through the hedge, but I killed the rabbit.'

However, Terry would never shoot a stag. He considered deer to be majestic and beautiful, so he never went stalking. He put hares into the same category. He watched many of these creatures in the grass fields beside the gallops. He regarded them as sacred.

Fortunately, during his time at West Lockinge he still enjoyed pheasant and grouse shoots and, of course, would constantly try to get rid of the rabbits on our schooling ground. They did unbelievable damage, not only burrowing into the soil and making holes for horses to put their feet into, but also getting into the fences and ruining the birch.

In the years I spent with Terry, I never wanted to spoil his love for shooting, but I seldom accompanied him on a shoot, which disappointed him. I'd spent many years as a child on shoots with my father, who the *Shooting Gazette*'s John Neville once described as, 'The finest pheasant shot that I have ever known.' Dad was certainly a brilliant shot and the envy of many. When I stood beside him during a drive, he seldom missed a bird. He had the most unbelievable eye, but because he died on a shoot, I always had a strange feeling about ever going to shoots again. Indeed, I often worried about Terry and prayed that his heart and health would stand up to a testing day with his gun.

As luck would have it I was often ultra-busy with the racehorses on the days Terry was invited to go shooting and, as a trainer, my prime duty was to watch the horses working at home, or travel to saddle them at the races. I had plenty of excuses, but I know Terry missed my company. On one of his rare entries in the game register book I gave him one Christmas, he wrote, 'A great day with Sam Vestey. The birds flew like rockets. Shooting was very good – a bit too good for me at times. I missed HEN – nobody to play with.' I don't quite know what he expected to do with me on a serious shooting day, but on reading this entry I do feel somewhat guilty that I was not by his side more often.

Sam Vestey vividly remembers the days Terry shot with him and has an amusing anecdote: 'When my sister-in-law, Henrietta, began sharing her life with Terry in 1994, he became a regular each year on our Yorkshire grouse moor, or shooting here at Stowell Park with me and my boys. Terry was a fair shot and always the life and soul of the party. I think he enjoyed the lunches most and always shot decidedly better in the afternoon. As the years progressed he enjoyed a glass or two of claret and broke away from his teetotal existence.

'One particular incident in Yorkshire I shall never forget. We always stayed in a neighbouring hotel/pub up there. Terry enjoyed it as much as any of us. On this occasion, after a long day on the moor, we had an equally tiring dinner. Everyone fell into bed. But at 2 a.m. the fire alarm in the *Fawlty Towers* lookalike started to go off, ringing with all its strength. It rang for what seemed like hours. Eventually, doors started to open out onto the communal landing; figures started to appear. The proprietor was not at hand to turn it off. Increasing noise welcomed Jimmy Lindley in his underpants; others were more decently clad. Then with a noise like a charging bull, Terry emerged from another room – in his birthday suit, brandishing his shooting socks and yelling, "I'll fix the fucker! Leave it to me!" Which I must say he did, ramming his socks into the whole offending apparatus. He always was as good as his word, was our Terry.'

When I first linked up with Terry and he moved to West Lockinge Farm, he was invited to shoot by many of his old friends. They were thrilled to have him back in their midst. Later on, he had some mouth-watering new invitations from a number of my owners and from their friends. It was on a shoot with Ken McGeorge, from Vodafone, that he first met Tim Radford, who was later to become one of our best-ever friends. His lovely wife, Camilla, who tragically died from cancer in 2015, owned some good horses in our yard. Tim is a remarkable man. Both he and Terry seemed to enjoy each other's company right from the beginning. They had many days shooting together either in Lincolnshire, where Tim lives, or on the grouse moors in Yorkshire. I habitually sent a loader with Terry when he travelled to these shoots. It always worried me that he didn't have enough help, especially when his hands, wrists and shoulders gave him pain, and I hated him driving long distances on his own. I protected him as much as I could because he was ultra-precious to me.

Dickie Tarran, who assisted us part-time on the farm, became a good friend and an excellent companion for Terry. He, too, enjoyed shooting and got on famously with 'The Boss' – which was extremely lucky, because Terry's ways were somewhat unorthodox. Dickie used to tell me that some of his days away were utter revelations. At times, when Terry got tired and his aches became unbearable, he would take a break and hand over his gun to Dickie, much to the surprise of his hosts. It is not usual for a loader to take a part in the shooting and certainly never normal practice on a big organised shoot.

Sending Terry off shooting, correctly dressed, was like sending a child to school in school uniform. On the night before a trip with Dickie, I used to spend considerable time putting out shooting clothes onto the bed in Terry's dressing room. I liked him to look good. He was hopeless at choosing his shirts, ties and sweaters. His colour-coding was appalling. Dickie always dressed immaculately and looked extremely tidy in his plus-fours, shooting socks and well-polished shoes. My man had to keep up with him. I always insisted that Terry take his mobile phone with him. It was well known that he hated using it, but at least he had it with him. It was switched off during the drives but, in between times, I liked to keep in touch with the two sportsmen and check on their progress. I missed Terry and frequently wished that I had broken my rule and gone with him.

When I asked Tim Radford for his memories of Terry on the Yorkshire grouse moors, he gave me two brilliant stories:

'We were all having breakfast in the dining room of the Yorke Arms in Ramsgill, near Pately Bridge. The Yorke Arms is a glorious old village pub, in an idyllic position in the centre of the small picturesque village of Ramsgill. The problem with the pub is that it has become terribly smart and now boasts a Michelin star. That would be fine in itself, but the staff have become extremely stuck up and very snooty. Well – you can imagine – we were a party of nine men, all excited about the day ahead and going up onto the moor. We ordered our full English breakfast and when it eventually arrived, a couple of the guests asked if they could have some brown sauce. You would have thought that we had committed murder – the girl (who I remember as being very pretty but extremely snooty) turned round and refused our request, reminding us that we were staying at the Yorke Arms, which, in case we hadn't noticed it, had a Michelin star. She turned her back on our table and walked back to the kitchen with her nose in the air – leaving us in stunned silence and disbelief – until Terry spoke up and said, "Well, I suppose a shag would be out of the question as well?" You could have heard a pin drop. The girl turned round and the table burst into laughter. The next person to arrive was the manager, who requested that we paid our bills and leave immediately! Terry's timing was absolutely brilliant, but we never did get the brown sauce!

'We eventually left the Yorke Arms – after much discussion with the management, as you can imagine – and we went up onto the moor. I had drawn peg number eight and was at the far end of the line, with only Terry to my right at peg number nine. I have often been at the end of the line on the first drive at Ramsgill and you can get some great shooting, as the grouse navigate the contours of the glorious hills. I told Terry to be on the lookout, as it was imperative to get the birds very quickly. As with most grouse drives, there was a thirty-minute or so wait before any birds appeared, and just when I was in conversation with my loader, I suddenly heard shooting to my right from Terry's butt. I looked around to see Dickie – who had accompanied Terry on that trip to help with the driving and was loading for him that day – reloading his gun before shooting again at more grouse moving out in the flank further to his right. I thought to myself: *Where the hell is Terry?* I could not spot him anywhere until my own loader pointed at a figure, squatting down some 20 yards behind the butt. There he was, having a shit in the heather, with his breeches down by his ankles! I have never laughed so much in all my life and have dined out on that story for years! I will never forget that sight.'

Although he had divorced Bridget in 1976, Terry remained extremely fond of his ex-wife and her family. His former brother-in-law, Bill Tyrwitt Drake, runs the most wonderful shoot at Bereleigh near East Meon, Hampshire. Over the years he invited Terry to shoot many times and by all accounts there were some excellent days. The shooting cards are exceptional – beautifully designed and illustrated. I have kept them all. Bill told me that Terry actually shot at Bereleigh every year from 1966 to 1982, and then again from 1993 to 2008.

'I presume he was self-taught but he had the ability to take a bird well out in front, which we all admired because most of us were much too slow. Just occasionally, this early shooting might have gone down as a touch greedy, because the bird could well have been heading for someone else. Luncheons were memorable because of his great enthusiasm and all those noises, which we well remember. He shot very straight and was a proper sportsman.'

Another of the shoots Terry loved was on the Bamford estate, at Wootton near Uttoxeter. It is here that the famous JCBs are made and organic meat and vegetables are produced for Lady Bamford's superlative farm shop at Daylesford, in Gloucestershire. Terry, plus his loader Dickie, were always flown by helicopter from Daylesford to Staffordshire. He adored his days with the Bamford family and told me that the pheasants were superb.

Sir Anthony Bamford has told me that Terry always had them laughing with his naughty jokes. 'He was so much fun. I always knew that we were going to have a good day's shooting when Terry was around.'

From the shooting cards I've kept, it appears that on 29 January 2005 the game total was 489 and on 11 November 2005 it was 445. No wonder Terry came back tired but beaming.

He was particularly fond of Alice Bamford, who was an excellent shot herself. He loved her company. She was always great with Terry and looked after him for me. After he died, she wrote these lovely words: 'I will always cherish my times with you and Terry. You were a truly incredible loving and funny couple. Sitting in your kitchen by the Aga, after being out on the morning gallops, was so much fun. I will always remember Terry's teasing. His excitement and skill out shooting were special. I absolutely adored him, with his warmth and naughty humour. Always a huge hug, a dirty deep laugh and that wonderful glint in his eye, which I can see right now.'

Tim Curtis was one of our best owners during the training years, and he used to invite Terry to shoot with him at Buttermere, near Hungerford. His overriding memory of shooting with Terry was that he was an astonishing shot. 'On the whole, he was shooting with people younger than himself, or with men who were generally known to be experts, but Terry usually outshone them during the course of the day. Underneath the jokes and the eff-ing and blinding, he took the shoots extremely seriously.'

In 23 December 2004, an article in the *Racing Post* featured Terry Biddlecombe on shooting. Terry was quoted as saying, 'When Tim Curtis's horse, El Vaquero, won a novice chase at Taunton, the owner was out shooting, but he got very nervous when his horses ran and he missed every single bird. It would have been a lot better if I had been out shooting and Tim had gone to the races.'

Terry was also invited as a guest to Simon Clarke's shoot at Dunstall in Staffordshire. Simon is the son of Sir Stanley Clarke, who did so much for racing and owned many racecourses, including Uttoxeter. Simon recalls those days: 'The key ingredient at a Dunstall Shoot is the people and the crack. Terry had that in spades and he kept us entertained with stories and jokes. One particular day comes to mind: when he was shooting here with Ginger McCain and Tom George. We discussed the excuses which trainers give to owners, like the race was "just too far" for him or the ground was unsuitable. The stories of racing and its people and the banter between Terry and Ginger were fabulous. We travel around our shoot in an old army ambulance, everybody crammed into the back. That day the old ambulance was rocking because we laughed so much and the only reason we came out was for air. It was one of the best days ever, with like-minded people enjoying good company and a good laugh.

'Now Terry could shoot. He would try to shoot the pheasants early. If he left them late, he would swing his gun so fast that we were not sure that he could stop, and I noticed that his loader would stand behind to catch him if he overswung! Terry will be fondly remembered by the Dunstall Shoot especially when stories are told of shooting days gone by.'

Although Terry always preferred to take part in organised shoots, he did from time to time practise his skills by shooting at clays and was extremely proud of his nephew Christopher – Tony's son – who is an ace clay-pigeon shot. Chris was World Junior Champion in 2001, as well as English Champion and the AAA English Open Sporting Champion in 2002. He has represented Great Britain in Europe and New Zealand.

With the clay-pigeon trap at home there were several memorable occasions, in particular when Terry gave lessons to jockeys before a charity clay pigeon competition at Goodwood Racecourse in 1996. Adrian Maguire, Johnny Kavanagh and Jim Culloty were among his pupils. There is a high bank up the farm lane and Terry fired the clays. Adrian had never shot anything before, but proved to be a complete natural. On that day at Goodwood, Terry shot in Josh Gifford's team, together with Nicky Henderson and Guy Harwood. Guy had always been a great friend. Both he and Terry had been together on several pheasant shoots in the past and when Guy was training racehorses, Terry had ridden winners for him. On that occasion at Goodwood, I accompanied Terry to the shoot. It was tremendous fun, but the jockeys beat the veterans. It was a pity that Christopher was too young, in those days, to join Terry's team.

Apart from shooting, Terry often drove with me to the horse shows when I was judging. I attended many each year, right from the day that I met Terry in 1993. The outings were usually during the summer months, and Terry would sit beside the rings, making comments to people around him who had no idea that he was my other half. 'If I was judging, I certainly wouldn't have put that horse first. Who is this judge?' He loved the shows, especially the big county ones, and we had some excellent days out.

Terry also enjoyed Hickstead, home of the late Douglas Bunn, one of his greatest friends. When I first judged there, Douglas was still going strong and both he and Terry had plenty of reminiscences. It was always a privilege to have lunch in Douglas's box. Sadly, after he died, the shows there did not have the same draw for Terry, although Roger Stack – another of his great friends – was still in charge of the hunter rings.

Hickstead was the last British show Terry attended. It was The Royal International Horse Show in 2013. By then his health had deteriorated drastically and he was in a wheelchair, but he spent the afternoon in a box overlooking the main ring. On that day I judged the final of the retrained racehorses and Terry watched the whole class. He really enjoyed himself and was still able to criticise my judging.

On the many days I judged hunter classes, Terry met up with a number of his old friends: in particular, Robert Oliver, whose stables in Gloucestershire border Tony Biddlecombe's farm. Robert is a renowned showman and a well-known judge of a horse. He had some good times with Terry during his racing days. Apparently, in the 1970s, Terry went to Harewood End in Herefordshire to try a horse for a client who was a racehorse owner. 'He was immaculately turned out in jodhpurs, highly polished boots and a flat tweed cap,' Robert recalls. 'He watched the horse jump two steeplechase fences, then, having ridden it himself over the same two obstacles, he turned it round and jumped the fences backwards. The tweed cap remained in place the whole time.'

I was also invited to judge on several occasions at the Dublin Horse Show. It is such a magnificent show and a great spectacle with a special atmosphere. We used to spend several days in Ireland and Terry loved the craic. On one occasion a fire alarm went off in the middle of the night in our hotel and all the guests had to evacuate their rooms. Terry and I went down the stairs in white dressing gowns to assemble in an area on the opposite side of the street. 'It's amazing,' said Terry, 'how awful some people look when they have to get dressed unexpectedly and their make-up has peeled off. They're almost unrecognisable. I certainly wouldn't want to wake up the next morning with any of them in the bed beside me.'

Although our days out each summer were mostly taken up with horse shows or holidays, there were other occasions when we were invited as special guests to dinners and lunches. We were frequently asked to talk at charity functions whether locally or further afield. Terry was never enthusiastic about giving these talks and it wasn't easy to drag him out. His ears were always flat back, like a bolshie horse. He hated public speaking and was surprisingly nervous. However, I devised a formula that worked well: I would write down some notes on a postcard, to which I briefly referred – and then ask Terry a series of questions. Once we got started and he got into the swing of it, he loved giving his opinions, coupled with reminiscences of the past. The audiences seemed to enjoy listening to us and were always most attentive. They particularly enjoyed it when we took each other on and had disagreements.

On one occasion in 2005, after the successes of Best Mate, we were guests of honour at the Lady Taverner's President's Dinner in the Long Room at Lord's Cricket Ground. Terry always adored cricket and had played a lot in his younger days. Whenever there was a Test match on television he would be glued to the screen. He was exceptionally knowledgeable.

One of Terry's greatest friends was David Brown, a regular player for England in the 1960s, who famously bowled brilliantly in the third Test in Sydney in the 1965–6 Ashes series. When Terry died, 'Browny' wrote to me and said, 'I loved racing and Terry loved his cricket and between both sports, we had a hell of a lot of fun together. I remember during the days of the National Hunt Jockey's cricket games that the Duke (David Nicholson) would manage to upset most of the opposition and it took all Terry's charm and drinking capacity to make sure that we kept the fixture for the next year. Terry and Josh came to play for an invitation XI at the County Ground during my benefit season, and knowing that T. W. B. found it virtually impossible to hit the ball on the offside of the field, I put all the fielders on the leg side. All I heard when he looked round the field was, "You bastard, Browny!" It was typical of him to support such benefit games and charity matches and his attendance always enhanced the occasion.'

On our visit to Lord's that June, we set off in a taxi. There was a huge gathering of people and Terry knew a lot of the guests, in particular our hostess, Rachel Heyhoe Flint. The Long Room is magnificent and we felt honoured to be seated in it. Fortunately, we did not have to make speeches and it worked out extremely well. We just sat up on a raised stage answering questions with Sue Mott. Neil Durdon Smith, Roger Easterby and John McCririck ran the auction.

It wasn't until it was time to go home that Terry went downstairs to the gents' loo, where he proceeded to have the most violent nosebleed. He had always suffered from nosebleeds, not just in the years that he was with me. He had apparently been vulnerable to them throughout his life and, as he got older, these bleeds became more and more difficult to stop, despite operations and cauterisations to the offending blood vessels. He was living on warfarin, which is a known anti-coagulant. On that particular night, I became extremely worried. I couldn't enter the gents myself, but people kept coming out and reporting that blood was pouring from Terry's nose.

Eventually, after what seemed like hours, he re-emerged, holding towels and rolls of lavatory paper. It looked as though he'd been in a boxing match. I could hardly see his face for blood. A taxi was waiting, but it was a scary journey back to the hotel and Terry was convinced that the bleed would restart at any time. We had a bad night and the minimum of sleep.

He still looked a mess the next morning, but we had to catch the early train home from Paddington. He would not let me sponge his face, nor touch it, so I just accompanied him with wads of cotton wool. I'm sure people thought we'd had a serious argument and that I had smacked him on the nose to shut him up. Poor Terry; he suffered so much from those nosebleeds and they were nerve-racking at times. They really frightened me.

CHAPTER TEN

Owners and Trainers

During my years of training racehorses and Terry's days as a jockey, we met a vast number of owners. They came from all walks of life and represented an extensive cross-section of society. Without owners, racing cannot exist. Many of them invest large sums of money into the game and they are the backbone of the sport, but they do vary hugely in knowledge and attitude.

Certain owners are easy to deal with. They fully understand racing and are good losers when their horses underperform or suffer injuries. Others, who are most likely new to racehorse ownership, may need educating and helping. Trainers need to spend extra time with them, explaining how the system works and what it takes to get a horse ready to run. It is a high-risk sport, not only for the jockeys but also for the horses. There is no such thing as certainty on a racecourse, which many punters find hard to accept.

We were not a gambling yard. I never backed any of our runners and Terry used to have tiny bets of £2.50 each way if he thought one of our horses would run well. Unfortunately, though, betting does play a huge part in racing and, since I was such a hopeless tipster, we lost a few owners to other trainers when their West Lockinge Farm-trained horses did not win.

The unexpected always happens in a training yard. No two days are ever the same, and those of us associated with the industry fully accept that we never stop learning. Training racehorses is full of surprises, as everybody connected to the sport learns to accept. It is essential to be open-minded and to be able to take the rough with the smooth. It was always great for me to have Terry by my side when I was training as he would help to soften the blows when unforeseen events occurred, beyond our control.

Both Terry and I recognised that it was vital to look after our owners. As a jockey, Terry had always loved his public. He had a special way with people. Des Lally, at Ballynahinch Castle Hotel in Connemara, once said, 'Terry realised that, no matter how important people thought they were, they were never any better than the rest of us. He treated queens, jockeys, waiters, barmen, lords, ladies, dukes, duchesses and sirs all the same.'

At West Lockinge Farm we had owners from many different backgrounds, but Terry treated them all alike. When we went racing he often spent time talking to the gate attendants, the car-park officials or the groundsmen. I would have to hurry him along to saddle up our horses because he was often wrapped up in conversation with racegoers. He never turned his back on anybody. Terry Court – current director of Brightwells – who helped Terry so much on his return to England from Australia and gave him a job with his firm, adored Terry and was one of his greatest friends. He, too, experienced Terry's love affair with his public. 'While Biddles was with me I used to carry out the selling races at Bath Racecourse, and in those early days of his employment, I used to get him to drive me to our various appointments.

'On this particular day, when we drove to Bath, I had already said to him that we would be having lunch in the directors' room, where they used to keep a little table for me behind the entry door. I told him we would pop in there for a bit of lunch before the seller. We pulled into the car park and when we got out of the car, three of the car-park attendants, realising that it was T. W. B. beside me, rushed up to greet him like a long-lost brother. They were obviously delighted to see him.

'We then approached the entrance gate where the same thing happened. Gate attendants left their posts and went over to shake him firmly by the hand, and a young lady, who was on duty, gave him a big cuddle and kiss before shedding a tear. We then walked approximately forty to fifty yards to the dining room and within that short distance he was accosted by a number of racegoers who were overwhelmed and thrilled by his presence. When we finally got to the dining room and went through the door there were between twenty to thirty directors and their guests who immediately, when realising who I'd brought with me, all stood up and greeted him to an amazing round of applause, which touched us both greatly. I finished up having lunch on my own. That was a reflection of the high esteem in which Terry was held by the racing fraternity and, remember, Bath is a flat racing track.'

Tim Russon, another good friend of Terry's, was directing for Central Television in Birmingham in the eighties and he remembers that, 'Dear Biddles was always friendly with everyone, and everywhere you went he was everyone's friend. One moment that captures the magic of the man came when we were sent filming to Ludlow to take in the excitement of a special race in honour of the Prince of Wales. There was a terrorist alert on up and down the country, and with Prince Charles at the races to present the prizes, the paddock and enclosures were swarming with Royal Protection Officers and Special Branch. Yet Terry boldly went where no other man would dare to go, marching through every security post and past every guard with camera crew in tow, to block the path of the Prince of Wales as he made his way to the Winners' Enclosure. The Prince greeted Biddles with the warmest of smiles and firmest of handshakes. They happily chatted away on camera for several minutes as the army of security men twitched and panicked for fear of breaching protection and protocol. But nobody dared do or say a thing because it was Terry Biddlecombe doing the talking and he was somebody special.'

Most of our owners knew about Terry's past and his love affair with his public and they greatly enjoyed being kept in the picture. Nobody was ever refused a visit, and every month I would write a newsletter. I have kept all of these letters on file and one day I might even publish them for my own interest because, looking back on them, they were extremely informative. Indeed, a number of our owners photocopied the newsletters and sent them on to their friends.

Terry and I were extremely lucky to have trained horses for so many interesting people. They trusted us and not only did they learn from us but we learned from them as well. We enjoyed their visits and our talks with them, either on the telephone, in the yard, on the gallops or at the races, but we did have a few set rules. Nobody was allowed to ring us up after 9 p.m. as we considered after that time it was far too late to have a lengthy conversation. Indeed, Terry and I had often gone wearily upstairs for a good night's sleep by 9 p.m., and if the telephone rang (on my side of the bed), Terry would unleash a tirade of swear words. He used to say to me, 'Why don't you ring that special number and find out what fucker is trying to ring us? Ring him back at 5.30 tomorrow morning and see how that goes down!' If we had worked a long day we needed a good night's sleep. We were often extremely tired.

In 2003 we had a visit from a television crew headed by Adrian Chiles. The BBC was making a film of Terry and me for a programme called *So What Do You Do All Day?* This was before Adrian hosted *The One Show* on BBC 1 and before he became such a famous sports presenter. Adrian arrived at the back door at 5.30 a.m. He shadowed Terry and me during the feeding, the riding out on the gallops and our day at the races.

It was a Cheltenham meeting that day and we ran a horse called Rosslea, which finished second. The film crew was introduced to a number of racing officials and we had lunch in the Royal Box. On the way home, Adrian fell asleep in the back of my car, totally exhausted by watching us work with horses from the crack of dawn until dark.

We had a lot of syndicates and partnerships. When they came to visit us, Terry would pick four or five people to take with him in the truck and leave the rest to me or to one of my helpers. He was in his element, transporting them up to the gallops. I dread to think what remarks he made or unprintable jokes he told. He loved to drive his truck as fast as he could across the grass fields and down the hills, finding it amusing if his passengers clung on to the sides or became over-anxious. They often returned to the house either shattered or giggling. How did he get away with asking one owner how she was coping with the change of life, or another hugely respectable lady, whether she had ever had sex over the back of a chair? No wonder they were ready for some refreshments on their return. We usually offered these in the house. Terry loved pouring out the drinks and was particularly proud of his homemade sloe gin.

For my part, I used to take many of the visitors into our dark-green double-decker bus, which was parked halfway up the hill, beside the gallops. This bus was Terry's idea and we bought it through the Internet. It was old but clean, and it had been well cared for. We bought it in 2003, after Best Mate's first Gold Cup win. From the upper deck, we could see the entire all-weather gallop and it was fun to watch the horses canter past. It provided a brilliant viewpoint and I often took flasks of coffee and tins of biscuits for elevenses with the owners. I also gave out lists of all the horses and sometimes we put numbered saddle cloths on them as well, for easier identification. Terry loved his bus, turning the relevant handles, until the number on the front read sixty-nine.

Sadly, after some years, it was spotted by certain undesirables from the local town of Wantage. Unruly teenagers walked across the neighbouring farmer's fields to play in the bus. These unwelcome intruders – totally beyond parental control – seemed set on performing acts of vandalism. They hurled boulders and stones at the outside of the bus and smashed the windows. They then pulled out the seats and left them strewn over the grass in the adjoining field. They also used the bus as a lavatory, which meant that I could no longer use it for owners.

When the police were alerted, they seemed to have little interest and turned a blind eye to this shameful behaviour. On one occasion Terry did catch a couple of the culprits. He shut them in the back of his truck and bundled them off to the police station in Wantage. After this incident we were given some of the offenders' addresses.

We tackled their parents, but they were most unhelpful and the vandalism continued. In the end, we decided that, because of the increased juvenile delinquency in our area, the bus would have to go and it was towed away by a local scrap merchant. Terry and I were sad to see it leave the farm. We felt that we had lost a friend – the field looked empty without it and many people in Wantage asked, 'What has happened to your bus?' It had become a local landmark.

The syndicate owners were usually more challenging than those who owned a whole horse or shared one with a friend. Many syndicate members were new to the game and it was difficult if they didn't know each other. Disagreements were not uncommon and certain individuals thought they knew more about racing than they did. The dangerous ones were those who chatted to their friends outside the yard and collected conflicting opinions as to how their horse should be trained or campaigned. In other words, they would go behind our backs and stir up trouble, but probably knew little or nothing about horses. Terry always said that if you employ an expert to do a job, then you should trust him to do it correctly: 'You don't go to a dentist to have a tooth taken out and tell the dentist how to do it.'

The extra-big syndicates were easier for us and less of a challenge. They were invariably run by experienced individuals, who made the final decisions and told their members how to behave. We trained for Million in Mind, Elite Racing and Axom and these well-established racing partnerships are superbly organised. Their members are well informed and travel to many different yards for visits, but the downside is that their visits are less personal. Terry and I seldom got to know individual members on a one-to-one basis and they were not allowed to travel up to the gallops with Terry's swear words ringing in their ears. We used to meet them for refreshments in our barn and on some occasions there were question and answer sessions with Terry and me seated on straw bales. The race planning for their horses was always done through their special reps. There was never any question of members querying decisions.

Sometimes owners came to West Lockinge Farm during the summer months to see their horses grazing in the fields. Brian Hartigan, a prominent member of Executive Racing became a very good friend. He wrote to me after Terry's death and said, 'I find it impossible to think of Terry without smiling. He frequently kept me laughing with his stories, I'm sure only slightly embellished at times, and his political incorrectness was a delight. One abiding memory is of a late summer's afternoon that we spent at West Lockinge Farm. We were joined there by a party of ladies of a certain age. Terry asked me to help him prepare his special-recipe Pimm's. For "special", read "lethal". To the Pimm's and the fruit he added an over-large amount of gin to take away the sweetness of the fruit.

Next was an equally substantial amount of vodka to remove the bitterness of the gin. The amount of lemonade we used to top up the jugs was something like two tablespoons. As the volunteer waiter, I was asked more than once if there was any more of the "lovely fruit cup".'

Ian Rees, who ran the syndicate for Executive Racing, had become interested in racing as a child. 'At that time,' he says, 'Terry Biddlecombe and Lester Piggott were my heroes. I was always more interested in jump racing, though, and despite only being seven or eight at the time, I loved Gay Trip and Terry Biddlecombe. I remember Terry winning the Mackeson (Gold Cup) on him and then being so disappointed when Terry was injured and couldn't ride him when he won the Grand National. One day, when I was a child, Terry was riding at Market Rasen and we parked our car in the middle of the course. At that time, the horses walked through the parking area to get to the start on the far side of the course and on the way to the start, Terry got dumped on the ground by his horse. As he sat there, without his mount, he looked up at all the people gathering round and said, "Well, I fucked that up, didn't I?"'

When Terry died, Ian gave me a rose for my garden called Golden Smiles. How wonderfully appropriate.

Then there were the owners who had jockey preferences. They were often difficult to please, since they had read about certain jockeys in the newspapers and had watched them ride on television. They had formed their own firm opinions and wanted their favourites to ride their horses. We always tried to match up our horses with jockeys we thought would suit their ways. Some horses need quiet riders whereas others need strong handling. At the height of our training years, Jim Culloty was our stable jockey, so he was handed the majority of the rides, but there were plenty of good, reliable jockeys who rode out for us at home and helped with the schooling. They, too, deserved their share of the spoils and often got the leg up in a race. A. P. McCoy was always top of owner Jim Lewis's list, and he rode some superlative races on Edredon Bleu. However, Jim did listen to Terry and was completely loyal to Jim Culloty when it came to choosing the jockey for Best Mate. Nobody else rode that horse as well. It was as though the two were made for each other.

When owners told us that they had bought the *Weatherby's Programme Book*, or had taken out a subscription to *The Racing Calendar*, our hearts usually sank. They would spot a race in one of these publications and then want to run their horse in it without having grasped the overall picture or understood the handicapping system. Many times the races owners chose were totally unsuitable – either the wrong distances or the wrong courses.

It was even more irritating when certain owners took it upon themselves to ring up the racecourses in order to get an update on the going. No racecourse official much likes being rung up by an owner, whereas clerks of the courses are always willing to talk to trainers. Imagine the chaos if the connections of all the day's runners on a race day started chasing after racecourse officials to get more information.

Apart from anything else, most owners have never even walked a course and certainly have never ridden a racehorse. They would not understand the true meaning of the words 'good', 'good/soft', or 'good/firm', going. The ground varies considerably from course to course, depending on the underlying soil structure, and even the clerks of the courses can be extremely inaccurate in their assessment of the underfoot conditions. They also tend to paint a better picture in order to encourage runners.

Wherever possible, Terry and I walked the courses ourselves before a race meeting began. In fact, I sometimes went off in the car and walked it the previous day. As far as the Cheltenham Festival was concerned, Terry traditionally walked the steeplechase courses on the preceding Sunday. He much enjoyed this, invariably carrying his long stick and was even photographed one year sitting on a fence to test the stiffness of the birch.

He was extremely accurate on ground and could predict exactly how the courses would ride. After all, he had walked and ridden enough of them in his days as a jockey. When he assessed the Cheltenham ground he was always closely questioned afterwards by the clerk of the course and members of the press. They valued his opinion, because nobody was more at home at Cheltenham than Terry. He had ridden numerous winners there and knew the course inside out. It was his favourite track and held a multitude of memories for him, both good and bad.

In concluding my observations on the habits of owners, I must say that it was extremely irritating to see owners push themselves into the weighing room. It certainly drove Terry mad. This area is the holy of holies and strictly reserved for trainers, jockeys and racecourse personnel. Weighing rooms are never large areas and to have them cluttered up by unwanted outsiders who have no business being there aggravates the officials and gives trainers a bad name. The jockeys need privacy and peace, and they are seldom in the mood to talk to owners prior to their rides. Matters of vital importance can be discussed through the trainers.

The best owners were always the ones who listened and cooperated with us, talking about their horses in a sensible and logical way. We knew that although the horses were there to win races, racing had to be fun as well. Owners need to have maximum enjoyment and feel part of a team.

Every autumn, usually on the third Sunday in September, we held a special open day for our owners. The horses were paraded in the little paddock behind our house while I provided the commentary. We looked forward to these days and spent many hours planning them. The horses always looked magnificent, because at that time of year they were three-parts race-fit and close to a run. They still had shining summer coats and the staff took huge pride in turning them out smartly, with all manes pulled and hooves oiled.

Terry spent hours tending to the grass in the parade ring. In the weeks leading up to the open days, he went round and round the paddock, as well as along the grass areas by the barns, on his sit-on mower. He was often naked from the waist upwards and got very sunburnt, despite wearing the huge wide-brimmed hat that he had brought back from Australia.

For the open days, we usually placed bales of straw round the edges of the viewing area and rows of chairs against the wall, close to the entrance gate. Occasionally, we positioned long flat-bed trailers, with further straw bales, on the other side of the perimeter railings, so that owners could sit higher and get a better view of the horses. When we had extra-big open days, we hired special tiered seats, but these were extremely expensive and we only ordered them in the years we could afford them. This was for the Best Mate Open Day in 2003 and the Hen and Terry Charity Open Day in 2004. Thousands of visitors turned up at the farm on these occasions. We were able to raise money for the Thames Valley and Chiltern Air Ambulance, as well as for The Injured Jockeys Fund.

I enjoyed sitting in my little caravan/commentary box during our open days. I got a bird's-eye view of all that was going on and I was never afraid to use the microphone to give Terry a ticking off, especially if he sent in the horses too slowly. He always preferred to be at the entrance to the parade ring and have his special friends around him. He used his long walking stick to give the horses a prod if they hung back at the sight of the crowds. Our guests seemed to appreciate the banter between myself and Terry. It made the occasion more light-hearted. On several days, one of our yard sponsors donated prizes for the staff. When this happened, I made sure that all the lads and lasses received an envelope or a bottle of wine. I approached certain owners to present the awards and there are some brilliant photographs on file recording these highlights.

When our open-day parades had finished, we opened the stables for our guests to explore. Members of staff were on duty in different areas and kept a close check on the horses to ensure that they did not get overexcited. They enjoyed talking to the visitors but found that they had to answer some strange questions. As well as the activity in the yard there was also an abundance of food and drink in our specially designated marquee in the garden, and although we issued our owners with special badges, there were always a number of gatecrashers on the lookout for freebies. Terry enjoyed sorting them out and he did not mince his words.

He also made sure that the waitresses kept the guests' glasses well filled. He mingled with everybody and was always the star attraction. It didn't matter whether he knew the guests or not; they all got the same treatment. Indeed, one of my owners, Ted Birchall, who only joined us in my later training years, wrote a lovely appreciation of Terry:

'Racing in Terry's day was still a sport and not being run for the benefit of the bookmakers. I was in the Silver Ring, looking in. Wishing! Many years later I could just about afford a small share in a partnership. I chanced upon Henrietta Knight and

West Lockinge Farm. With Hen came Terry, who was the added bonus. I only met Terry a few times, as unfortunately his problems often kept him confined to his box. However, I did sit with him for a while in the garden, during the last of Hen's owners' open days, where we discussed the old days and put the world to rights regarding the modern racing scene. Terry asked me about myself and my wife, Dorrie. He took an interest in our comparatively mundane careers. We were ex-fire officers. I realised that, despite our totally different backgrounds, there may have been some empathy somewhere, maybe even mutual respect. I certainly respected Terry, if that is another word for hero-worship. When I was driving home, I then knew that I was no longer in the Silver Ring. I am extremely proud to have made his acquaintance and, dare I say it, maybe even for a short while, been his friend.'

At the end of every open day, the owners and guests were given entry forms for the Five To Follow competition. They needed to select five horses from the yard to follow for the season for an entry fee of £5. First prize was usually £500. The competition became extremely popular. Each horse got points for being in the first four in any race and we sent out monthly updates. Everybody became involved and the entrants got to know more about the horses and how they were performing.

The open days were such happy occasions and Terry's presence made them double the fun. He used to get extremely tired walking around and talking to owners, but he never complained and never admitted how much his arthritis was hurting him. He supported me through and through. During these days, the geese and ducks would also wander around in the farmyard, but they never caused any problems. Nor did the pond beside the stables. Only once did we put barriers around it to satisfy the Health & Safety inspectors and the insurers.

It was a particular honour to train several horses for the Queen and even more exciting when one of them, Harvest Song, ridden by William Kennedy, won a hurdle race at Fontwell in 2010. Mostly, the Queen's jumpers are trained by Nicky Henderson, but a few with physical problems ended up at West Lockinge. Her Majesty visited the farm and I well remember driving her up to the gallops to watch her horses. We still had the bus at that time, but No. 69 was no longer visible on the front. The Queen was a wonderful owner. I used to telephone her at Windsor Castle or Buckingham Palace to discuss the well-being of her horses and I always spoke to her after a race. She is unbelievably knowledgeable about horses and racing. It was always a great privilege for my staff to take her racing colours into the weighing room and watch the jockeys come out into the paddock wearing the royal silks, with the black velvet cap and gold tassle.

———

I began training racehorses for the Brashers – Chris and Shirley – due to an unusual meeting in the weighing room at Wolverhampton in 1992, when that course was still a jumping track. There was a call on the tannoy: 'Would Henrietta Knight please go to the weighing room.' These messages are worrying for trainers, because it often means that the stewards want to interview them about the running or riding of a certain horse. On this occasion I couldn't see that there had been anything untoward with the way our horses had performed. Apprehensively, I put down my sandwich in the bar and walked to the weighing room. It was there that a middle-aged couple introduced themselves and said that they would like to talk to me about buying a racehorse.

At the time, I didn't realise how famous these two future owners were. Chris Brasher had not only won that Olympic gold medal in Melbourne in 1956 and started the first London Marathon in 1981, but he had also made sporting history by helping Sir Roger Bannister run the first four-minute mile in 1954. Shirley Brasher had been a top-class tennis player under her maiden name of Bloomer. In her prime, she had won the French Open. She explained to me that she liked lady trainers and female horses. Could I find her a nice young mare for sensible money? A few months later, I came across a strong bay filly by King's Ride that was being sold privately by Mark Dwyer. Shirley bought her and named her Princess Hotpot. We had a great deal of fun with this mare, including several wins. Shirley even rode her herself, a few times, when she visited the yard. Hotpot had a fantastic temperament and was a brilliant jumper.

Val McCalla was another interesting owner. He was Jamaican by birth, highly intelligent and the founder of *The Voice*, a newspaper aimed at Britain's black community. He answered an advertisement for a horse for sale that I had put in the *Racing Post*. We had plenty of successes for Val and he was unbelievably generous. When his four-year-old, Stompin by Alzao, won the Glenlivet Hurdle at Aintree in 1995, he had clearly had a substantial bet. Two days later, he rang me to say that he was sending me a present for training Stompin. I expected that this would most probably be a case of wine or champagne, because Val loved to drink. Imagine my surprise when a brand-new Volvo arrived in the yard with the personalised number plate, M11 HEN. I was speechless, but gratefully accepted it and I still drive Volvo cars today – with that same number plate.

As our years with Val progressed, he sponsored races at Kempton every February, one of which was the Adonis hurdle. He held pre-racing receptions in a large box overlooking the track and invited many famous people. Terry's eyes were on stalks when he came face to face with the beautiful Naomi Campbell. Val often took us out for lunches in smart restaurants with his charming wife, Linda, but sadly, as his health gradually deteriorated, he was no longer well enough to go racing. He died in 2002 and both Terry and I were greatly saddened. We missed him.

A few of my owners bred their own horses and were rightly proud when they won races. The Wyatt family, from Snetterton in Norfolk, were great enthusiasts and had a thoroughbred mare called Ardenbar, by Ardross. She produced numerous winners and when her son, Muhtenbar, won a race at Ascot in 2009, it gave Tim and Anne Wyatt a day to remember. Terry always enjoyed teasing their daughter, Cherry, who had eye-catching hair with black and blonde streaks. Terry called her 'the Friesian': just one of the many nicknames he gave my owners. He seldom remembered their real names. Many a time I had to think twice before realising to whom he was referring, and when he was asked to write down a telephone message, the names were often impossible to decipher. It was as though they had been written down in code.

Terry christened one of my long-standing owners 'Brandy'. Stephen Smith, who had several horses in our yard, used to work for Seagram, the parent company of Martell, the Grand National sponsor. The fact that Martell was actually a very fine cognac, and not just a brandy, was a subtlety lost on Terry, but he always enjoyed the lunch at Aintree, particularly as it was prepared by top chef Albert Roux. Our biggest wins for Stephen were with a horse called Harris Bay, which needed to go right-handed and loved Ascot, where he won a £50,000 handicap in November 2007 and the United House Gold Cup the following year, under a masterful ride from Timmy Murphy.

———

Lord Cadogan – Charles, whom I have already mentioned in previous chapters – was a great supporter of Terry's. He was Lord Chelsea in Terry's racing days, but the title changed after his father died. Both he and his father were great National Hunt enthusiasts and had some very good horses. Charles was an excellent owner at West Lockinge Farm and was a big support to me when I began training. For many years he was deputy senior steward of the Jockey Club and director of Jockey Club Estates. At one time, he had seven horses in the yard and he was one of the easiest owners I ever encountered. He thoroughly understands the game and has been a Jockey Club steward at many racecourses.

Recently, he told me about an amusing incident dating back to the 1960s, when Terry was asked to ride a horse of his, trained by Verly Bewicke. He was a big black youngster from Ireland called The Black Moth, by Black Tarquin. At home he was a superstar on the gallops and jumped superbly, but on a racecourse he continually disappointed and would not take the proceedings seriously. He did not try a yard. Terry was given the leg up in a novice hurdle that day at Worcester in order to assess the horse. The ground was heavy. Beside the starting gate was a huge puddle of water and other parts of the course were flooded.

In the paddock, Charles told Terry not to trust his mount at the start because he was a playboy and to keep him on the move. He told Terry not to take him behind the gate where the floodwater was lying. As it so happened, the start was delayed due to a horse being resaddled, and without thinking Terry wandered over to the water puddle, where The Black Moth went straight down and began to roll. Both the jockey and horse were soaked.

The Black Moth completed the race, but made little effort. On dismounting, Terry was not amused; as well as being drenched, his clean white breeches were covered in mud. A few years later, the same horse was given to Captain Tim Forster to lead his string, a job that he did well, and then he won six or seven point-to-point races, but it's a story that always sticks in Charles's mind. Fortunately there were few puddles at Letcombe Bassett – except along the Ridgeway, and everybody was well warned.

The staff in the yard loved it if Terry gave them a nickname. At one time we had two Bens working for us. Terry called one of them 'Bendy Ben' because he was the middle one of triplets and walked slightly lopsidedly. This was Ben Arthey, now doing well as a trainer in Northern Ireland. The other Ben was called 'Ben Cock', because he always cocked up the schooling sessions. This Ben – Ben Rivett – went on to be a successful point-to-point rider in East Anglia and is now a much-respected estate agent.

Jim Lewis, of course, had many horses at West Lockinge Farm, including Best Mate, Edredon Bleu and Impek. Inevitably he was known by Terry as 'Lucky Jim'. Jim was extremely superstitious, and always took a toy black cat with him to the races. One season, he only visited West Lockinge Farm once, on the owners' open day.

This was the year before Best Mate's first Gold Cup win, so ever afterwards we thought it brought us more luck if he stayed away.

Jim often muddled his horses up when he saw them on a racecourse, partly because most of them were bay. He always enjoyed making Terry laugh with this story against himself. 'It was Boxing Day in 2002. Best Mate and Lord Noelie were both running in the King George VI chase. As usual, I accompanied Terry to the pre-race saddling boxes. The low sun was in my eyes and my varifocals were very dark. Nervous as hell, I dutifully followed Terry into the box and put my hands on this beautiful horse's neck – "Go well, Matey," I said, "and come home safely." Terry doing his best to stifle a laugh said, "Jim, this is Lord Noelie, you daft bugger. Go back and have another Guinness."'

Trevor Hemmings was an exceptional owner. He had horses in a number of yards and it was a privilege to train for him. Funnily enough, it was during that unusual holiday at the Sheen Falls Hotel in Co. Kerry in 1998 that I received a telephone call from Trevor. At the time we were driving round the beautiful countryside in our hired car when my mobile telephone rang. Over the next ten years we trained plenty of winners for him, including Chives, which was upsides Best Mate in the 2003 Gold Cup at the top of the hill, only to fade in the closing stages due to a broken blood vessel. Then Southern Star won the Warwick Classic Chase in 2004, ridden by Graham Lee, a jockey whom both Terry and I always believed in wholeheartedly, and Glasker Mill won several good chases, including one at Cheltenham in 2007.

Trevor also owned a horse called The Vicar, which he claimed to have named after Terry. He won us a few races, but was somewhat unpredictable and nobody ever knew what he would do next. Well-named?

It was great when Trevor won three Grand Nationals with Hedgehunter in 2005, trained by Willie Mullins, Ballabriggs in 2011, trained by Donald McCain Jr, and Many Clouds in 2015, trained by Oliver Sherwood. He lives close to Aintree and from childhood had always dreamt of winning races on the Liverpool course. He has a great sense of humour and I always enjoy talking to him. When I was training, he often rang me up on a Sunday morning and we would put the world to rights.

One of my more unconventional owners, Jan Johnson, came from Wales. Her husband, Victor, bought her an unraced three-year-old – later named Lord JJ – as a birthday present. Jan arrived at the yard as always in amazingly high-heeled shoes and promptly got her heels stuck down one of the grids covering a drain. Terry seized the opportunity, lifting up and stroking her shapely legs to free her from the trap – just like a farrier picking up a horse's leg to shoe it. Many years later, when Terry and I were on holiday in Mull, Scotland, with Tim Radford, Victor and Jan joined us and Jan announced that she would like to go pony-trekking, which involved scenic rides along the beaches of the island. However, because she had barely ridden before, she did not enjoy the experience. It frightened her and she felt decidedly weak at the knees afterwards. Terry said, 'Jan, I suggest that at your age you give up the idea of riding four-legged animals and concentrate on riding the ones you understand: the two-legged ones.'

During the many years Terry and I went racing together, we came into contact with a large number of fellow trainers, both in England and in Ireland. Terry got along well with most of them and they respected him. In 2011, we stayed a night with Martin and Carol Pipe at Nicholashayne, Devon. We were looked after like royalty and had the most wonderful time. Not only did we have a superb tour of the yard and the gallops, but we were taken to the local pub for a fun dinner and evening. Terry always got on extremely well with Martin and there were plenty of jokes. When we went to bed we found that Martin had placed a blow-up doll on Terry's side of the bed. Terry was highly amused and immediately picked her up and cuddled her, while Carol Pipe and I doubled up with laughter.

After Terry died, Martin wrote this: 'I can remember coming home from the dentist (which I hated) when I was 16, then going into our red sitting room at home and watching a horse win on the television, owned by my dad's friend, Sid Billing. It was at Sandown on 7 December 1961, and the horse was Fisherman's Song, trained by Eddie Reavey. It was ridden by Terry Biddlecombe. We were all very excited and little did I know that, later in life, I would become a racehorse trainer and meet my then-idol many, many times. Terry was a swashbuckling jockey, a supreme athlete and ahead of his time. He lived life to the full and could still have ridden successfully beside today's jockeys. Terry and Hen came for an overnight visit a few years ago and we had a delightful time together – great fun. It was so nice to see them so happy: "best mates" together.'

Terry always respected Paul Nicholls and enjoyed talking to him at racecourses. Paul said, 'Terry was a larger-than-life character who always said it like it was. I remember one of the first times I trained a winner he said to me, "I'm glad you can fucking train, because you couldn't fucking ride!" I was incredibly fond of Terry and he always had time for a chat, even if it was nearly always regarding a colourful subject.'

One of the trainers Terry rode for at the end of his riding career was Richard Head. He told me that he has memories of a party at Newbury Racecourse, given by Derby-winning trainer Dick Hern in about 1970, when Terry was absolutely at the top of his riding career with Fred Rimell. 'He came into the room looking like a Greek god: slim, golden-haired and walking tall. He exuded confidence, optimism and bonhomie. Everybody's heads turned. He had terrific charisma and he charmed the room. I was so impressed by his presence at the time that I have never forgotten it.'

CHAPTER ELEVEN

A Passion for Cheltenham

When Terry and I began to share the training of our racehorses, we were rewarded by plenty of winners. Looking back, people will say that we were primarily known for the training of Best Mate to win three Cheltenham Gold Cups, and Edredon Bleu to win the Champion Chase and the King George VI Chase. However, we did achieve many other successes with horses of varying degrees of talent – maybe not stars, but, nevertheless, consistent and rewarding at their own level.

However, right from the beginning, it was the victories at Cheltenham Racecourse that gave us the greatest thrills. It is the mecca of National Hunt racing and had always been Terry's favourite course. He had a number of victories at Prestbury Park, as well as his fair share of down days. The racecourse is set like an amphitheatre beneath Cleeve Hill, and on festival days the atmosphere is electric. It mesmerises racegoers. The excitement and thrills are so addictive that fans return to see the action year after year.

Terry was Gloucestershire born and bred and he always had a host of local well-wishers. Even when he returned to the racecourse in his later years, his public still welcomed him with open arms, and Cheltenham pulled Terry to it like a magnet is pulled to an iron bar.

However, its significance to me was slightly different. It was at Cheltenham races in October 1993 that I spent that memorable day with my future husband. The year I fell in love with him.

In my teenage days, I remember seeing Terry's name – T. BIDDLECOMBE – on the old number board beside the weighing room, painted in bold white letters on black wood. There were no electronic screens in those days. When Terry retired from racing at Cheltenham in 1974, he was given that board and I now have it hanging up in my office at West Lockinge Farm. I will treasure it for ever. On that historic day when Terry hung up his boots, his last race was aboard Amarind in the Cathcart Chase. He was a big, strong chestnut horse from the USA, trained by Fulke Walwyn. He finished fifth. Richard Pitman won the race on Soothsayer, a gorgeous-looking dark-bay steeplechaser also from America trained by Fred Winter. Richard remembers walking down the chute to the main racecourse. It was lined with Terry Biddlecombe well-wishers, so he took a pull on his horse and let Terry lead the runners out onto the track. The crescendo of cheers from both sides of the course was deafening, like a Mexican wave. Many thousands of racegoers had stayed behind to witness Terry's retirement ride. He was the A. P. McCoy of his day. The public adored him.

———

Back in 1967, Woodland Venture won the Cheltenham Gold Cup with Terry in the saddle. The horse was trained by Fred Rimell. It gave Terry a day to cherish for the rest of his life, but the race had almost been a non-starter for him, thanks to a bad fall the previous day from Glenn in the Cotswold Chase. He had been kicked and badly trodden on. Andy Turnell, a top-class jockey and a good friend of Terry's, remembers, 'His breeches had been all but ripped off him. He had lacerations to his bollocks and was bleeding profusely. He was in a dreadful state and the remains of his breeches were red. However, in typical Terry fashion, he got the skin stitched up by his favourite Irish doctor, Doc Wilson, who also gave him an injection for a badly bruised knee. So effective was the injection that, the next day, he went on to win the Cheltenham Gold Cup. He was a tough man, but how he got through the pain barrier, nobody will ever know. On the day of his fall he must have been in agony but he even rode in the next race: the Champion Hurdle.'

Nowadays, Terry wouldn't have been allowed to ride with a local anaesthetic in his knee. Painkillers are strictly monitored. In fact, most of his contemporaries in the sixties and seventies would have failed dope tests and the breathalyser as well.

After Terry died, I had many wonderful letters, and one, in particular from Mike Newman, Josh Gifford's cousin. He later became head groundsman at Huntingdon Racecourse and was always a great ally. 'I would like to recall an early experience with the boys at Cheltenham in the sixties, the year Josh rode What a Myth. We all met in the car park: Josh, Terry, David Nicholson, "Tumper" Lehane, Macer Gifford and John Gamble. We went in through the old western entrance. On entering the paddock, we approached a small door at the bottom of the main stand. Josh knocked, and lo and behold, we were ushered into the Cellar Bar, with the steward saying, "Usual sir?", upon which, a bottle of Bollinger and glasses were duly provided. We all sat on beer barrels and enjoyed more than one bottle – and this, I assure you, was only five hours before Terry went out and won the Gold Cup! I remember it clearly.'

Arthur Moore – the well-known Irish jockey and Tommy Carberry's brother-in-law – also remembers an occasion from the Cheltenham Festival. Terry shouted across the room, 'So where are you staying tonight, Tommy?' to which he replied, 'With the Queen.' Not, of course, to be taken literally. It referred to where many of the jockeys stayed and partied – in The Queen's Hotel in Cheltenham. But Arthur said it was a highly amusing answer at the time. He often witnessed those fun days on the racecourse and the post-race parties.

It was with the knowledge of Terry's incredible Cheltenham background that I set forth to secure my own festival winners. Nobody knew better than Terry how the racecourse should be ridden.

In 1997, Karshi won the Stayers' hurdle at the big March meeting. He was trained from West Lockinge and he provided me with my first festival success. It was an emotional day. Karshi was owned and bred by my brother-in-law, Sam Vestey. My sister, Ce, who had suffered that life-threatening stroke in November 1995, had somehow managed to get to the racecourse to watch him win. It was unbelievably exciting, especially since jockey Jamie Osborne made virtually every yard of the running. This victory gave me a taste for further festival success.

When Jim Lewis sent us Edredon Bleu from France at the end of 1996, and then bought Best Mate in Ireland in the spring of 1999, we had no idea that from then on right up until 2004 these two horses would cement our arrival into the big time. Blue and Matey, as we nicknamed them, stood out as our stars because of their amazing consistency and soundness. Neither horse ever missed a season. They were clean-winded and had wonderfully strong legs. They never let us down. Both horses shone at Prestbury Park.

Edredon Bleu provided us with our second festival win when he was victorious in the Grand Annual Chase under A. P. McCoy in 1998. He was also second in the Queen Mother Champion Chase the following year, to Call Equiname, but it was his victory in that prestigious race in 2000 that will go down in history as one of Cheltenham's most exciting finishes of all time. A. P. rates that victory as number five in his top-ten successes, but for Terry and me, it was number one.

In that race, Edredon Bleu gave a demonstration of breath-takingly quick jumping and showed not only courage but also the utmost determination – both of which are great attributes in a steeplechaser. He simply would not let his opponent, Direct Route, beat him, even though he was headed between the last fence and the finishing line.

I couldn't watch it live – it was too much for me. I just walked round by the weighing room and under the number board to listen to the commentary. Even then, there were times when I had to block my ears, and waiting for the result of the photo finish seemed to take an age. To win Queen Elizabeth the Queen Mother's own race, and for her to be there to present the trophy made it a surreal day. She was such a great supporter of National Hunt Racing and I had known her personally for over thirty years.

From the late seventies up until 1992 I was privileged on many occasions to have been one of the Queen Mother's houseguests at the Royal Lodge in Windsor Great Park. Every July, she held a big weekend party for the famous King George VI and Queen Elizabeth flat race at Ascot Racecourse. She would invite about five married couples, plus four or five unattached friends. My mother and father knew Queen Elizabeth extremely well. She visited their house, Lockinge Manor, each summer for lunch and knew I was passionate about racing. We had many talks about her National Hunt horses. She even personally wrote some treasured letters to me about her horses – one of which was reprinted in William Shawcross's book, *Counting One's Blessings: The Selected Letters of Queen Elizabeth the Queen Mother.*

It was a great honour and privilege to be invited to stay with her, but I needed to be on my best behaviour and make sure that all my clothes were clean, well ironed and neatly packed. Each year I bought new white underwear for those weekends because the guests' suitcases were unpacked by members of the staff at Royal Lodge. I used to have a shop-up at Marks & Spencer every June and buy new knickers, bras and petticoats.

My bedroom was the same one each year: a lovely big room with a huge double bed and an adjoining bathroom. The windows looked out over the garden. Before I changed into a long dress for dinner each night, a clean bath towel was draped over the back of the chair in the bathroom and a lovely hot bath was run for me. The bedroom was full of flowers – mostly roses – but these were removed every night and put on a table on the landing, because flowers give off carbon dioxide in the dark. It is probably why, nowadays, no patients are allowed flowers in hospitals.

The dinner parties were memorable and we each had a handwritten menu. There were liveried waiters and superb food and wine. After dinner the women invariably left the men and went to the drawing room. I often sat beside Her Majesty on a big sofa and discussed racing. She loved music, and later in the evening one of her guests would play the grand piano and we would have a sing-song. Sometimes Queen Elizabeth would put some old 33 rpm records on the gramophone and there would be dancing. Looking back, they were amazing weekends – days that will go down in history.

It was only when I met Terry and he started living with me that I was taken off the guest list, but we both continued to be invited to Royal Lodge each year to the cocktail party after the Grand Military Race at Sandown Park in March. I was able to show Terry exactly where I had stayed during my single years. Like everyone else, he adored Queen Elizabeth the Queen Mother, and was lucky enough to ride horses for her on many occasions – in particular, Game Spirit, on whom he finished third in the 1974 Cheltenham Gold Cup. Later, she sent him two signed photographs, which I had framed. They hang in the hallway of the farmhouse. When Her Majesty lunched with my parents, Mum always invited Terry and me to attend and there were plenty of good racing memories.

After Edredon Bleu's victory in the 2000 Champion Chase, there was the excitement of the prize-giving and Queen Elizabeth's presentation of the trophies. It was an unforgettable occasion. When Jim Lewis and his wife, Valerie, had received the owner's winning cup, I walked up onto the rostrum with A. P. McCoy behind me. Luckily, I had no trouble with my curtsey, but I was amused to see on the replay later that the winning jockey also executed a curtsey. It was a brilliant day and what a race to win. My mother was there too, and had lunched in the Royal Box. She was understandably extremely proud.

Two races later we had our second winner of the day. Lord Noelie, with Jim Culloty in the saddle, won the Sun Alliance Chase for his hugely enthusiastic syndicate. We immediately became part of another round of joyous celebrations. Terry and I hugged each other again and again. We could hardly believe that we had trained two festival winners on the same day.

There was no Cheltenham Festival in 2001 because of the foot-and-mouth outbreak. Racing was not allowed. The disease was a disaster for the country and for farmers. It also represented a considerable financial loss to those who relied on the festival to provide a large proportion of their yearly income; hotels, guest houses and restaurants were particularly hard hit. For our part, as trainers we were bitterly disappointed that we could not run Best Mate in the Arkle Chase. He was ante-post favourite and Terry and I both felt sure he would have run well. We had to wait until 2002 for our next taste of festival glory, but from then on our fortunes in the blue riband of steeplechasing – The Cheltenham Gold Cup – rose to giddy heights. Best Mate won his first Gold Cup in 2002, then repeated this victory in 2003 and 2004. Even after his first win, our lives began to change. We had a horse in our midst that everybody wanted to own. We were in possession of a precious jewel and it was now our duty to keep him safe.

During those early years which marked the beginning of the new century, Best Mate's popularity soared to colossal heights for a steeplechaser. Racegoers love a rising star, and the Best Mate fan club had begun. Best Mate's admirers constantly clamoured to come and see him, or get news of his day-to-day life. At that time neither Facebook nor Twitter existed. If people wanted updates, they had to telephone, write a letter or send a fax. Yet, it wasn't only the racing public that took an interest in our new phenomenon; the press did as well. Best Mate was photographed and filmed like a movie star.

I was deeply touched by all the attention and had never before experienced anything like it. I wanted to reply to everybody and acknowledge the kindness of our supporters. When we went on holiday in Ireland during June 2002, I packed an extra suitcase and filled it with fan mail. I stayed indoors for several days and answered letters while Terry tried, unsuccessfully, to catch a salmon. I sent small individual photographs of Best Mate at Cheltenham to everybody who had sent their congratulations.

We did not spend long away from West Lockinge Farm during the summer of 2002. We didn't feel properly relaxed leaving the horses behind and preferred to be at home to watch over our new wonder horse.

In July of that year, I was approached by Channel 4 with a view to filming Best Mate during the build-up to the 2003 Cheltenham Gold Cup. Being superstitious, I was hesitant at first, fearing that filming might jeopardise his chances of a second win, but in due course the film crew moved in and we spent some extremely happy days working with them. Best Mate's victory in the 2002 Cheltenham Gold Cup left me in a state of bewilderment, but Terry had always believed the horse would win. It is true that Best Mate had been ultra-consistent in his races, never finishing out of the first two placings. Yet, for me, it was hard to believe that the little farmyard at West Lockinge had been able to turn out a Gold Cup winner. It's the race everybody dreams of winning – the pinnacle of steeplechase racing – and it has eluded many top trainers.

The excitement of that first victory remains crystal-clear in my memory. I hadn't watched the race with Terry, but when I ran down the pathway from the paddock to the racecourse I found him sobbing with joy beside the railings where the horses walk back. I threw my arms around him and we hugged each other tightly, unable to hide our emotions. My blue suit and Mum's pearls had turned out to be lucky, as had Terry's yellow tie and battered old trilby hat. Out of superstition, we wore the same outfits in 2003 and 2004 for the next two Gold Cups. We kept everything the same and, by 2004, I had perfected my run to meet Terry.

Best Mate undoubtedly made my career and certainly brought Terry and me into the public eye, while in our private lives, the Cheltenham Gold Cup victories brought us even closer together. We lived for each other and we lived for Best Mate. It always amazed me that Terry never showed a hint of jealousy, although I was officially Best Mate's trainer and he had twice been refused permission to train when he had retired from race-riding. We shared our successes equally. It was always a joint effort; Terry never cared about paperwork, it didn't bother him that it was my name on the licence. He was unbelievably supportive, and after a notable win would often say, 'Hen, this is your big day.' Having experienced numerous such days himself, he just seemed proud that I could have my days in the sun as well.

With Best Mate, Terry and I had both been given a huge responsibility. We structured our lives around him but he was a pleasure to train. The longer we had him, the more we loved him. His charisma and charm were always apparent. He was a real showman and a horse who always wanted to please. He really enjoyed his work. Indeed, rather like Terry and me, he got bored if his holidays were too long. He thrived on action and adventure. Racegoers called him 'the people's horse' and he thrived on the adulation. The nation adored him. He was good for racing and thoroughly deserved to win jump-racing's Horse of the Year award twice in 2003 and 2004.

In the summer of 2003, Terry and I were invited to Yorkshire for the annual Timeform Dinner. This is a charity evening and there is always a high-class auction. These dinners started in 1971. By the end of 2014 they had raised over £6.5 million, mostly for Macmillan Cancer Relief. Terry was not enthusiastic about the idea, even though he knew that plenty of friends would be there. He reckoned that travelling to York on a Friday afternoon just for a dinner was something he could easily do without. He hated long evenings. At home he liked his supper in the kitchen at around seven o'clock, before going upstairs to bed to watch his favourite television programmes. As he got older and was in more pain, he used to get extremely tired in the evenings, but still insisted on getting up at 5.15 a.m. every morning to feed the horses.

However, I managed to persuade him that it would be difficult to refuse this particular invitation, since Reg Griffin, Timeform's chairman, was a great friend. Both Reg and Jim McGrath had put in a huge amount of time and work over the years to organise these evenings, and our neighbour, Charles Cadogan, would also be attending. For twenty-five years, he had sponsored one of the races on Timeform's charity day at York.

As we took the lift up to the restaurant on the racecourse, we met trainer Peter Easterby. He said to me, 'Whatever are you and Terry doing here? You must be getting some award.'

He was right. After the hugely successful auction, Reg Griffin announced that Terry and I had jointly been chosen to receive Timeform's Personality Award for 2003. This was a complete surprise and a great honour. In the past presentations had been made to famous racing personalities including John Francome, Peter O'Sullevan, Lester Piggott, Vincent O'Brien, Henry Cecil, A. P. McCoy and Martin Pipe. I could not believe my ears.

We felt extremely humbled and privileged, and a short film was shown on all the restaurant televisions of Terry and me celebrating the victory of Best Mate in the 2003 Cheltenham Gold Cup, including the big hug I gave him when I ran down the shute to meet him on the racecourse. The Timeform racing personalities are traditionally presented with an engraved carriage clock. Mine still has its place of honour on the dresser in our kitchen.

Other awards also came our way during those golden years: I won the Horserace Writers' and Photographers' Association Derby Award for the National Hunt Trainer of the Year in 2002 and Channel 4's Racing Personality of the Year in 2003. Then I was voted Lanson Champagne Lady of the Year in 2002 and received seven Guinness Awards at the Cheltenham Festival from 2002–04. These prizes were a huge boost to us, validating our training methods and further cementing our special partnership.

They were unforgettable, fairy-tale years, and after the 2003 Gold Cup, I decided to write the Best Mate story. It was not easy to isolate myself, let alone collect and transfer my thoughts onto paper, and at times, Terry felt left out, especially when his dinners arrived later and later. Fortunately, I have always enjoyed writing – a legacy from my university and teaching days – and *Chasing Gold* became a best-seller. Later, after Best Mate won the 2004 Cheltenham Gold Cup, I updated and renamed it *Triple Gold*.

Although Cheltenham gave Terry and me our greatest training successes, Best Mate was also successful at Aintree over hurdles in 2000, and at Sandown in the Scilly Isles Chase in 2001. He then won the Peterborough Chase in 2002 and the King George VI Chase at Kempton the same year, as well as taking the Ericson Chase (now called the Lexus) at Leopardstown in 2003. His first chase victory came at Exeter in October 2000, and then he won the Haldon Gold Cup at that course twice in 2001 and 2004. There is a special room dedicated to Best Mate at Exeter, with photographs displayed on the walls. Racegoers there always took him to their hearts, and it is a lovely tribute to him.

Meanwhile, Edredon Bleu always seemed in his element skipping round Huntingdon racecourse and won four consecutive Peterborough Chases there from 1998. He was also victorious in the King George Chase at Kempton in 2003. It was some achievement for a chaser to win the Queen Mother Champion Chase at Cheltenham – over two miles – and then prove his versatility by winning over three miles at Kempton. He was a diamond of a horse and, like Best Mate, hugely popular with the public.

The Peterborough Chase proved an extremely lucky race for West Lockinge Farm and we ended up winning it eight times. Camilla Radford's Racing Demon won it twice, and Impek, another of Jim Lewis's French imports, was victorious with A. P. McCoy in 2005. The racecourse always gave us a great welcome when we ran our horses on the Cambridgeshire track, and no other trainer has ever registered as many victories in its feature race. Yet, despite many happy days at Huntingdon, there was one occasion in 2001 when I felt nothing but sadness.

My mother took special pride and pleasure in the successes that Terry and I were experiencing. When Best Mate first arrived from Ireland, in 1999, he was stabled in her yard at Lockinge Manor. She used to talk to him every day and watch him leave the stables on his daily exercise. She realised that he was potentially a top-class racehorse and she witnessed a number of his early victories.

On 24 November 2001 I had both Edredon Bleu and Best Mate due to run on the same day: Edredon Bleu at Huntingdon in the Peterborough Chase and Best Mate at Ascot in the Amlin Chase. I had decided to go to Huntingdon since Terry had opted for Ascot. Norman Williamson was scheduled to ride Edredon Bleu and on Wednesday morning he came to West Lockinge to jump him over the fences.

After the schooling session we all gathered in the farmhouse for breakfast, but, as we sat down for a chat, I received a telephone call from the village postman. He said he had just opened the front door at the manor to find my mother lying on the floor at the bottom of the stairs. Both Terry and I dropped everything and drove up to Mum's house at the other end of the village. We were appalled by what we saw.

She had obviously fallen down the stairs with her breakfast tray. She always took it up to her bedroom at around eight o'clock in order to drink her coffee, eat her toast and read the papers. On this occasion she hadn't made it. Her three dogs – the yellow Labrador, the nervous collie and the cheeky long-haired dachshund – were wandering about aimlessly. Crockery was strewn all over the hall floor and Mum was lying unconscious among the debris, having hit her head on a skirting board jutting out at the foot of the staircase. It was a shocking sight. I had only spoken to her on the telephone twenty minutes earlier; she had been in great form and was looking forward to coming racing with me on the Saturday. Terry feared the worst straight away and told me to dial 999, then we both sat on the sofa in the sitting room, waiting for the ambulance. There was nothing else we could do. Eventually Mum was put onto a stretcher and taken off to the John Radcliffe Hospital in Oxford, but it didn't look good.

We had five horses due to run that day at Kempton Park Racecourse. I did not know what action to take, but guessed that Mum would still want them to fulfill their engagements. Somebody had to go to the races to look after the owners and Terry volunteered, even though, deep down, he wanted to stay with me and drive me to the hospital. Tragically, Mum did not survive her accident and my sister came down to the Oxford hospital from London. It was shattering for both of us.

Extraordinarily, we had three winners at Kempton. Jim Lewis's Stars Out Tonight, plus my own horse, Red Blazer, and my sister's horse, Maximise. It was as though Mum had willed her daughters' two horses to win. Terry told me he had been utterly miserable at the races and that he had sat on his own for a lot of the time, on a bench at the far end of the members' enclosure. He hated being separated from me and he adored my mother. When we met up again, later in the day, he was comforting and affectionate, but he was as heartbroken as the rest of us. It was one of the strangest days of my life, but together, Terry and I handled the tears. The following day we had two more winners at Wincanton, but neither of us attended. On Saturday Best Mate was beaten into second place at Ascot by Wahiba Sands, but Terry saddled a young mare called Returning to win the Novice Chase.

Edredon Bleu duly won the Peterborough Chase and was, as always, the star of the day. I watched him in a daze, still in deep shock from Mum's death. As a racehorse trainer, however, I had to pull myself together and keep the show on the road, especially as all the horses were running exceptionally well. In fact, in eight days we had a total of ten winners. It was an extraordinary month, but looking back it saddened me that Mum never lived to see any of Best Mate's Gold Cup victories. She would have been so proud.

At her funeral, Terry was upset because I made him wear a coloured tie – Mum hated black ones. He was annoyed with me for not letting him wear his customary funeral tie and felt that he was the odd man out. It was a deeply moving day and the church at Lockinge was crammed. An extra tent was put up outside. Queen Elizabeth the Queen Mother attended – she was extremely fond of Mum – and I sat next to her in the church. I read one of the lessons and when I came back to my seat she touched me and said, 'That was beautifully done.' I was close to tears, but her words have remained with me for ever. I believe this was the last occasion that she ventured out on a public engagement. She was 101 years old.

Despite personal tragedies such as this, Terry and I were unbelievably fortunate to have been entrusted with so many lovely horses during our days together. They gave us countless memorable days and highlights that were unrepeatable. I experienced magical moments that I could never have believed possible. No one could have written the script in advance. It just happened.

CHAPTER TWELVE

The Other Side of the Coin

Training racehorses may look straightforward from the outside, but, as in all walks of life, there are always downsides. Terry and I experienced some unforgettable highs and many glory days, but we had our fair share of misfortunes as well. Despite outwardly being tough and carefree, Terry was, underneath, unbelievably soft and sentimental. He genuinely cared for people and for animals. It took very little for him to dissolve into tears if something upset him. The everyday ups and downs he could take, but if there was a tragedy to deal with, then it hit him hard.

Terry was an extremely loving man and Elain Mellor, wife of former champion jockey Stan, was one of many who witnessed his gentle side.

During his jockey days, Terry apparently called in to the Mellors house at Middleton Stoney, near Banbury, late one Friday afternoon for a cup of tea and a talk with Stan. When he arrived, Elain was about to set off to Gloucester with their two-year-old daughter, Linz, who was going to stay with her grandparents in Wales. The handover was to be in the car park at Gloucester Market. Since Terry was going back to his own home in Gloucestershire, he offered to take the child with him. Linz was put into the passenger seat of Terry's car, with no seat belt, and off they went. When Elain's mother arrived in Gloucester to collect her granddaughter, she spotted Terry's Jaguar in the market car park but could see no sign of the driver, nor the child. On closer inspection, to her amazement, she found Terry fast asleep with his seat right back and the child asleep on top of his chest. They both looked so peaceful that she found it hard to wake them up.

Terry was always haunted by the deaths of horses – or any animals he loved. In 1959, as an amateur, he had ridden one of his father's horses, a lovely French-bred hurdler Or Massif, at Cheltenham. This horse tragically broke its foreleg when falling at the last flight. Terry was only eighteen at the time and was heartbroken. Although he became more resigned to tragedies as he got older, whenever he rode a horse that had to be destroyed it hit him hard. One horse that he particularly liked was Red Thorn, on whom he won the Great Sefton Chase at Aintree in 1964. I have a lovely oil painting in my bedroom of Terry jumping a fence on this beautiful white-faced chestnut. He believed Red Thorn could have won a Grand National, but in 1965 the horse broke his leg at Doncaster in the Great Yorkshire Chase and couldn't be saved.

When at West Lockinge, both Terry and I had plenty of black

days. Some people would say that we were sentimental with our horses and dogs, but we treated them all like members of the family and knew them as personal friends. Every one had a different personality and they were our children. We hated to see them injured or suffering from pain. However, if one trains horses, one has to expect accidents. They are fragile animals – like human athletes. When highly tuned, the injury risks are high, but unless they are hard-trained and raced on the tracks, nobody ever knows what ability they might possess.

During my years of training, we had several tragic accidents at home. A beautiful grey French horse of Lady Bamford's, Faucon Bleu, broke his fetlock on the gallops, and Silverbar, belonging to the Wyatt family, snapped a hind leg when cantering between fences in our schooling field. He, too, was grey and a brilliant jumper. These two accidents were shocking for the connections of both horses, but they were completely unforeseen. Neither horse had ever had a fall nor shown any signs of lameness in previous months. One winter, an employee of mine fractured her shin bone dismounting from a horse in the yard – a simple accident, but she must have landed awkwardly. The same must have happened to these two lovely horses – if you put your foot down incorrectly, you can shatter a bone. On both occasions Terry was superb. He comforted me, he talked to my staff and he reassured the owners that there was nothing anybody could have done to prevent these tragedies.

In 1997, we trained a stunning looking big bay horse called Wild West Wind. He belonged to Sam Vestey and he won some decent races, including a couple of steeplechases. He was one of the nicest, kindest horses we ever had in the yard. Terry adored him and fed him every morning. Indeed, everybody loved him. But one weekend he became ill. Initially, we thought that he had contracted a form of colic. He wouldn't eat and looked miserable but he did not thrash around rolling, nor did he have any temperature. The vets were mystified. Early on the Tuesday morning, Terry opened the door to feed him and found him lying dead on the straw. It was one of the saddest moments of my training career. Terry was completely shattered and couldn't even stay in the yard, but left me to deal with the knacker van and autopsy. It transpired that the horse had died from a ruptured abscess in his intestines. He had been given plenty of painkillers on the previous day so we hoped that he had not suffered too much, but I will never forget that morning – such a waste of a gorgeous animal.

On another day, in 2001, Terry again showed the sensitive side of his nature. We had a famous retired event horse in the yard called Sir Wattie. When ridden by Ian Stark, he had won the Badminton three-day event twice, in 1986 and 1988, and had represented Great Britain in the 1988 Olympic Games in Seoul. Wattie was given early retirement at twelve years old – not because he was unfit to continue his eventing career, but because his owner thought he had done enough competing and needed a happy home. He was sent to West Lockinge to teach the young racehorses how to jump and for me to ride out with the string. He became our yard mascot, but was hopeless on hacks, because he was afraid of traffic and terrified of tractors. Ian told me that he had always been the same, yet never incurred a cross-country fault in all his eventing days and jumped some of the strangest-looking fences, including a fence made up of two cars at Badminton. When Sir Wattie was in his mid-twenties, arthritis set in and he became very lame. Therefore it was decided that he would have to be put to sleep.

He was always spoilt and came into a stable every night. When the vet arrived, one sunny summer afternoon, Terry bravely announced that he would hold Wattie for me. I certainly didn't want to do this myself; I loved him too much, and I was grateful for Terry's offer. After the horse had been put down both Terry and Roger Betteridge, the vet, returned to the house in tears.

I have never seen two grown men in such a bad state. They were crying like children and Terry took two days to get over our loss. It was as if one of his best friends had died. It hit me hard, too, but I needed somebody to console me and back me up – I didn't need Terry to be sobbing in the kitchen. How I wish that we did not get so attached to our animals. They can be such heartbreakers.

Sarah Griffiths, who used to help in the office during my training years, got on exceptionally well with Terry and she told me that, 'Although Terry was able to be outrageous and shock everyone, he was never afraid to show his emotions either. I remember him being as upset as anyone on that day when Sir Wattie had to be put down. He was the first visitor to see my daughter, Molly, at the Wantage Hospital after she was born. He arrived at 8 a.m. straight from the gallops in his wellies with a huge tin of chocolates. No visitors were allowed in before 10 a.m., so I always wondered how he had talked his way up to my room, I assume he had just charmed all the nurses.'

In 2004, following his third Gold Cup victory, Best Mate had his customary summer holiday during the months of May, June and July. Nothing was changed. He went out as usual into the field everyday with his best friend, Edredon Bleu, and at night they both came in to cosy, straw-bedded stables in order to be given extra food. Jim Lewis never liked his horses to spend nights outside, in case there were thunderstorms. In mid-July all our horses came back into steady work. They walked and trotted for several weeks in order to recondition their muscles and harden their legs, but still enjoyed their daily turn-outs in the fields. Best Mate looked magnificent – he had summered really well. He was such a handsome horse: a horse to feast one's eyes upon. He could have won in the show ring. His conformation was faultless.

We had held the Best Mate Open Day in 2003 and due to its success, we had decided to hold an even bigger open day in 2004 – The Hen and Terry Charity Open Day. We knew that a large number of racing enthusiasts would flock to West Lockinge Farm to see the triple Gold Cup winner and it was an ideal opportunity to raise money for our chosen charities. The 19 September was a lovely sunny day. The horses looked superb and a bumper crowd of 7,000 people flocked to the farm. Everybody wanted to pat and stroke the champion and we built a special enclosure so that he could be viewed and photographed from every angle.

After that memorable Sunday, we decided that Best Mate would have his first outing for the new season at Exeter in the Haldon Gold Cup on 19 November. He duly won this race with Timmy Murphy riding, because Jim Culloty was out of action but, whereas he had won the same race in 2001 by twenty lengths, this time he only beat Seebald by a short head. It was a nerve-racking occasion and at one moment it looked as if the favourite would get beaten.

Maybe, following Best Mate's third Gold Cup victory in 2004, we had been too easy on him at home and given him less work than usual during his preparation. We had installed a Martin Collins gallop during the summer months and the horses had cantered easily on the new Ecotrack surface. Perhaps the effects of winning three Cheltenham Gold Cups were beginning to tell. Who knows? Terry and I asked ourselves plenty of questions. We didn't feel that the horse was at his best at Exeter, even though he jumped superbly and there was a huge crowd present to watch him run. We had lengthy discussions afterwards with Jim Lewis and it was decided that Matey's next race would be the Lexus Chase at Leopardstown on 28 December, where he had sparkled in 2003. The course had obviously suited him, and Jim Culloty would again be available to ride.

Unfortunately, everything seemed to turn against Best Mate on that particular Irish trip. During the journey over on the boat, he hit his head on the inside of the horsebox and cut himself above one eye. It was a nasty gash and required veterinary attention. Butterfly stitches were inserted, but he seemed quite happy and ate well when he arrived in the Emerald Isle. Terry and I hoped that he did not have a headache and that there would not be too much swelling the following morning. Fortunately, all seemed well and the course vet pronounced him fit to run. On the day of the race, it rained and rained. The going changed from good to soft to soft, heavy in places. This was exactly what we did *not* want, because Best Mate always preferred a sound surface. Despite the change in ground, it was decided to let him take his chance but he ran flat and was beaten into second place by Beef or Salmon. He had a hard race and didn't show any acceleration on the rain-softened turf. Naturally, we were deflated, especially as Best Mate had started at odds on and had been expected to win. In previous races, Beef or Salmon had always finished behind him.

When Best Mate returned from Ireland, at the end of December 2004, he was a sick horse. He was running a temperature and was off his food. He looked a shadow of his usual self. It took him several weeks to pick up again. He had obviously contracted a virus and the race had also left its mark. We gave him a long holiday and plenty of special tonics. Gradually he started to regain weight and perk up. For most of January he was not ridden, but was led out to graze and when the weather was good, we turned him out into his favourite field. His coat began to shine again and his appetite returned. He looked brighter and happier. He even started to push Terry out of his way each morning to get to his breakfast. He always did this when he was feeling well.

There were two-and-a-half months between Leopardstown and Cheltenham and we just prayed we would be able to get him there for a fourth Gold Cup run. However, he had to show us that he was 100 per cent fit and well. February passed by and his work programme was increased.

At the beginning of March, we took him to West Ilsley to Mick Channon's lovely grass gallops. Mick is an excellent friend, and this former well known international footballer would generously welcome our champion for his pipe openers. Matey had worked there in previous years as well in preparation for his three Cheltenham Gold Cup wins and the gallops had been a good place for us to assess his well-being. On that occasion in 2005, I drove up to the Downs on my own to watch him while Terry stayed at home to supervise our other horses.

After a quiet warm-up canter on the all-weather surface, all seemed well, and the horses walked down to the start of the long grass gallop known as Gilbert's. It provides an uphill climb and is a stiff gallop. I remember Major Hern, who trained three Derby winners at West Ilsley, saying to me that if a horse gets to the top of Gilbert's and is still full of running, he is fit and well.

In the final furlong and going around the left-hand bend, Best Mate faltered and dropped back. Something was clearly not right.

His two work companions both pressed on to the end. The former champion was left trailing in their wake. I rushed up to the horses to see what was wrong and was horrified to find blood streaming out of one of Best Mate's nostrils. He had broken a blood vessel – probably due to the effects of the virus a few months earlier. We would have to pull him out of Cheltenham. There would be no more glorious festival days.

I immediately rang up Terry who, for once, answered the car phone in his truck, and I telephoned both Jim Lewis and the Press Association. Our dreams of possibly winning a fourth Gold Cup had been shattered, but at least our champion was still in one piece and did not seem even slightly distressed when he got back home.

Following on from this black day, we gave Best Mate a long holiday and another lovely summer in his field. As always, he looked superb during the months of June and July. He restarted his daily ridden exercise in early August.

At our 2005 open day in September, he was once more the centre of attention and nobody would ever have known that he had experienced training problems in March. Terry and I were smiling again, because Matey had been working brilliantly at home. We told his followers that he would race at Exeter on 1 November. It was one of his favourite tracks.

On that fateful day, when Best Mate returned to the racecourse he loved, nobody could have foreseen the tragedy that was to unfold. Thousands of fans were there and attendance numbers were exceptionally high. It was business as usual; everybody was longing to see the former wonder horse. Terry and I did the saddling up, as we always did, and we felt happy with our star. In the designated box, while we positioned his tack, his ears were pricked. He was trembling with the excitement of the occasion and he intently watched everything that was happening around him.

As he absorbed the atmosphere, Best Mate stared across to the racecourse with his usual eagerness – and when he walked around the paddock, he strode out as though he owned the place. He had never been beaten at Exeter and this was his fourth visit. He loved playing to his public and was a proper show-off. The only difference that day was that he was being led up by his new lass, Gemma Bennett. His former minder, Jackie Jenner, had left our employment at the end of April. There were some outstanding photographs of Best Mate in the preliminaries that day and Gemma had turned him out superbly. She was rightly proud of her new charge. Jim Lewis and his supporters thronged the centre of the parade ring wearing their customary Aston Villa scarves. This was Jim's favourite football club and Best Mate's racing colours were maroon and pale blue.

Terry legged up the jockey, Paul Carberry, who had been invited to ride Matey that day. Jim Culloty had retired from race-riding and the two other jockeys who had previously ridden and won on Best Mate were unavailable at Exeter. Timmy Murphy rode Contraband for David Johnson and A. P. McCoy rode Ground Ball for J. P. McManus.

After watching Best Mate canter down to the start on that November day, I remember thinking how magnificent he looked.

There was no hint of anything amiss. He strode out majestically and his coat gleamed in the autumn sunshine; even his dapples showed up. In keeping with tradition, I then walked down the racecourse to watch the race unfold and listen to the commentary close to the last fence. I could see the action from there without being among the huge crowd of racegoers. The grandstand was packed with people. My nerves were tingling with anticipation, but I was pleased with our horse. He had never looked better. I felt proud to be training him.

There were eleven runners in the Haldon Gold Cup in 2005 and, as they streamed over the fence in front of me, Best Mate looked happy, he was up with the pace. He jumped with his usual fluency and glided through the air. Then the runners disappeared around the corner, out of my sight and I could no longer clearly hear the commentary. I waited anxiously for them to approach the final bend and held my binoculars to my eyes with shaking hands. Would I see Best Mate close to the front? On the two occasions he had previously won the race, he had always been prominent when they had turned into the straight.

All of a sudden I spotted the runners. They were closely bunched, but there was no sign of Best Mate among them. Then I saw him: on the inside of the course, pulling wide of the fences. Instantly, I knew that something must be horribly wrong. My heart sank. He hadn't been pulled up in any race since that very first point-to-point in Ireland. Indeed, on every other occasion, in the twenty-one races he had contested, he had finished in the first two. He had either won or been second.

In a flash, I was under the railings and making my way further down the track. Best Mate was approaching me in a trot and his stride appeared normal, but as he got closer he faltered and his gait changed. He veered across the course towards the outer railings, close to the last fence. There was a lack of co-ordination in his hind limbs and his eyes were glazed. As he wobbled further, Paul jumped off in the nick of time, just before his mount gently keeled over on his right side onto the beautifully manicured green grass. I was with him instantly, but I knew immediately that his life was ebbing away. Some years before, I had been riding my treasured three-day event horse when he had suffered a heart attack and his behaviour had been exactly the same. The end was quick. Best Mate would have felt no pain. It was as though he was in a coma. He took his last breath and lay motionless. There was no struggle. His death was extremely peaceful.

A sudden numbness came over me. Was this for real, or a bad dream? In no time at all, I was surrounded by scores of spectators and members of the press. A new stand had been erected that day, beside the final fence. It was crammed with racegoers – most of them Best Mate fans. He had died in front of their eyes and they had seen everything first-hand. The shock was indescribable. There was an eerie silence as people gathered around the fallen star, and then the dreaded green screens were put up so that the racegoers could no longer see him.

I took a grip of myself and remembered what my darling Mum had always instilled into us as children: don't cry in public. I tried to blank out the full horror of the occasion. At least the horse hadn't suffered – it would have been far worse if he had broken a leg. But his supporters in the racing world had lost their idol. He had acquired a massive fan club and he could not possibly have lost his life more publicly. The race had been televised and millions of people had watched his dying moments. I needed to pull myself together and face up to the truth.

Terry came down the course as fast as he could to find me. He had watched the race unfold on the big screen beside the paddock. He put his arms around me and his eyes were full of tears, but we had a job to do and it was not the right time to mourn. People wandered about on the track in disbelief. Jim Lewis and his wife Valerie were totally shattered. There were wet eyes and handkerchiefs everywhere.

For my part, I went straight to Paul Carberry and kept the crowds away from him. I walked back beside him to the weighing room and he carried Best Mate's saddle. It was a solemn walk but I needed to return to the buildings, as we had another runner, Racing Demon, in the following race. It was his first chase and there was no reason for him not to run. Racing had to continue. The gallant victor of the Haldon Gold Cup – Monkerhostin – was being greeted by his own supporters in the unsaddling enclosure, but the crowds were noticeably subdued.

I was approached by many people – they came up to me from all angles – but I managed to stay calm and talk sensibly. I even did a television interview on a racing channel. It wasn't easy, but I stressed how lucky we were to have trained such a wonderful horse and I explained that he was born and bred to race. He had died doing the job that he enjoyed and thankfully he had not suffered. I remembered the words of Byron, 'Those whom the gods love, die young.' I remember saying to the press that all horses have to die sometime – we all have to go – but it's doubly tragic when it happens so unexpectedly.

Racing Demon, with Timmy Murphy, duly won the novice chase. This, too, was an extremely moving occasion. As I walked to greet the horse, Timmy put out his gloved hand and gave my own hand a tight squeeze. When he walked into the winner's enclosure, the crowd gave Demon a huge reception. There were massive cheers and I remember saying to Timmy, 'This is unbelievable.' He said, 'They do have hearts, you know.' I will never forget that demonstration of affection. It touched me immensely.

It was a strange, sombre journey back to West Lockinge Farm. Neither Terry nor I spoke much, yet my mobile telephone never stopped ringing. I ignored many of the calls and I dreaded getting back to the yard to see Best Mate's empty stable. Fortunately, a couple of my staff had decided to put Red Blazer into his box so that it would be less of a shock for Terry and me to walk across the concrete the next morning and not see our champion's head over the door. When my travelling staff got home, they put Best Mate's rugs into the washroom and his special head-collar, with his brass nameplate, in the house. No horse has ever worn it since, and I will treasure it for ever. It still hangs up by the back door.

The tragedy on Exeter Racecourse was broadcast that night on the national news. The next day, all the newspapers were full of Best Mate's death, with some unpleasant and distressing photographs recording his last minutes on the front pages of several of the tabloids. When he won his third Cheltenham Gold Cup, he was on the front page of *The Times*. When he died, he hit the headlines and took centre stage again. Best Mate had captured the imagination of the public. He was often called 'The People's Horse' because it seemed that so many of his fans thought that they owned him. His intelligence, beauty and courage were exceptional. Certainly, I knew when he died that we would never train another horse like him. He had huge ability and was such a proud individual.

Terry was hit hard by Best Mate's death. He used to feed him every morning and he treated him like a close friend. In all the years I lived with him, I never saw Terry in such a bad state as he was on the evening of that disaster. He drank several glasses of whisky to drown his sorrows, but since he had barely touched alcohol for over twenty years, those drinks noticeably affected him. He cried and cried. It was utterly tragic. I remember finding it extremely difficult to get him upstairs to bed. He was shattered and very much the worse for wear.

Fortunately, by the next morning he had come back to his senses and was able, as usual, to help me feed the horses in the yard. However, he was noticeably subdued. He knew that he shouldn't have had a drink, but his emotions and the bottle had got the better of him. From then on he was brilliant and gave me huge support. We had a lot of attention from the press and there were numerous interviews. I needed him to be fully *compos mentis* and he did not for one moment let me down.

After Exeter, Jim Lewis was naturally devastated but he did not want a post-mortem examination. Looking back, it seems clear that Best Mate had either had a heart attack or ruptured an artery. There were no outward signs of blood and both his nostrils were clear. Jim wanted his star to be buried at the racecourse and the officials were happy for this to happen, but his wish wasn't granted, thanks to certain crazy regulations brought in by the European Parliament. His burial plans became entangled in red tape and in the end, civil servants at the Trading Standards Office of Devon County Council refused Exeter's request. The Environment Agency and DEFRA had passed the buck, so that the final decision rested with this office. It hinged upon whether, as a racehorse, Best Mate was classified as a pet or a commercial animal.

The definition of the former seems to be an animal nurtured by humans but not normally eaten, but of course, horses are eaten on the Continent. Therefore, Europeans regarded racehorses as commercial animals. The head of Trading Standards declared, 'Since foot-and-mouth disease and BSE, it is illegal to bury fallen stock. They have to be disposed of in approved ways.' When those in charge were asked what possible harm there could be in burying

211

a racehorse many feet underground and miles from anywhere, they merely replied, 'We are here to enforce the law and not to bend it.'

When questioned on the matter, poor Jim replied, 'I understand that they had to close various gaps in the law after foot-and-mouth, but horses are not cloven-footed. They do not get the disease nor do they carry it. It's political correctness gone mad.'

Instead of being buried, Best Mate was cremated and at a later date his ashes were placed by the winning post on Cheltenham Racecourse. There was a moving ceremony at Prestbury Park, courtesy of the racecourse officials, who later further recognised the achievements of this outstanding horse, by renaming an area on the far side of the track opposite the grandstand as the Best Mate Enclosure. Some months afterwards, a bronze statue of Best Mate, which had been cast from the original by Philip Blacker, was positioned close to the Cheltenham paddock. It is life-size and identical to the one that stands on the village green in Lockinge.

It was my uncle, Christopher 'Larch' Loyd, who commissioned the first statue, because he wanted Best Mate's greatness to be recognised close to where he was trained. The measurements for the bronze are exact and were taken when the horse was still alive. Philip came to West Lockinge Farm on many occasions, not just with his tape measure, but also with his camera. At that time, he had his studio close by in Faringdon, in Oxfordshire, and both Terry and I watched the sculpture unfold. We often drove over to look at it and make comments. It was a work of art.

———

Looking back on the life of Best Mate makes me realise just how lucky Terry and I were to have trained such a special horse. Many racegoers have memories of him, but most will agree that his magnificent appearance and flawless jumping set him apart from his contemporaries. It was a privilege to have had him in our midst. I wrote several letters to the newspapers in order to thank his fans for their support – it would have been impossible to have replied to every letter and card. I am reprinting here the one that I sent to *Horse & Hound*. This weekly magazine, one of my favourite publications, had always given the horse maximum publicity and often featured him on its cover. I wrote:

I have been surrounded by horses and ponies all my life. There have been plenty of wonderful moments, but inevitably, tragedies as well. One learns to enjoy the highs, but it is important to accept the lows, too. Yet nothing could have prepared me for the shock of losing Best Mate, suddenly, at Exeter Racecourse. It was a poignant and unbelievably sad day, not only for everybody connected to this brave and beautiful horse, but also for his thousands of admirers. He became a household name and won the hearts of the people. We received an amazing amount of flowers, letters, cards, e-mails, faxes and calls. We have been overwhelmed and deeply touched by so much kindness. Your support and sympathy have been hugely helpful, but we must not dwell on his tragic death and should be thankful, as well as honoured, to have been part of his life – part of the life of a great horse who inspired a nation and did so much for the sport he enjoyed. He was a talented athlete with a great temperament. He loved the crowds and responded to them by

213

giving them memories to cherish. Thank you, Matey, for always being yourself and for being such a special person. You will never be forgotten.

Later in 2005, I was at Cheltenham Racecourse, in Sam Vestey's box, when renowned racing poet Henry Birtles came in and asked if he could read out his poem on Best Mate. After Best Mate's death, I had received many poems, along with letters and cards, but Henry's was the best by a long way. It was beautifully framed and illustrated and I now have it hanging up in my sitting room. Even Terry agreed that it was exceptionally good. Each year on Cheltenham Gold Cup day, Henry recites it to the crowd, beside the Best Mate statue. It reads as follows:

A call to arms, upon us fast, that week in March now looms.
When thousands gather for the craic, when spring smites winter's gloom.
When stories get wheeled out again, those great Gold Cups of old.
It's minus two without the gale, yet no one feels the cold.

And so this year we'll celebrate a recent hero's past.
A horse whose place in Cheltenham lore not just in bronze we've cast.
A horse who proudly holds his own with legends of this track.
A kindly horse with looks and style and quality to match.

Now factor in his entourage, a most unlikely team.
Led by a former schoolmistress and harnessed by her dream.
A dream she shared with Biddlecombe, fine jockey of his time.
A dream they lived to realise, once they'd put aside the wine.

The owner, good Jim Lewis, vintage Brummie through and
  through.
His songs the only downside, his silks claret and blue.
The colours worn by Villa when they last brought home
  The Cup.
Engrained in racing folklore now, with Jim Culloty up.

They played an almost comic role, when cameras stopped
  to call.
But mark me now and mark me well, for him they gave
  their all.
They taught Best Mate that what he had was handed to the few.
They honed his power, they understood they showed him what
  to do.

And when unleashed in combat, though she couldn't bear to
  look.
Preferring racecourse car parks, where with head in hands she
  shook.
He always brought her running from behind the heaving stands.
To welcome him, victorious, clinging tight to Terry's hand.

Step forward, Henrietta, racing's first reluctant Knight.
And take a bow with Terry now for getting it so right.
For giving us the memories of a truly noble horse.
Whose early death remains the only reason for remorse.

A death that robbed a nation, but upon it we won't dwell.
Let's celebrate the life of one who served his sport so well.
Best Mate, you never let us down, you lived up to your name.
You ran your rivals ragged, showed 'em how to play this game.

He won with ease and nonchalance; he won with craft and style.
He won the hearts of England and the mighty Emerald Isle.
He gave us what we'd waited for, a Gold Cup crown retained.
An undisputed champion, a king who proudly reigned.

Don't judge him upsides Arkle, if you don't judge man by God.
But see him as a winter king, who never spared the rod.
Who poured it on at Prestbury Park, with smiling Jim aboard.
And left this world with three Gold Cups, Best Mate by all
  adored.

People say that losing a relation, a friend, or a horse, is character-building, but if that is the case, my own character must have been built many decades ago. I have witnessed numerous disasters in my life, but death does not get any easier to handle. One never gets used to it.

With racehorses, trainers have to brace themselves against hardships. Yet, I often wonder whether, without Terry, I would have continued training on my own. Terry was my rock, and I constantly turned to him for reassurance and advice, even though at times he, too, needed to be held up.

It is all about teamwork and trust. I consider that at West Lockinge Farm, we experienced both of these in abundance.

CHAPTER THIRTEEN

Casting Back

Looking back over the life Terry led during his racing days and assessing his contribution to the National Hunt scene make it easier to understand the reasons for his declining health in later years. His body was hammered in so many ways – not only as a result of racing falls, but also by his wild lifestyle. Many would say that it was an amazing feat for him to have survived for as long as he did. Nowadays, due to vast technological developments that have occurred worldwide over the last century, there have been colossal changes within the racing game. Current Health and Safety regulations, together with more and more red tape, have definitely prevented jockeys in this age from living like they did in Terry's era. The structure of racing has altered beyond recognition and I find it extremely interesting to pinpoint the changes.

It was no mean feat to win three National Hunt Jockeys' Championships in the 1960s, but Terry achieved this. He was successful in the seasons of 1964–5, 1965–6 and 1968–9. From 1958 until 1974 he rode over 900 winners. By contrast, on his retirement in 2015, A. P. McCoy had ridden over 4,000 winners and captured twenty championships. Why the difference? In Terry's riding days, there was far less racing and no summer jumping. Racecourses used to apply to the National Hunt Committee for fixtures. Nowadays, courses put on as many race meetings as they can, for greater betting opportunities and larger turnover. Fifty years ago, the jump season ended in May and didn't resume until the end of July or early August. Everything happened at a slower rate. Instead of trainers making entries for their horses five days in advance, as they do today, the entries were made six weeks before a scheduled race. There were no jockeys' agents, no mobile telephones, no computers and no overnight declarations. None of the daily races was televised and there were no closed-circuit televisions on the courses.

It was decided some weeks earlier where a particular horse would run and, in most cases, which jockey would ride it. Terry used to say that he would look down the entries in the Racing Calendar and be able to work out where he would be going thirty days later – provided, of course, that the horse was fit to run. The whole pace of the day-to-day racing was slower and less cut-throat. Jockeys seldom rang up trainers to ask for rides. The trainers rang the jockeys, but the top riders had a good life and plenty of fun.

The riding fee for a National Hunt jockey in 2015 is £162 and the valet fee paid by the jockeys is £16 a ride. In 1960 professional jockeys were paid £7.10s per ride, with no percentage of the prize money, and they paid their valets £1 for each horse they rode.

In 1969 the jockeys' fees went up to £13 a ride. When Terry was asked how much he earned in a year, he said that he reckoned it was £6,000, if he was lucky, and this included a £600 retainer from trainer Fred Rimell, but the day of getting slipped a tip by an owner had gone and he had to pay all his expenses out of his earnings, including travelling and tack.

A. P. McCoy and I have often compared racing today with racing in the sixties and seventies. He acknowledges the achievements of jockeys in Terry's era but mostly approves of the changes made in racing during the twenty-first century. Yet he thinks that, where jockeys are concerned, there was a greater strength in depth in the olden days. There were more top-class jockeys riding and many more jockeys who had been brought up through the ranks. They were tougher and were proper horsemen.

Indeed, if one looks at the list of jockeys in the sixties and seventies, there are many famous household names. In the present-day statistical charts for the Jockeys' Championship, there are certainly at least a dozen well-known ones at the top of the list, but then the famous names peter out. There are undoubtedly some good young riders, but I doubt whether too many will make racing history.

Nowadays, a lot of the jockeys have had less overall riding experience as children than they did in the last century. Many have not even come from horse-orientated backgrounds. A number of the modern younger jockeys graduate from the British Racing School, but this can never equal the experience of riding one's ponies in childhood. In Ireland, there is much to be gained from pony racing or 'flapping', plus showjumping and hunting. The young would-be jockeys have a huge advantage because horses are in their blood from day one. No wonder many of the top jockeys are Irish.

Terry's best friends in his riding years were probably Michael Scudamore, who lived locally and gave him plenty of advice; David Mould, the dapper, stylish jockey to whom Terry was like a brother; plus Josh Gifford, another champion jockey, who was an outstandingly fearless rider and later became a top trainer. His brother, Macer Gifford, who tragically died young from motor neurone disease, was also a good friend. Michael Scudamore rode Linwell to win the Cheltenham Gold Cup in 1957 and Oxo to win the Grand National in 1959. He was older than Terry, but a wonderful mentor. David Mould rode many horses for Queen Elizabeth the Queen Mother and he told me that, during his days with Terry, life 'just flowed'. 'We shared everything,' he said. 'We shared money and we shared fun. We spent a lot of time together and we lived for racing. Terry never minded what he said to anyone – including the stewards – but he always got away with his outrageous remarks. Everybody looked up to him and respected him.'

Johnny Lehane was another amusing mate of Terry's and rode many winners. Then there was the legendary Dave Dick, who partnered numerous top horses for the eccentric Dorothy Paget. He also won the Grand National on Mrs Carver's ESB in 1956. Dave's stories had to be heard to be believed. He was a unique man and the most wonderful company. When I took Terry to his memorial service in Newbury in 2001, he was visibly shaken, and it greatly upset him. From then on Terry vowed that he would never again attend a funeral or service for any of his best friends. He cried his eyes out on our homeward journey. When Josh Gifford died in 2012, Terry stayed at home. Josh's death hit him hard.

In his riding days, Bob Davies, who married Terry's sister, Sue, was one of Terry's arch-rivals but they got along well. They often fought out the spoils until the last day of the season to win the Jockeys' Championship. In the late sixties, before he got married, Bob used to stay with Terry. 'We often went racing together,' he recalls, 'but we both struggled with our weight and were often in the Gloucester Turkish baths. In the 1960s Cheltenham always gave a dinner for the Champion Jockey at the Queen's Hotel on the Friday night of the Mackeson meeting, now The Open. This was for men only, with the champion paying for a separate dinner at a later date for fellow jockeys, wives and girlfriends. When Terry and I shared the championship in 1969, that dinner was, as usual, in November. We had a very good evening, with a late night, which of course necessitated a morning in the baths before we rode in the afternoon. Julian Wilson had arranged to interview us that day on the roof of the main stand, which was then the BBC presentation area. It was about an hour before the first race. When we arrived, his first words were, "I hope nobody you know is watching this in colour." Colour television had just begun and we must have been looking exceedingly rough.'

Brough Scott, who rode with Terry, remembers that Tuesdays used to be ladies' day at the Gloucester baths, but Terry would charm himself into the steam room early on and an hour later, a rollicking Gloucester voice saying, 'Hello darling,' would scare the non-existent pants off the first naked lady to venture in. 'One year we spent the morning before the Midlands National sweating in the Turkish baths in Stoke,' Brough told the *Racing Post*. 'Once dried, off we set towards Uttoxeter, he the champion, me the acolyte. Halfway there, he directed me into a pub and ordered two sharpeners to set us right for our four-mile and 24-fence journey. They were Babycham and brandy. "Yes," said Biddlecombe, with majestic persuasion, "the bubbles will give us sparkle and the brandy a bit of kick." As it happens we both fell on the far side and he swung me up on the back of his remounted horse and we cantered back as a tandem.' (*Racing Post*, 6 January 2014).

Of course, this would not be allowed today. No horses can be remounted after a fall, let alone by two jockeys.

In Terry's era, there were no saunas at the races. In order to lose weight before they rode, the heavier jockeys spent many hours in the Turkish baths around the country. A. P. McCoy spent plenty of time sweating when he was riding, but he told me that, during all his days as a jockey, he never saw the inside of a Turkish bath. I told him about some of Terry's experiences in these buildings and especially when the jockeys attracted the attention of some other, less desirable, inmates. I think he is relieved not to have been on the scene in those days.

In Terry's own autobiography, *Winner's Disclosure*, he described the hours he spent losing weight.

'As well as the Gloucester baths and my own little box at home, I should think that I've visited every Turkish bath in the United Kingdom. There were some amusing and weird incidents in these unusual surroundings and over the years I met some colourful characters.'

When Terry started racing, he would go to the Turkish baths in Gloucester at seven o'clock every morning. 'They were usually deserted, but the steam room would be ready, so I would switch it on and then weigh myself. I could lose six or seven pounds in a couple of hours – sometimes more, moving from the steam room to the hot rooms, ending with a quick dive into the cold plunge pool. At about 9.30 a.m., Bill, the manager, would come in and ask me if I wanted anything. I would ask for "the usual" which consisted of a Worthington "E" and a port and Babycham. I would pour out exactly half of the beer before going back into the baths and repeating the same routine. When I came out, I would finish the beer, have a quick shower and take off in the car to the races.

Once in the car, I would sip my port and Babycham, which made me feel great. I never stopped to dry myself but in all the years that I kept up this routine, I never had a cold.'

Terry maintained that if he had not rigidly stuck to his routine at the baths, he would never have been able to carry on riding, but the sweating took its toll and seriously affected his health in later life. Having damaged a kidney in 1970 through his bad fall at Kempton, the remaining one had to work overtime to get rid of excess fluid and was considerably weaker in later years. The torture that Terry endured in the Turkish baths is hard to comprehend nowadays.

Terry's favourite baths were the Savoy Baths in Jermyn Street. Apparantly they were totally different to those anywhere else. In *Winner's Disclosure*, he stated:

If I was staying in London overnight with other jockeys, we would perhaps go to a club, or to the pictures and then return to the baths to lose weight for the next day's racing. The management was appreciative of tidy people, and I think most jockeys come into this category; if you were there in good time they would keep some cubicles for you, each with two bunks inside. Having secured these, we would go down for a sweat and ask the man in charge to give us a tap on the shoulder in the morning at about 5 o'clock or 6, so that we could have yet another session. To stay in London was expensive, but at the Savoy Baths we had marvellous service for about £1 10s., which included a doss

224

down in the bunks, the use of the steam and hot rooms and a
shave in the morning from old Bill, the barber. The masseurs
there were all good, but one of them was outstanding. If I was
too tired to sweat I went into a steam room to get really hot and
then to the massage room. There they had slabs of marble, which
were sprayed with hot water to keep your temperature up and
the masseurs would get to work. This particular man had an old
sock which he put on his hand before beginning to rub my back,
my backside, legs, thighs and stomach for half an hour, non-stop.
The sweat used to pour out of him and I would lie there, half
asleep and think to myself, I'm in the wrong job, I should be
doing that! In half an hour he would rub up to three pounds
from my body.

Richard Pitman remembers accompanying Terry to the Turkish
baths in Swindon. As usual, Terry was extremely hard on himself
and turned up all the knobs to make the rooms as hot as possible.
Richard could barely stand it and felt decidedly wobbly. Then he
heard Terry's voice saying: 'Don't worry, Pip. I've got something
that will revive you.' He duly went to the cold pool where a bottle
of Moët champagne could be seen dangling from a string. It was
lucky there were no breathalysers at the races in the old days. After
an evening out and hours in the Turkish baths, jockeys could still
be inebriated when they rode at the races the next afternoon.

The sweat box Terry acquired from Dave Dick had belonged
to Bryan Marshall – a top National Hunt jockey in his day. It had
been designed for a small flat jockey, Charlie Smirke, so was not

that easy for Terry to fit into. The heat was generated by a number of bare 150-watt bulbs with special bamboo filaments. Apparently he often burnt his bottom on these bulbs and it was extremely uncomfortable to sit in. Terry would be in a deckchair wearing his customary sweatsuit and goggles, but the temperatures often became unbearable and he would stick his head out of the lid on the top of the box and take in some fresh air. He could lose almost a stone in eighty minutes. The heat must have been stifling. Terry was filmed in this sweat box and nowadays can be seen on the Internet – on YouTube (under 'Terry Biddlecombe HOT-BOX').

Richard Pitman's years as a jockey spanned from 1960–76. Fred Winter was his boss. Richard remembers that all the jockeys looked up to Terry and that they lived in awe of him. 'He was like a god – a big, blond bombshell,' he says. He recalls his first time in the stewards' room with Terry. The officials called most jockeys by their surname – including Richard – but not Terry, who was addressed by his Christian name. Everybody respected the champion, and what Terry said was what mattered. On one occasion when there was a race day at Stratford, the racecourse had apparently slyly incorporated a trial plastic fence and placed it on the far side of the track without telling any of the jockeys. However, Terry had walked the course and seen this monstrosity. It had a metal frame, filled with stiff plastic birch bundles. It was a dangerous obstacle. Terry went back to the weighing room and said to his fellow jockeys, 'We're not riding in any chases today. The plastic fence is unsafe.' Many of the jockeys were longing to ride as it was probably their only ride of the week, but they listened to Terry and agreed to stand by him. After this demonstration and the jockeys' refusal to ride, the racecourse officials ordered the fence to be removed and it was taken away with a tractor and trailer. Racing continued and all the jockeys got their rides.

Terry considered Stan Mellor to have been in a category all of his own and always a danger. He was chuffed to have overtaken him and Stalbridge Colonist on the run-in when winning the 1967 Cheltenham Gold Cup on Woodland Venture. Like Terry, Stan won three National Hunt Jockeys' championships. He often reflects on the good times they enjoyed together, even though they rode in opposition. It always amazed him that Terry was so hard on himself. 'He was totally dedicated but seemed driven to ride as many winners as possible,' Stan says. 'He lived life in the fast lane and loved a challenge. He was the leader of the pack.'

Stan recalls that the jockeys in his day had a completely different style. 'They were horsemen and rode with a proper base seat. They sat deeper into their horses and had good hands. Nowadays, many jockeys ride with their reins too long and have what we called snake reins. We were always taught to ride with a straight rein and keep contact with our horses' mouths. Present-day jockeys shoo their horses along and use too much of the whip. They don't push or squeeze them through their legs and knees. We never rode with our toes in the irons. We rode with our feet well into the stirrups. We never looked between our legs to see horses behind us and we certainly did not watch races on the big screens, as there weren't any. Many modern-day jockeys bump up and down in the saddle and sit too heavy on their horses' backs to get them to go forward. Amateur riders used to do this in my time, which is why National Hunt flat races were called "bumpers".'

David Nicholson was a long-time mate of Terry's and rode with him as a jockey in the sixties and seventies. In later years he really cared for Terry through all his hardships and always rang him up on Christmas Day, even when Terry was in Australia. David was a tough, hard man on the surface with a bombastic nature, but had a soft heart and looked after his friends. Graham Thorner, another champion jockey in the seventies, was considerably younger than Terry but always had great respect for him. 'Terry was hard to beat in a race when he was going well,' he says, 'and he would never give an inch to anybody. He was exceptionally tough, but had wonderful manners, having been brought up the right way in a proper farming family.'

Graham says that, even when narrowly beaten in the jockeys championship, as in 1970–71, or in a race like the 1972 Grand National, Terry was always the first to congratulate the winner with a shake of the hand. Terry often told me that when Graham pulled up after winning that Grand National on Well To Do, beating Terry on Gay Trip, he had tears in his eyes. So Terry said to him, 'I can't think what you are crying about. It should be me that's crying as you've just beaten me!'

There were some good younger jockeys riding in Terry's era and these included Michael Dickinson. He later became a top trainer both under National Hunt rules and on the flat in the USA, and saddled the first five horses home in the 1983 Cheltenham Gold Cup. 'When I started riding, Terry Biddlecombe was champion jockey and of course we rookies all held him in great awe. However, I remember one occasion when, in a chase against him at Wolverhampton, my excitement got the better of me. Terry was riding an 11-year-old with top weight and well past its best, but I was on a good horse with bottom weight and just starting on its upward trend. I came upsides with Terry at the third last and I was cruising! As I flew past him, in my excitement, I yelled "I've got you! See you later!" – not the way to speak to your idol. After the finish Terry came into the weighing room and told his boss, Fred Rimell, "That Michael Dickinson's a cheeky bugger." Despite my remarks, Terry remained as good-humoured as ever. He was a big help to all us young ones, giving us good advice and knocking us into shape. He rode much shorter than anyone else. He was extremely brave. Any steeplechase jockey who falls in a race always says, "I'm all right. I want to ride in the next race and again tomorrow." On one occasion, Terry and I were both laid up in Walton General Hospital, having fallen at Aintree. Terry was in a lot of pain, but he was tough. I much enjoyed watching the great champion guilefully persuading the doctor that he was fine and perfectly fit to ride the next day. He should have gone into movies.'

Terry always gave advice to jockeys even in the days when he was riding. James Delahooke – one of the best judges of horseflesh that I have ever met – remembers riding against Terry in his amateur days. 'We all worshipped him,' he recalls. 'I was lucky enough to spend time with those boys in the sixties – on the trains, in the bars and in the weighing rooms. In spite of being a celebrity, Terry was always helpful, friendly and encouraging to a very moderate seven-pound claimer. We all loved him for it.'

Towards the end of his career, Terry rode for Fulke Walwyn. Ron Barry – 'Big Ron' – was a top jockey but mostly rode in the north. He was very strong. In 1973 Terry had been booked to ride Charlie Potheen in the Cheltenham Gold Cup, but Fulke was looking for someone to ride his other runner, The Dikler, in the race, so he asked Terry for advice. Terry told him about Ron Barry, who he reckoned would be well suited to the horse. Fulke contacted him and arranged for him to school The Dikler a few days before the Festival.

In the meantime, there had been a jockeys' showjumping competition at Stoneleigh in Warwickshire, which was rather unfortunately televised. Fulke settled down to watch his prospective jockey, but a bet had been laid between the riders to see who could get round the course in the quickest time, irrespective of how many fences were knocked down. Ron duly won the bet, but demolished most of the obstacles. Fulke was horrified at the prospect of this man riding his horse at Cheltenham. History does not relate exactly what he said to Terry about it – it was most probably unprintable. However, Ron had the last laugh when he won the Gold Cup on The Dikler and Terry only finished third on Charlie Potheen.

Way back in the last century, fences and hurdles would never be omitted from a race because of the brightness of the sun. Indeed, it was unheard of to take out any of the obstacles. Bob Champion, who rode with Terry in his later years and partnered Aldaniti to win the Grand National in 1981, told me that all the jockeys would have at least a dozen different pairs of goggles with varying colours of Perspex lenses. They wore orange ones if it was a dull day and dark-green ones to block out the glare of the sun. He never saw any horse fall due to the position of the sun and nobody ever complained. He says that the fences were always discernible in the last few strides, whatever the weather, and the horses coped perfectly well.

Nowadays, because of strict Health and Safety rules, the powers that be think differently. Races are ruined when the jumping element in National Hunt racing is reduced. Many chases are more like glorified flat races. Fences are not omitted on eventing cross-country courses due to the sun's rays, nor are show-jumps taken out of a competition in bright sunshine. Showjumpers compete in all weathers and during all hours of the day. Times have changed and probably not for the better.

Bob Champion has fond memories of Terry or the 'Blond Bombshell', as he was often known. Terry always walked into the weighing room carrying a bottle. 'Everybody looked up to him and when he rode around the paddock, his many fans lined the rails to watch him – such was their adoration for him,' Bob says. 'He was like the Elvis Presley of that era.'

The first time they rode against each other was in a novice chase at Ascot in 1968. Bob was an amateur then – Mr Bob Champion – and he rode a horse called Glide Scope. Terry rode a big horse called Domacorn, which was prone to making mistakes, but was extremely talented and jumped soundly on this occasion. Bob followed Terry into the last fence and was amazed by his strength – with his whip held high he gave Domacorn one whack on his hindquarters on the take-off, one smack in mid-air and one as he landed, but then he never touched the horse again and it flew right up to the line. Terry always maintained that if a horse did not go forward from three cracks of the whip, it would not improve with any more. He deplored the way that jockeys are so whip-happy today. Bob says Terry's strength came from his legs and the squeezing up that he did with his knees: 'Not like most of the present-day jockeys, who ride with their toes in their irons

reeting Terry after winning the Cheltenham Gold Cup, 2004.

Right: Terry with Henry O'Toole at the Ballyconneely Pony Show in 2008.

Below: The Hen and Terry Charity Open Day, 2004. Terry Court auctioneering the Best Mate rocking horse.

...rry fishing at ...llynahinch, ...nnemara, ...th Cyril ...ggins 2000.

...st Mate in ...e Cheltenham ...ld Cup, 2004.

Hen and Terry at an owners' open day, 2003.

Flowers for Hen from Terry at another West Lockinge open day.

Terry and John Oaksey at Best Mate's Open Day, 2003.
Photograph © Jean Ashdown-Coates

Terry and his five children at his 70th Birthday Party in 2011. Left to Right: Laura, Robert, Lucy, James, Libba. Photograph © Matthew W

Terry and Hen at their official wedding at Didcot Register Office, 201

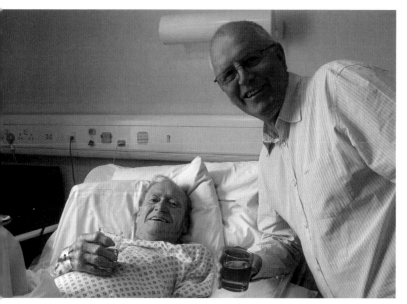

Terry in hospital with Mick Channon, 2013.

hn Francome, Hen and A. P. McCoy at Terry's Memorial day at
heltenham Racecourse, February 2014. Photograph © Matthew Webb

Hen and Nigel Twiston-Davies arriving
at Terry's funeral, 17 January 2014.
Photograph © Matthew Webb

and have no balance. They are forced to sit too far back and bump the saddle on their unfortunate horses' loins.'

The top Irish jockeys in Terry's era included Pat Taafe, who rode Arkle; Willie Robinson, who partnered Mill House; Tommy Carberry, who won the Grand National and Cheltenham Gold Cup on L'Escargot; Dessie Hughes, the father of Richard; and Eddie Harty, who won the Grand National in 1969 on Highland Wedding. After his retirement and looking back on his riding days, Eddie reflected that he rated Terry as the best jockey he had ever seen. Timmy Hyde, who rode Kinloch Brae for the Duchess of Westminster, was another Irish jockey with whom Terry rode. He was a good friend. They were a great bunch of skilled professionals and, like their English counterparts, thoroughly enjoyed life.

In his race-riding days, Terry shared some of the best times with Bill Smith. Despite being ousted by Bill as stable jockey to Fred Rimell in 1972, they remained friends. Bill gave a humorous speech at Terry's memorial service and Terry would have chuckled at the stories he told. This – which did not appear in his speech – is one of the best.

'In 1973 we were both riding in the Irish Sweeps hurdle at Leopardstown on the day after Boxing Day. For some reason we had both been to Wolverhampton on Boxing Day that year – not to Kempton. We flew to Dublin out of Birmingham Airport. As was the norm in those days, we then got stuck into miniature bottles of spirits, which were the only drinks we could get on the plane.

'Once in the hotel, we carried on with the minibar in the room – something of a novelty back then – and to Terry's way of thinking only put in for him! The phone rings and it is Fred Rimell, who demands to know where I am, as I am riding Comedy of Errors for him the next day. I was told, in no uncertain terms, to get over to his hotel. Terry started trying to sober me up – holding my wrists under the cold tap and making me drink water – not that he was going to drink the stuff himself!

'After a rather tricky dinner with Fred, Mercy and several owners who had runners the next day, I was ordered by Fred to stay in bed on the morning of the race and not ride out anywhere. Later, I left for my hotel with some of the other diners. One of my companions was the daughter of an owner in the big race. The rest is a little hazy, but I can only assume that Terry, who was in the bar on our return and suggested a nightcap, may have got a little distracted on the way back to his room. In the morning, I do remember that there was the owner's daughter in our bed and next to her, TWB!'

Despite this rather wild evening and night, Comedy of Errors won the big race the next day.

Apparently on another occasion, when Fred Rimell won The Midlands Sports Personality of the Year, both Terry and Bill were invited to a big lunch with Fred by the owners of Comedy of

234

Errors. 'I stayed the night before with Terry at Corse Lawn and we drove to Birmingham for the lunch in my car – an Alfa Romeo sports car that had been lent to me. The lunch was very boozy and when we left to drive home all I wanted to do was sleep. Terry took the wheel and I remember waking up to see that we were doing 70 mph-plus on the motorway and were passing traffic on our right-hand side, with none on our left. Terry had taken to the hard shoulder and was speeding along, remarking that there was no traffic on it and the other three lanes were blocked!'

When they returned home, Terry decided that Bill must help him break in a pony. He wanted it done then and there. 'This was before Monty Roberts and Join Up. After it had buried me for the fifteenth time, it finally gave in and by the end of the day Terry had us jumping over a pole on top of a couple of barrels.'

Way back in 1969, John Francome rode in a number of races with Terry, and afterwards they always remained close friends. In the late seventies and early eighties they played tennis together, when Terry lived at Corse Lawn, near Gloucester, and John was a fantastic back-up to me when Terry's health drastically declined in 2013. He constantly visited his old friend at West Lockinge Farm and supported me. Apart from using the same valet – Jo Ballinger – when they were jockeys, John also used to change next to Terry in the weighing room where, apparently, the jokes and the laughter brought renewed inspiration to fellow riders. John still vividly remembers watching Terry's shocking fall at Stratford in 1961. On that day, Terry was riding Hydra Dor and his foot got stuck in the stirrup iron when the horse hit the ground. As it got to its feet and set off in pursuit of the other runners, Terry went with it. From that day onwards, Terry always had a horror of people being dragged by loose horses and always deplored children riding ponies with stirrups that were too narrow for their boots or shoes. He used to tell me that for years he suffered nightmares about that fall at Stratford and on the day, he had visions of his leg being wrenched from its socket if the horse had jumped the next fence while he was underneath its tummy.

His head had already been bumping the racecourse turf for 200 yards and he'd been deafened by the noise of Hydra Dor's hooves hammering his crash helmet. He approached the obstacle upside down and with no control whatsoever, but miraculously the saddle suddenly slipped right round as the horse gathered speed. Somehow, Terry was able to extricate his foot before the fence.

John could never believe that after this horrifying incident, Terry stood up, vaulted over the rails and returned to the weighing room, as if nothing had happened. Alarmingly, he was allowed to ride in the next two races, despite suffering from delayed concussion. The whole incident showed just how tough the jockeys were in the last century. Despite the pain that day, Terry never moaned or complained. This attitude typified him right up until he died. When he fell from Hydra Dor, he was not even wearing a back protector.

Of the amateur jockeys who were successful when Terry was riding, I have singled out three. They became special friends. John Oaksey – then Lawrence – who won the Hennessy Gold Cup on Taxidermist in 1958 and was second in the Grand National in 1963 on Carrickbeg, was one of them. He later became a founder trustee of the Injured Jockeys Fund. Chris Collins was another. He was Champion Amateur rider in 1965–6 and again in 1966–7. He also won the Pardubice Chase in Czechoslovakia on Stephen's Society in 1972.

Chris owned the Goya Perfumery business and one of his products, Cedarwood, was said to, 'Give a man character.' Terry and Chris posed together in their crash helmets and racing colours for a photograph to promote Cedarwood. It was shown in all of London's Underground stations. Chris remembers that the advertising agency came up with the idea that this poster should feature a footballer, but he vetoed it because racing was his sport. They produced a weedy male model who looked like a fish out of water when dressed in jockeys' colours, but Terry was more than happy to pose with Chris.

'After a good lunch at Wheeler's, Terry and Josh's favourite restaurant, we went along to the studio and spent some time being photographed,' Chris explains. 'Terry did it as a friend and the only fee was lunch. Rather different from today!' I never saw Terry look so serious in any other picture, but it became a famous photograph. Goya cologne sold for 8/6 and the aftershave for 7 shillings. A print from the poster hangs on my kitchen wall.

Chris recalls that it was always the greatest pleasure to see Terry in action. 'He had a most attractive seat on a horse,' he says. 'In those days I used to watch nearly every race from the last. Terry steaming into it was magnificent. During all the time I spent with Terry and Josh – weighing rooms, Turkish baths, lunches on days off, etc. – money was never once mentioned. They rode to win and for the sport of it.'

The third amateur was Richard Tate, son of the legendary trainer Martin. Richard was champion in 1968–9 and 1969–70. He and Terry had many good times together, including holidays abroad – in particular on Elba. In the fiftieth year of the Bollinger Awards he was on the team when Terry attended the trip to France. It was a celebration for professional and amateur jockey champions and they stayed in a French château and went down into the champagne cellars in Reims courtesy of Madame Bollinger. They all had a great time. Richard also remembers his first ride at Warne Hunt – now a discontinued racecourse. He had no proper equipment that day and no riding clothes. Terry lent him all his kit. He was unbelievably helpful to his fellow jockeys, even the amateurs.

Terry enjoyed watching the changing styles of riders after his retirement. Even during the week before he died, he watched races on the big television screen in his bedroom, and focused on the younger jockeys. He singled out several up-and-coming riders and they are already proving his judgement correct. Of the established jockeys, he always adored A. P. McCoy and spent many hours discussing racing with him. He was Terry's idol and they had a huge amount in common. When riding, A. P. was driven by a determination to win, and fellow jockeys say that Terry was the same. He hated finishing in second place.

There is no doubt that Terry was a fantastic champion jockey in his day, but he admitted that he had a style all of his own which would have been difficult for anybody to copy. He was five feet eleven inches tall but rode with extremely short leathers. He would take a lot of weight through his knees and almost knelt on his horses, which kept him off their backs and especially off their loins. As well as riding with short stirrups, he rode with short reins. He had superb balance and beautiful hands, but always kept a contact with the horses' mouths. He maintained that a horse's head was its balancing pole and that a jockey should always keep a good hold of the reins in order to give his mount confidence and support.

Terry emphasised the importance of getting horses to race with a rhythm and he deplored jockeys who rode with long, looping reins and approached the fences with no contact. Of course they needed to be ready to slip their reins over an obstacle if the horses made mistakes but they had to be quick to pick them up again on landing. Terry would say to jockeys, 'Sit into your horse. Keep an even contact and ride forward. Don't look for strides, but let the fences come to you.' 'The memory I guard closest is of Biddlecombe at the last fence. He would send a horse at and over the obstacle with a dash and belief and compulsive commitment that I never saw matched before or since,' Brough Scott wrote in the *Racing Post*. Interestingly, when walking around at the start, Terry never showed a fence to his horse. It was the same at home when we schooled the horses. He never let the jockeys go up to the fences before they began jumping, 'The buggers will see the fences soon enough when they get to them,' he would say. He was probably right; after all, three-day-event riders and showjumpers never show the first fence to their horses.

Peter O'Sullevan wrote about Terry during the 1968–9 season: 'After he had won on King Candy at Warwick, the stewards told him that he was too brave. He had ridden into the last as if it were not there and his nearest rival had hit the deck while upsides. The stewards lectured him because they considered his forceful riding had caused his opponent to fall.'

Yet, very few people knew that Terry had his own idiosyncrasies. He habitually kicked with his right leg only and was never any good at changing his whip from his right hand to his left. This technique is regularly taught nowadays to young jockeys, when they are trained by professionals and they constantly practise on mechanical horses or Equicizers. Although it would have been hard to imitate Terry's unique style, many young jockeys admired him and tried to mirror him. Enda Bolger, the cross-country king from Ireland and champion point-to-point rider over there on many occasions, remembers a day out hunting as a child in Co. Kilkenny. He was trotting along a road on his pony when Mrs

McCalmont, the Master, rode up beside him and said, 'You are riding ridiculously short, young boy. Put your leathers down!' 'I'm trying to look like Terry Biddlecombe,' retorted Enda.

Brough Scott also wrote, 'On a horse Terry had incredible balance and power. Off it he had an engaging farmer's boy charm. One day at Ludlow these two qualities combined to effect a treble as unique as it was cheekily outrageous. After winning the opening hurdle race, T. W. Biddlecombe was not engaged again and so joined a group of us down at the last fence for the second. Also there were a couple of young ladies to whom Biddlecombe and the splendidly named Johnny Gamble got chatting, and no sooner was the race over than the desperate duo were seen driving off to a local farmhouse in the young ladies' car. The other races came and went with no sign of the champion, and it was not until saddling had started for the last that Terry came crashing through the back door of the Ludlow weighing room. As he duly cruised past the post, the commentator called out, "A splendid second winner for Terry Biddlecombe." Who else knew it was actually a third?'

Day-to-day life for the jump jockeys in Terry's era seems to have been considerably tougher than it is today, even though it was slower and less of a rat race. To get to the races they often travelled by train, where they would play cards and have a round of drinks. There were no motorways, and car journeys were tedious and slow. During the 1965–6 National Hunt season Terry travelled some 80,000 miles along the old roads in order to capture the championship. On the racecourses, there was little regard for a jockey's well-being. Concrete posts held up the railings around the courses and when jockeys fell, they could be thrown against these lethal uprights. Indeed, when Terry's brother, Tony, a top amateur rider and champion in the 1961–2 season, was riding at Wincanton in 1957, he was catapulted into the rails and posts on the far side of the course after his mount, Ascension, slipped on the bend. Terry, who had led up the horse, caught her when she was loose but their father, Walter, whipped off the saddle, vaulted onto the mare and galloped back across the course to find Tony, who was in a very poor state, with a badly broken leg that kept him in hospital for three months. There was no doctor attending him. Nowadays, all the uprights and railings are plastic and Terry's father would never have been allowed to ride bareback and hatless down the course to find his stricken son.

In days gone by, if a jockey had a fall, somebody had to find the doctor and the medical team and this might well not have been until some while later. Today, doctors see injured jockeys almost immediately. None of the jockeys wore body protectors and there were no proper crash hats. Instead they wore cork helmets, which looked more like halved eggs. They did not have chin straps to secure them and the helmets often came off in a race. If a jockey was concussed he was not necessarily stood down. If they felt OK, they rode again shortly afterwards. Nowadays, a jockey is not permitted to ride for at least seven days and has to pass a hospital concussion test.

At home, I have several photographs of Terry riding in races that would make the hair of present-day medics stand on end. There is a picture of him winning a hurdle race at Cheltenham with his arm in plaster – the cast is clearly visible at the bottom of the sleeve on his colours.

'What happened here?' I asked him.

'Oh, I had a small break in a bone in my arm and the hospital put it in plaster to protect it.'

He won the race and nobody seemed in the least bit concerned. There is also a photograph of Terry riding round at the start at Hereford in a neck brace. 'Oh yes,' he said. 'I had a hairline crack in a vertebra but I felt fine to ride, so I just gave my neck some support.'

The racecourses had no hard-surface inside tracks in Terry's era. Vehicles did not drive round beside the runners. No ambulances followed the jockeys, and if a jockey had a bad fall it could often be missed from the stands. In February 1970, Terry had an extremely bad fall on the flat, in the last race at Kempton. It was on the final bend. The ground was heavy and badly cut up. It was nearly dark. Terry was towards the back of the field and not going particularly well when his horse stumbled and went down onto its knees. As it struggled to keep its feet, it knelt on him with its full weight and kicked him. Terry always remembered the excruciating pain and how he somehow rolled under the rails, but nobody saw his fall from the grandstand and he was left in agony on the cold, wet grass. It was not until several other jockeys returned to the weighing room and saw Terry's clothes hanging on his peg in the changing room that one of them said, 'Where is Biddles?'

An ambulance was finally dispatched to look for him and he was taken back to the medical room. He was badly hurt and his blood pressure had risen alarmingly. He was coughing up blood. He spent many weeks in Ashford Hospital and was taken there from the racecourse with a police escort and sirens blaring. He had split a kidney and had crushed his ribs. His whole riding career hung in the balance. The injury to that kidney was to give him trouble for the rest of his life. It never worked again, and during the final years of his illness the remaining kidney failed on several occasions. Renowned author and racing journalist Jonathan Powell said, 'I can remember visiting Terry in hospital after that fall at Kempton and shaking my head in disbelief that he ever intended to ride again.' It was due to this horrendous fall that Terry missed the winning ride on Gay Trip in the 1971 Grand National. He never forgot watching the race from his home on the television. It was bittersweet. He loved the horse and was pleased that it won, but he longed to have been riding him.

Among some of the senior jockeys who helped me during my training years, I will treasure the support I received from Dominic Elsworth, Mick Fitzgerald, Graham Lee, Jamie Osborne, Paul

Moloney, Timmy Murphy, Sam Thomas and Andrew Thornton. They often used to come to West Lockinge Farm and ride out. They did plenty of invaluable schooling. They all rode winners for the yard, which gave me immeasurable confidence. They remain great friends, Andrew and Dominic were especially supportive in the final months of Terry's illness.

Dominic always remembers the trick that was played on him on his first day at West Lockinge. Sam and Timmy ushered him into the kitchen for breakfast and told him to sit in the chair at the end of the table, the back of which was covered by a jacket. Terry came in and saw him sitting there. He growled loudly, 'Get out of my chair! Nobody ever sits in it, bar me. Can't you read?' He pulled off the jacket to reveal white initials T. W. B., painted on the wood. Nowadays, we still have that chair but I keep it in the conservatory so that nobody will misuse it. It is usually bedecked with damp washing as I don't much like people sitting in it. It holds too many memories.

Mick Fitzgerald rode a number of winners for us but wasn't always the polished jockey he later became. 'When I was in my first year as stable jockey to Nicky Henderson, I made far too many mistakes, just because I was desperate to get it right. I was second jockey to Hen at the time, behind Jamie Osborne. Terry had not long been on the scene, but it's fair to say that his reputation as a brilliant jockey was not lost on Nicky and he enlisted Terry to coach me. We spent a few evenings in the sitting room at Hen's house, all of us mind, not just me and Terry! I felt like a schoolboy as the videos were played, some of them were shocking and Terry in his inimitable way just said, 'Sit still boy.' I remain indebted to him for giving me his years of experience as a champion jockey and big race winners for nothing, because most of all he wanted to see me do well. I did not feel like a schoolboy anymore when I left Lockinge after those evenings and because of that I am now a jockey coach. I hope in some small way I can give young jockeys a helping hand, just by taking the time to speak to them, and making them realise that we are all too keen at times, yet it is not always the best way. I try to model myself on Terry and I am eternally grateful to him for all his help.'

Apparently Terry's race-riding instructions were renowned for being straightforward. Timmy Murphy found that he was incredibly sound and helpful, but kept everything simple, 'If one had to change a plan and had to ride differently as the race developed, Terry usually understood why his race instructions had not been followed,' he says. 'He always supported the jockeys, and he understood our reasonings and where we were coming from. He was great with his advice. If ever I went to ride out at Lockinge and I was in pain from a fall, I never dared mention it to Terry, because he had suffered far more himself. He never complained but was just annoyed that he could not do the things that he used to do fifty years before.'

It seems that all the regular jockeys at our yard really enjoyed the talks at breakfast time. Paul Moloney in particular was often spellbound by the stories of Terry's riding days. 'Having been such a successful jockey, it was fascinating to hear the day-to-day happenings in the olden days,' he recalls. 'It was a privilege to school horses at West Lockinge Farm and get helpful advice afterwards from Terry.'

Warren Marston never rode out for us at home, but he was always most reliable when we secured his services on a racecourse. His feedback after a race was invaluable and he really knew the game. He used to say to his agent, Chris Broad, whom Terry called 'Squeaker', 'If Hen has a horse that she wants me to ride and I am not otherwise engaged, please put me on it, as her horses are always well schooled and are good jumpers.'

One of the most professional jockeys we ever had riding out was Graham Lee. Everybody adored him and he had such a wonderful way with people and horses. Terry thought the world of him and was exceedingly proud to have seen Graham change from being a National Hunt jockey – he won the Grand National on Amberleigh House – to riding so successfully on the flat. I asked Graham for his memories of his days at Lockinge and he started off like he always does: 'They were happy days,' he said. 'With Terry, it was always an honour to be in his company and I was privileged to ride for a man who had everything – experience, knowledge, humour, class and presence.'

Although Terry accompanied me to the races less and less when his arthritis progressed and he became less mobile, I will always cherish memories of our earlier training days, when he walked courses in order to assess the ground. He always paid attention to the way in which the fences were built and presented. In his own jockey days, he walked every racecourse. He continually moaned about the laziness of his modern counterparts, very few of whom bother to look at the going and walk round before they ride. So much can be gained by noting the ground on the take-offs and landings and getting a feel for the course on a racing day.

Terry always gave clear and simple instructions to the jockeys before our horses ran in their races. He would explain where to lie-up and where to drop out – in other words, where a jockey could afford to let his mount take it easy and get into a better rhythm and where losing any ground meant losing a race. As a jockey, Terry used to encourage his horses to relax, and this was often close to the back of the field. He maintained that they conserved energy. Yet with novice chasers he always liked the horses to be handy. It was largely due to Terry's meticulous attention to detail that in 2004 Jim Culloty was able to keep Best Mate on the inside of the course on a fresh strip of grass that had not been used on the previous day and provided the best-possible going. The horse had a beautiful action but always needed good ground.

Terry rode at virtually every racecourse in the UK except Fakenham, and he only ever visited the place once when we had a runner. In his days there were racecourses at Birmingham, beneath Spaghetti Junction, Bogside, the venue for the Scottish Grand National, Buckfastleigh, in Devon, Hurst Park, near Kempton, Manchester and Wye. It is sad when racecourses close;

DIS WASHER

CLEAN

XX DAD

2 AM

Nottingham and Windsor were great jumping tracks, but since the nineties they, too, have gone. Folkestone and Hereford were lost as well in 2012.

Finally, in Terry's riding days it was not unusual for jockeys in a race to snatch or borrow a whip from another rider who was, most probably, going less well. On 12 March 1964 Terry rode The Pouncer for Eric Cousins at Stratford. 'During the race I dropped my whip,' he remembered. 'Turning into the straight I asked one of my fellow jockeys if I could borrow his whip. He said, "No." "I'll give you a tenner for it," but "No," was still the reply, so I grabbed the whip out of his hand and sent The Pouncer on to win. After the race, the jockey came and asked me for the tenner and I said, "I offered you ten pounds during the race and you let me down, so you're not having it now!" I think I won by a head, but I should have won by about ten lengths – I was lucky.' (*Winner's Disclosure*).

Nowadays, it is strictly forbidden to take another jockey's whip in a race and there are severe penalties. On 4 December 2014, Davy Russell received a ban for borrowing Phillip Enright's whip in Ireland – and the horse did not even win. Terry would have applauded him for his ingenuity. He was an admirer of Davy Russell's, ever since the jockey spent a month at West Lockinge Farm during his early riding days.

CHAPTER FOURTEEN

Downward Spiral

From about 2007 onwards, Terry's general health and mobility began to deteriorate alarmingly. There were many simple jobs that he could no longer do, yet he remained in good spirits and was as outrageous as ever with his remarks. Arthritis, from which he had suffered for numerous years, took a stronger hold and his joints noticeably began to show the wear and tear from his racing days. No jockey who had experienced the crunching falls that Terry suffered in the sixties and seventies, resulting in forty-seven fractures, could have expected to make it into later life without aches and pains. He had punished his body in his youth and it had taken an unreal hammering. On top of this, medical care and attention in the mid-twentieth century was nowhere near what it is today, nor were the medicines.

Terry's hands and knees were his most badly affected joints. It used to upset him when he could not unscrew the tops off jam jars, or climb up the farmhouse stairs without a struggle. On many occasions, he would delay going up the staircase to bed at the end of the day until I was ready to steady him on the steps and walk behind him. His bravery knew no limits, although I often used to think how much easier it would have been if we had lived in a bungalow.

It was typical of Terry, however, that he would not give in to setbacks and he never wanted to let me down in the yard. We continued to feed all the horses at 6 a.m., even though it became an issue for him to undo the latches on the stable doors, especially if there had been a frost during the night and the bolts were jammed. I often had to open the doors for him. The breakfast feeding took a lot longer and it became more and more difficult for Terry to bend down and feel the horses' legs.

Not only did Terry's wrists look unsightly, and at times red and angry, but the skin on his hands was paper-thin. He constantly knocked them, cutting them and slicing off the top layers of skin. He bruised easily and bled freely, largely due to living on warfarin tablets for his heart and poor circulation. His wrists had been broken umpteen times and in the past had been constantly plastered and bandaged. When Terry rode in races he used to wear special supports. The left wrist was the worst. It had seen four fractures – and he had broken five fingers as well on that hand.

He also suffered from gout, and there were numerous deposits of uric acid crystals on his fingers: hard-looking lumps, which never improved and worsened whenever he ate certain foods that were high in purine. When I drove Terry to see a gout specialist in Oxford, he was so shocked by what he saw that he asked for

Terry's permission to photograph his hands and wrists to use in his lectures to the university medical students.

Despite the poor blood supply to his hands, Terry's fingernails grew at an alarming rate and it was always my job to cut them. He told me I would have been a hopeless manicurist and in turn, he was a rotten patient. He never kept still, but constantly grumbled and swore at me, because he thought that I was going to hurt him or cut him. I was better at filing the nails with emery boards and he tolerated this approach. This brought back memories. In my twenties I had owned a special blacksmith's bag full of farrier's tools for paring and rasping the Shetland ponies' feet on my mother's stud – but they were a lot easier to work with than Terry. Not only did we visit the gout expert in Oxford, to no avail, but also a top consultant in the hand unit at the Wellington Hospital in London, where once more, he was told that his wrists were beyond repair and that the pain could only be temporarily alleviated by a couple of cortisone injections.

Gradually, Terry did less and less outside. He gave up shooting because he could no longer lift the gun to his shoulder and his fingers were not able to operate the trigger or load the cartridges. It was a struggle for him and he missed these days out enormously. Fortunately, he could still watch our horses on the gallops. He continued to drive his battered old truck across the fields and would sit for hours at the top of the gallop, waiting for riders to appear. He never missed any of the horses, and if the staff or jockeys were riding badly he would tell them in no uncertain terms.

As well as being on the gallops, he kept up his feeding of the ducks and pheasants up the lane. He still watched the red kites and buzzards in the sky and he still listened to Radio 5 Live throughout the morning, to keep up-to-date on news. Our horses continued to run well, even after we lost Best Mate in 2005, and we had some lovely young chasers to train. We kept enthusiastic for the future, despite Terry being less and less keen to go to the races. He preferred to stay at home and watch the various racing channels. There was too much walking to do on the racecourses and he could no longer get a grip of the leather straps, to tighten the girths, when we saddled up our runners.

The 2005–6 National Hunt season had produced some pleasing winners for us, although fewer than in previous years. In November 2005, Impek won the Peterborough Chase under A. P. McCoy, and in the spring of 2006, Harringay was victorious in the Mares' Novice Hurdle final at Newbury under Timmy Murphy. Terry came racing that day and gave brilliant instructions to Timmy, telling him to hug the inner on the better ground. In the autumn of 2006, Racing Demon easily won the Peterborough Chase with Graham Lee. Yet, despite these wins, owners could see that Terry's health was on a downward slide and we no longer went to point-to-points in Ireland or to horse sales.

I think that a number of people reckoned we had seen our best days, and sadly, a number of our horses were not replaced when they were retired or injured. Owners either decided to withdraw from the sport, or else asked younger trainers to find them new recruits. Jim Lewis sold off his less successful horses and his one remaining French horse, Oumeyade, was moved to Paul Nicholl's yard at the beginning of 2008. Jim did not own the horse in full and his co-owners wanted a change and a chance to be with the champion trainer, but it was a sad day when the horse left West Lockinge Farm.

I had trained horses for Jim Lewis since the early 1990s and the departure of Oumeyade marked the end of an era. The two sets of blue and maroon colours, hanging on coat hangers in the attic, were packed up and posted to Paul Nicholl's office. Jim's decision hit me hard. If only he had kept just one good horse at our yard; after all, we had never done anything wrong for him with the good horses that we trained and he had experienced an amazing run of luck. Fortunately, we still remain friends, but I will never forget that final telephone call and the disappointment that went with it. Nowadays, the once Lucky Jim does not have any National Hunt horses in training, although he still enjoys his days out at Cheltenham, where he meets his old friends and admires the Best Mate statue. The golden years with the Aston Villa colours were unforgettable, and had Jim not sent us horses like Edredon Bleu, Best Mate and Impek to train, we might never have climbed so high up racing's ladder of success.

———

Although our horse numbers dwindled, there was a plus side as well. Terry and I could spend more time together and switch off from racing. We lived for our holidays and we continued to travel to Ireland, mostly to Connemara, but I dreaded the airports and wheeling Terry about in his chair. He liked the wheelchair, because it meant that he could get to the head of the queues and sit closer to the front of the aeroplanes. At one time, he insisted on having a race with a fellow wheelchair traveller across the tarmac at Cork Airport. Admittedly, it was far safer having him on wheels than on his feet, but he would often prod passengers in front of him with his long walking stick if they annoyed him, or got in his way; he would then turn away pretending that it was an accident and I would get all the flak.

The stays at Ballynahinch Castle were as magical as ever and we went for plenty of drives around the country, exploring the beauty of Connemara and visiting our friends, or attending the Sunday pony shows. We also spent many hours with Cyril Biggins, fishing on the river by the hotel, but he was careful only to take us to places with the minimum of walking for Terry and where we could find him somewhere to sit. On occasions, Terry would fish from a chair. His casting was not great, but he loved it and, as usual, spent hours trying to entice a salmon onto his line.

On the rare occasions that I was lucky and caught a fish, I would have expected him to be jealous, but that was never the case and he was just as thrilled for me as he would have been if he had landed the spoils himself. I am not much of a fisherwoman, but I love it. I find days spent on a river therapeutic and fascinating. It is a wonderful way to appreciate the beauties of nature and switch off from the day-to-day realities of life.

Some of the other holidays Terry and I took were on the Isle of Mull, off the west coast of Scotland. We travelled on several occasions to this amazing island and I usually drove Terry in our car; although it was a long, tiring journey and often took upwards of ten hours, it was well worth it when we got there. We were invited to Mull by Tim Radford, who owns the beautiful Benmore estate on the island. His Knock House, where we stay, is big and comfortable. It looks out across sandy beaches to the sea. The Scottish scenery is stunning, the wildlife in Mull is breathtaking and I was always intrigued by the sea eagles. When Tim is not in residence, the house is let out commercially and, not surprisingly, there is a waiting list for it. The housekeeper/estate secretary is Kim Bissett. She is most efficient and loves riding. She has a horse of her own, which is kept nearby in one of Tim's fields, and now there is a magnificent all-weather arena for other riders on the island to enjoy as well. Kim's husband, Donald, is the head keeper. Not only does he organise the fishing and the stalking, he also drives the boat that takes guests sea fishing or sightseeing to surrounding islands, including Iona: a fascinating place with a big history. There is an abundance of good salmon fishing on the estate, either on the picturesque little rivers or on the vast Loch Ba, where you fish from a rowing boat. I was lucky with my fishing rod in Mull and Terry enjoyed sitting on the banks when I cast my line into the rivers. On one afternoon I caught two salmon and he posed beside me for a photograph with the fish.

In February 2011, Terry celebrated his seventieth birthday at the Eyston Arms in East Hendred. He had absolutely no idea that a party had been arranged in his honour and thought that he was just going out to dinner with my sister Ce, fellow trainer Charles Egerton (Edgy) and me. The first person he saw as we walked up to the bar was his brother, Tony.

'What the hell are you doing here?' he exclaimed, and then the secret was out, as other guests began to appear from every corner of the pub. Ce hosted the party and all five of Terry's children were present. It was a great evening and very moving. Terry was in excellent form and looked wonderfully happy in all the photographs. It was a special party, but sadly, this was the last time that he ever saw all his children together under the same roof.

The summer of 2011 was an especially good one. Terry and I spent some more memorable days in Mull at the beginning of July and on Monday, 25 July, we were officially married at the Didcot Register Office. We had talked about getting properly married for several years and I finally tracked down Terry's missing divorce certificate in the January of that year through Her Majesty's Courts Service at Gloucester County Court. We adored each other and it would have been tragic if Terry had suddenly died and we were not legally joined.

Our visits to the register office prior to our official wedding were short and sharp, but we both signed all the relevant papers. The lady in charge seemed highly amused by Terry's sense of humour and the stage was set. Our four witnesses were Terry's middle son, Robert, and his wife, Gemma, plus my secretary, Dawn Graham, and her boyfriend, Tony Breakspear, who worked for the post office in Oxford and who Terry called 'Postman Pat'.

It was a lovely sunny day and the service only lasted for twenty minutes. Afterwards, we had a memorable lunch beside the River Thames at the Boathouse Restaurant in Moulsford. Both Terry and I were indescribably happy. Seeing the photographs afterwards and Terry's smiling face still brings tears to my eyes. At last I was a properly married woman, even though it had been a long wait – I was finally and legally Mrs Terry Biddlecombe and I was immensely proud of my new status. I had never ceased loving Terry since the day that we met in 1993 and the bond between us had become even stronger as the years had passed by. At the beginning of August we had our proper honeymoon in Connemara and it was a perfect holiday. As in previous years, we went to the annual Connemara Pony Show in Clifden. It was a fun day and had the usual festival atmosphere. Terry met numerous friends and happily sipped his glasses of Guinness outside the Station House Hotel, which overlooks the showground. It was not until we got home that some strange accidents befell him. Looking back, these may well have been forerunners to his stroke in October.

———

Every morning, after we had finished feeding the horses, Terry would drive off to the newsagents, Rowes, in Wantage to collect the newspapers, which included his copy of the *Daily Sport*. He enjoyed trundling off to Wantage in his old truck and he met many people in the shop. They exchanged local gossip and put the world straight. Everybody knew Terry. He always came back smiling, but on one occasion in September, at about 8 a.m. he walked into the farmhouse kitchen, covered in blood.

He told me he had tripped on an old carpet in the shop – but there was no carpet. He guiltily put his head round the door and said, 'I've had a fall.' His hands were badly cut and skinned. His nose and face were also bleeding. It took me at least thirty minutes to clean him up and he was extremely sore and shaken. I bandaged his poor old hands and applied ointments – mostly aloe vera gel. We stopped the nosebleed and I washed his face. He was already painfully stiff in his knees and by the evening, he could barely walk.

Thinking back, I am certain that Terry had suffered a blackout that morning and had momentarily lost consciousness. He had then fallen head-first onto the shop floor. Knowing what I know now, this was most probably a mini-stroke. It was a miracle that he managed to drive home. During the days that followed, he appeared normal and his wounds gradually healed, but he never did remember exactly what had happened in the shop.

The second mishap that befell Terry that autumn was in the yard at West Lockinge. At the time his feet were playing up more than usual. He was suffering bad attacks of gout in his toes and also in his ankles. He often wore sandals, because they put less pressure on his feet when he walked. After watching our horses on the gallops, he always parked his truck beside the house at the top of the driveway. On this day in September, I was in the office overlooking the yard and it was after the second lot, at approximately eleven a.m. I looked out of the window, to see Terry's vehicle slowly running backwards down the slope towards the stables. He was sitting in the driver's seat, but seemed to be making no attempt to stop it. Obviously the handbrake had not been applied, nor did he have his foot on the brake pedal. The Daihatsu rolled for about sixty yards and then veered left-handed, crashing straight into the outside wall of a vacant stable.

At the same time, there were horses in the yard returning from exercise and used saddles were lying on the gravel. At least five members of staff were preparing to lead their horses to the wash-down area. Thankfully, nobody was hit by the truck and even the saddles escaped its wheels. I think the jolt of the vehicle as it hit the brickwork must have brought Terry back to his senses, but the whole episode can only have been caused by another blackout. He calmly got out of the side door and looked at the damage, which was significant. 'That was lucky,' he said. 'My sandal got caught under the pedal and I couldn't use the brake.' He always had an answer and at the time everybody believed him, but when I examined his shoes, I saw that there was no way they could have been to blame.

Finally, at the end of September, when Terry was driving up the old runway to the top of the gallops, he failed to turn left along the track and crashed his truck through the wooden fence that divides our farm from that of the neighbouring farmer. The rails were smashed to pieces, but unperturbed, he reversed, returned to the farm and merely complained that the steering had locked up on his Daihatsu. We all thought that this was strange as it had recently passed its MOT and he went up that pathway most days. Fortunately, he was driving very slowly and nobody was in his way. I could not help feeling how lucky that this mishap did not happen in the village, or on the busy main road at the top of the farm.

I remember thinking to myself that these incidents with the truck were strange, and Bob Bullock said to me in the yard one morning, 'I don't think Terry is very well. He's not behaving normally.' Obviously I watched him even more carefully after that, but he seemed to be alert and enjoying all his normal television programmes, as well as swearing at everybody around him. He was in far better shape than his truck, which, after the accidents that autumn, had become even more battered and dented than usual.

Our last open day was held on 26 September 2011. At that time, we had thirty-eight horses in training. Terry, even though wobbly on his legs and moaning about his gout, was in sparkling form throughout the day. Instead of standing and organizing horses into the parade arena, he was happy to sit on a chair by the entrance gate, surrounded by his friends, but there was plenty of laughter and I made my usual references to him when speaking through my microphone from the little commentary box. That year we had a smaller marquee in the garden but an excellent pig roast. There was plenty of alcohol, plus the usual tables and chairs, so that the owners could sit around and chat. Terry told me that he enjoyed the day, but it saddened me to see him noticeably less mobile.

After that day in September, due to the ever-increasing problems Terry had with his hands and wrists, plus the obvious difficulty that he had with his walking, I decided that it was best for me to feed the horses every morning on my own – sometimes with the help of my head lad, Andy Fox. Terry did not object to this and rather enjoyed being left in bed to sleep a little longer. However, he usually started getting dressed at around seven a.m. and after my rounds in the yard, I would return to the house and help him with his shoes and socks; he could still do most other tasks on his own. On that fateful day, 9 October 2011, when I looked across to the house from the yard at 6:45 a.m., I was surprised not to see the light switched on in his bathroom. I went straight upstairs to see if he had overslept. I knew that he had not had a good night and had been up and down out of the bed to visit the lavatory on several occasions. Indeed, he had woken me up a couple of times to say that he had a pain in his tummy, but as I was such a heavy sleeper in those days – I am not now – I had not really taken in the gravity of his problems. When I went up to the bedroom to rouse him, he was sprawled, naked, across the bed and in a dreadful state. He appeared semi-conscious and was sweating profusely.

I remember talking quietly to him and asking him what was wrong. He mumbled some unclear words, rolled about on the bed, and then lay back on his pillows. His bad turn seemed to have happened during the hour I had been in the stables. I had left him at 5:45 a.m. and at that time he was sleeping peacefully. I did not suspect anything particularly serious, because I was used to Terry's problems and he was often uncomfortable, but I do remember saying to him, 'So you're not getting up then?' to which he replied, 'No.' I straightened up his legs and body to make him more comfortable and pulled a light sheet over him. He went back to sleep.

On that particular morning, we were supposed to take four horses to work on Mick Channon's gallops. The hired horsebox was due at 7:45 a.m. and Dominic Elsworth had arrived to ride one of the horses. I remember coming down to the kitchen and saying to Dom, 'You will have to be in charge of these gallopers. Terry is not at all well and I'll have to call the doctor.' My first instinct was to ring my loyal and dependable vet, Roger Betteridge, who is just as knowledgeable and helpful with human ailments as he is with horses. I told him exactly what had happened and he suggested that Terry might have had a stroke.

My heart sank and my mind momentarily blanked out, as it had so often done in the past when I had received a shock, such as on the day Best Mate died. However, I pulled myself together, despite all sorts of things flashing through my brain, and dialled the NHS emergency number. It was answered quickly, even though it was a Saturday morning. In a short while, a team of paramedics arrived with an ambulance. The men were highly efficient. By the time they got to the farm, Terry was able to sit up and I had given him a gentle sponge to clean and freshen him up. I had also put a T-shirt on him and he was looking a lot better when the helpers went up to the bedroom.

However, his mind was still confused. He answered a few simple questions and uncharacteristically did not object to the various tests that were done – blood pressure, pulse rates, etc. Yet my worst fears were confirmed when the paramedics told me that they, too, suspected he had suffered a small stroke. He was stretchered down the stairs and into the ambulance, which I then followed to the John Radcliffe Hospital in Oxford.

Whatever people say about delays in A & E, the nurses and doctors were brilliant that day – even though it was a weekend. By midday, following further tests, Terry was admitted to the stroke ward. It was a tense morning and I felt very much alone. I never left his side, except when he was wheeled off on a trolley to have some essential scans. He was very quiet, but he knew I was with him. He did not remember anything that had happened at home and was soon lying in a hospital bed, with tubes inserted, and sticky pads attached to his body, wiring him up to the monitor machines that bleeped constantly. Not being accustomed to hospital wards, I found the whole experience unbelievably scary.

Fortunately, Terry was put into a side room on his own. I remember ringing his brother, Tony, and telling him what had happened. As always, Tony was brilliant and supported me to the hilt. He drove from Gloucester to the hospital and was an absolute star. My sister, Ce, was also extremely helpful. She explained the medical procedures to me – she had, of course, been a top-class nurse and hospital sister in London in the seventies and had suffered a bad stroke herself in 1995. She instantly recognised all the signs and complications associated with a diminished blood supply to the brain. A few days later, I was told that Terry's stroke had been caused by an embolism – a small blood clot somewhere in his body. Mercifully, his brain scan was clear. As he had lived on warfarin for a number of years, the clot was somewhat surprising, but blockages can never be ruled out with patients suffering from heart defects.

Every time I visited Terry in hospital, he began to look a little better and was soon able to walk – albeit in a wobbly fashion and holding onto my arm – to the bathroom for a shower. I am hopeless with showers and never use them. We have none at West Lockinge Farm. I remember getting myself utterly soaked while trying to help Terry wash himself. I sat him on a stool under the shower-head but kept turning all the knobs in the wrong direction. It was a nightmare.

Terry's children from Gloucester – James, Robert and Lucy – also visited him. Sometimes they came with Tony. He had a lot of support and gradually brightened up, even though he had no real interest in what was going on outside the Radcliffe and did not remember the name of the hospital. He never once asked me about the horses at home, which was most unusual, but I spent plenty of time talking to him. I would hold his hand and tell him what was happening. There were get-well cards to pin up on his walls and plenty of enquiries as to his well-being. His stroke had been mentioned in the *Racing Post*. He barely watched the television in his room, as his eyesight was blurred and his speech still shaky. He also found it difficult to swallow, but luckily suffered no paralysis. I made him numerous vegetable soups and he would drink them. He always enjoyed my soups. Above all, he kept smiling.

While Terry was in hospital, I made sure that my wonderful golden retriever, Tiger, was well looked after at home. Annabel Scrimgeour, who expertly schooled many of the horses on the flat each week and always looked after the farmhouse if Terry and I were away, offered to look after Tiger during my visits to the hospital. She loved him as much as I did. He was my shadow and the best dog I ever owned. He was almost human and seemed to sense that I was worried. I found him very quiet in the evenings, but I thought this was due to me having left him all day. I did not suspect that he, too, was ill. He still ate up his food and came out with me to feed the horses in the early mornings but then, all of a sudden, on one of the days after he and I had been up on the gallops, he jumped out of my car and collapsed on the concrete beside the back door. I could not get him up, even though he wanted to stand. Two of my staff helped me carry him into the house and I drove him to the vet in Abingdon. Whatever next? Terry was in hospital and Tiger had been admitted to the veterinary surgery. Imagine my horror when I was rung later in the day and told that he had died. I cried and cried; I adored him so much. He had suffered an internal haemorrhage to his lungs, caused by cancer. He was only seven years old and I still miss him dreadfully. I have never wanted another dog since that day, especially as I am told that nowadays many pedigree dogs are susceptible to cancer due to a decrease in the size of the gene pool.

After about eight days, Terry was allowed to leave the John Radcliffe Hospital. I was still in a daze myself. I had lost Tiger and Terry had suffered a stroke. I was lent a wheelchair to take home and the hospital staff gave me several walking frames, all of which proved extremely useful. The nurses were most helpful and had enjoyed Terry's humour, which luckily began to return after a week's confinement. I remember driving him back to West Lockinge Farm on my own, but I had been assisted in Oxford by the hospital paramedics, who had lifted him into the passenger seat of my Volvo fourtrack. There were plenty of supporters to greet him at home. Bob pushed the wheelchair up to the front door and in later months made a special ramp over the step. The next day, we received a wonderful basket of fruit that had been sent by two of my favourite owners, Andy and Wendy Sole. Fortunately, despite swallowing difficulties, I managed to feed him on plenty of soft foods. At last I could see light at the end of the tunnel and Terry seemed to be on the mend.

Gradually, Terry got back into his normal regime at home, but he never drove another car nor did he ever smoke another cigarette. He did try, on one occasion, to drive my Subaru in a field but it frightened him and he did not feel he had any control. He said to me then and there, 'I don't ever want to drive again. You can chauffeur me anywhere that I want to go.' He remained true to his word.

The stroke had left its mark and it took away a lot of Terry's independence. I continued to watch over him carefully and took him back to the hospital for tests on several occasions, but his recovery was remarkable and he soon began, once again, to curse and swear at people in the yard and give his special vocabulary a good airing. Yet he did listen to what I told him and would often ask for help with his walking. He had obviously given himself a big fright.

From that day onwards, I began teaching myself to be his carer, due to his needing so much more everyday help. It was not easy to train the horses and to mind Terry, but I had a great back-up team and numerous offers of assistance. We had a good autumn and winter, with Calgary Bay winning two good races: one at Cheltenham and one at Doncaster. Somersby also won the Victor Chandler Chase at Ascot in January 2012 and Terry was well enough to attend that day. I was delighted to get him to the racecourse and he thoroughly enjoyed the occasion. He was given a great reception but, as usual, was in floods of tears after the victory.

At the end of February 2012, Terry and I were invited to a select dinner party in London at Le Gavroche, run by Michel Roux, Jr. Our host was Wilson Dennison from Northern Ireland, from whom we had purchased many good racehorses in the past. Wilson was due to be presented with an OBE the next day at Buckingham Palace, for his services to industry in Northern Ireland through his company, Dennison Commercials, which primarily deals in Volvo trucks.

We travelled to London in a hired car, because Terry was apprehensive about spending the night away from home. He was placed that evening next to Wilson's daughter, Katrina. They had always got on well together and she fully understood Terry's humour. It was a memorable occasion. Katrina wrote a letter after Terry died, and reminded me of the celebration:

'I had a great chat with Terry when we had dinner in London. I remember telling him that Dad had brought me back his autobiography from Cheltenham when I was about twelve. I also remember saying to Terry it was time for him to write another one. He just laughed! And then I asked him, if he did do a second book, what would be the highlight of it. In reply he just pointed to you across the table. My heart melted, because, when I looked up, you and Dad were laughing and by the look on his face I knew it was a lovely moment for him. It will always stick in my mind, especially as Terry then went from being that romantic man to roaring at a waitress about not having any wine! He made me laugh a lot.'

At this time, I was allowing Terry to enjoy a few glasses of wine and the doctors told me that it would do his health no harm.

Terry's mobility got a little better during the winter months and my sister helped me to get a stairlift fitted into the farmhouse. This proved a great asset and made everything so much easier for him. After his stroke, I had bought a new double bed and put it in our drawing room, in case he preferred to sleep downstairs on his return from hospital. However, at the time, he was disgusted by the idea and still insisted on sleeping in our own bedroom. He did sometimes agree to have a rest on the new bed in the afternoons, provided that I would do the same. I hardly ever lie down during the day and I was not overjoyed by his idea of an afternoon cuddle while watching racing on the big flat-screen television. I would have preferred to have been busy outside, but I went along with his wishes. He was precious to me and so I did everything I could to make him happy.

After the Cheltenham Festival in March 2012, I realised that it was time to have a proper rethink about the future. Would I ever be able to get our training operation back to its top level on my own? Even though the horses were of great importance and we had some wonderful owners, it was Terry who meant everything to me. After much deliberation and discussions with my sister and Sam, I decided to hand in my licence at the end of the season and concentrate on looking after him full time. He was on chirpy form, but needed all the attention I could give him. I knew that his arthritis and internal problems were giving him a lot of aggravation. He was living on special pills and probably, on borrowed time. He regularly attended the local surgery and visited consultants at the Oxford hospitals. I realised that every time I went out into the yard, or onto the gallops or travelled to the races Terry would be on his own in the house and this was not fair. He hated being alone and I loved being with him more than anything else in the world.

It was a hard decision to quit training and it upset Terry as much as it upset me, but looking back, I know it was the right move because I was able to give him almost two more years of life that he might not otherwise have had. The reaction to my retirement from the training ranks was colossal. The newspapers were full of it and the racing journalists wrote some lovely pieces. *Horse & Hound* magazine even did a special feature and sent a cameraman down to West Lockinge. I realised that I would miss the press as much as they would miss me. In the past there had been many memorable days entertaining them at our yard, and a number of them had become special friends. At home both Terry and I shed many tears. We had come to the end of the rainbow, but there would be no pot of gold, no more dreams, no more fairy stories. Our racing adventures had been magical. We had shared everything and we had jointly trained many winners. Our lives would never be the same again. The curtain was ready to come down for the last time.

Having decided on my future, one of the toughest tasks was breaking the news to my loyal staff, some of whom had been with me for many years. I knew they would be upset, because they loved their horses and lived for their days out at the races. I informed them at the same time as I told my owners and the press, because I wanted everybody to know within the space of twenty-four hours. Two of my favourite employees, Jo Castle and Carol Titmuss, came into the kitchen afterwards in an emotional state. They were visibly shaken by the announcement and extremely surprised. Terry gave both of them strong drinks. Both girls were top-class team players and Terry adored them. Indeed, when he was so ill in 2013, and I had to go out, they took turns to sit with him. They would do anything for Terry and not only did he totally trust them, but he also discussed his problems with them. They were always understanding and considerate.

At the time of my retirement, as well as Jo and Carol, there were several other loyal members of staff on the payroll. In particular Bob Bullock who had been at West Lockinge for fourteen years and Dave Reddy who had worked for me since 1996. They were shocked when I told them that there would be no more horses trained from our yard. They had both been invaluable to me during my training years and Bob had led Terry up at the Cheltenham Festival in 1974 when he rode Bumble Boy, trained by Bill Marshall, on his last ever hurdle race ride. Both men got on famously with Terry and they shared many jokes. If I wrote up on the staff notice board that I was giving a £10 reward for lost scissors, head collars or leading reins and Bob found them, he would refuse to take my money but, apparently, Terry would say, 'Take her tenners. You can give them to me, she'll never know.' Dave had always accompanied Best Mate to the races on his big days and would habitually walk beside the horse in the paddock. He loved discussing the pros and cons of good looking girls with Terry.

When I relinquished my licence, it was important that my employees were not left in the lurch. I tried to work out ways of giving the older ones different jobs in the yard and I assured them that I would continue to employ them at the same rate. Jo stayed on for a while, but her hips gave her a lot of pain and they badly needed operations, so she found it difficult to ride out. In the autumn she had a simple fall and fractured her ankle. When she recovered she decided to begin a new career. She started working in an accountancy office, dealing with computers and now she is the manager.

Carol, too, had a good think about her future and while on her annual holiday, decided to give herself a change as well. She no longer works full-time with the horses. Fortunately, she still helps me part-time in the office and in the stables, when we are particularly busy. Her input is invaluable. There were plenty of existing jobs left for Bob and his tractor – harrowing, rolling or topping the fields, as well as levelling the gallops. He is still with me and continues to tread in and fork over all the divots in the schooling field. Dave remained part of the furniture too and drove to West Lockinge every week day morning. There were still a number of horses for him to ride and he seemed happy to carry on as part of the new team.

At the end of the 2011–2012 National Hunt season, we still had plenty of horses in the yard and many of them stayed on for the summer to enjoy their holidays in the paddocks. Gradually, however, I changed over my business from training racehorses solely for the tracks to pre-training them and teaching young horses to jump. This has been a success and the gallops, as well as the schooling fences, are still meticulously managed and maintained. As well as using them myself, I hire them out to fellow trainers and event riders, which is extremely popular. Many children, interested in pony racing, also use the gallops and get special instruction from the likes of John Reid, the retired flat race jockey, who knows so much about the game. As a hobby I have continued with my Connemara pony stud, which I share with my sister. For a number of years I stood a successful stallion, Lecarrow King, which Terry and I found in Connemara and imported to England in 2005. In 2009, when ridden by Sam Roberts, he was Connemara Pony of the Year at the Horse of the Year show.

In the autumn of 2012, most of Camilla Radford's National Hunt horses were transferred to Mick Channon and although she has sadly died, many of them are still being trained by him at West Ilsley. They spend their summer holidays at West Lockinge Farm and my staff begin riding them in July. They usually go into full training in September.

Although my twenty-three years of training with a licence may have come to an end in the spring of 2012, my involvement with racing did not and certainly never will. During the remainder of that year, Terry and I did not disappear to another land and put racing out of our minds; instead we spent even more time together discussing the sport. We both needed to be kept busy – me because I loved so many different aspects of the horse world and the countryside; and Terry, in order that he could wake up in the mornings with something to look forward to and take his mind off all his nagging pains.

In the June of 2012 I judged a Mountain and Moorland Pony Championship at the South of England Show at Ardingly in Sussex. I took Terry with me and we hired a mobility scooter for him. It was the first time he had driven one and he loved it. I will always remember him visiting a stall in the trade stand area, where two pretty girls had set up a table for wine tasting. He was in his element and soon had everybody laughing.

After this expedition, we decided to invest in a scooter for Terry. He would whizz around the farm, or yard, on it and frighten everybody. Once he turned it over, when going up a bumpy lane where I had forbidden him to go. He was quiet after this episode: it had taken him half an hour to right the scooter again and drive it back to the farm. He got a schoolmistress lecture from me, when he confessed where he had been. We had all been searching for him and were extremely worried. As usual he had refused to carry a mobile phone. Yet, the mobility scooter gave Terry a much needed boost, because he could once more go places on his own and it restored some of his independence. He had always liked to drive around the locality by himself and do his own thing.

We did not take Terry's scooter to Mull, when Tim Radford kindly invited us there in July 2012. It was probably just as well, because he might have driven it into the sea, or got it stuck in the sand. Nevertheless, I often used to put the scooter into the back of my Volvo when we went racing and Terry drove it around several racecourse enclosures.

We had another lovely holiday in Scotland that summer and, as usual, during the evening dinner parties Terry was the centre of attention. However, during the daytime he did not go on many boats because he was worried about getting in and out of them. He always dreaded slipping and falling over and I fully sympathised. If he had broken any more bones, it would have been disastrous. He enjoyed the mackerel fishing, however, and loved putting his line over the side of the boat into the sea, but when it was laden with fish he found it hard to pull it back onto the deck. His hands were, once again, playing up badly.

It was a particularly long journey that year, driving up to Scotland, and I found it exceedingly tiring without a co-driver. Terry never once left the passenger seat, on the ten-hour trip, except when we got to Oban for the ferry. We had collected two of our fellow guests, Tom and Avia Costello, from Glasgow Airport and fortunately I had put a fold-up wheelchair in the boot of the car. This proved very handy and Tom duly wheeled Terry onto the passenger deck.

Back at West Lockinge, during the rest of July and part of August 2012, Terry was well preoccupied by the Olympic Games. He barely missed watching any event and was exceptionally well clued up on all the different sports. During his riding days, he had often been on the television show, *A Question of Sport*.

Life at home was quieter that autumn. Without our training responsibilities, Terry and I had more time to meet up with our friends – many of them were ex-owners. We often went out for lunches in the local pub and the conversations stimulated Terry's brain. There were certainly plenty of jokes and reminiscences. They were happy days.

When I went shopping in the local town of Wantage I would drive Terry to meet his mates in The Cellar, a small downstairs bar in the old Post Office Vaults beside the marketplace. By now he was enjoying a pint of Guinness or a glass of whisky on a daily basis. Again, the doctors told me that a small amount of alcohol would do him no harm. Terry adored his hours spent in The Cellar and sat on a stool at the bar, chatting to all the local characters. Pete New was barman for many years in The Cellar during Terry's visits. 'Terry always sat on the same stool in the bar,' he says. 'If a local person was on the stool when he came in, he would give it up for him. If a stranger was on it, he would be told in no uncertain terms that it was Terry's seat but, due to his arthritis, Terry could never use the gents' toilets, as they were outside the building and meant a long walk, so he always used the Ladies' loos. This did lead to some embarrassing moments with the female customers, but Terry took everything in his stride and there was always plenty of laughter.

'From a personal point of view, there are numerous accounts of Terry in The Cellar Bar that I could not pass on, and a number of them are unprintable, but they are still high in the memories of all those who had the privilege to meet him. He held court every time he entered the room, because people knew what he had achieved and what he meant to the sport of racing. He usually had two halves of Guinness in small glasses, because his hands would not allow him to hold a pint glass. Occasionally I put in a shot of Jameson's Scotch as well, and he used to say, "If Hen comes in, Pete, drink one yourself before she sees it." Terry was always asked his opinion on a horse's chances in races, especially the big ones. On one occasion he was asked which horse would win the Grand National and he said Mon Mome. Goodness knows why, as apparently he never backed it himself. It won at 100/1 and several of us were much better off after his tip.'

Several other regulars from The Cellar have stories about Terry. One, known to his friends as Sweaty, worked in Henry Candy's yard and used to cycle over to Lockinge to see the horses and talk to Terry. On one occasion while looking at some horses in the field, Terry said to him, 'Come in and have a look at this one,' but did not tell him that the fence was electrified. Sweaty said that it was a 'shocking result'. Lee Reiber told Terry that his first bet was on a horse called Fisherman's Song, which won at big odds. Terry said to him, 'I know. I was riding it!' A lady set up a Facebook page called 'Faces of Wantage' and asked Terry if he would mind having his picture taken sitting in The Cellar. He duly obliged and the picture had more likes than any other face that she included.

Pete went on to say, 'Personally I miss him as much today, in 2015, as I did when he passed away. We have customers who met Terry only once but still recall the experience when they revisit us.'

The year 2013 started well. The young horses that we were pre-training in the yard looked good and I was kept busy on a daily basis, watching them on the gallops and supervising the riders. I continued to do all the feeding at breakfast time. Terry still suffered a massive amount of pain in his wrists and knees, but was in good spirits. In early March, he was driven to London to have special injections in his knees by Jonathon Lavelle at the Fortius Clinic, just off Park Lane. His pain was definitely alleviated by this medication.

On 10 March, I drove Terry to Oaksey House, the rehabilitation centre funded by The Injured Jockeys Fund, where he joined many of his old friends at a reunion for those who had been associated with Fulke Walwyn's training years at Saxon House in Lambourn. Many photographs of Terry were taken that day and I will always treasure the ones of him surrounded by his jockey friends. It was the last time many of them ever saw him, although he did meet up with a few ex-jockeys on his one and only day at the Cheltenham Festival a few weeks later, when we were invited to lunch in the Cheltenham Racecourse marquee. On this occasion, we took Terry's mobility scooter and he much enjoyed driving around on it with his hand on the bleeper.

In May 2013 we flew from Heathrow to Shannon to stay in Co. Clare and yet again view horses with the Costellos. Tim Radford travelled to Ireland at the same time. Terry picked out a lovely three-year-old by Presenting, who was a half-brother to Racing Demon – a good horse I had trained for the Radfords. Tim did not buy the youngster on that occasion, but later in the year decided to add him to his string. He is now called The Last Cavalier, after Terry. We had an excellent trip and, as usual, saw some lovely young horses. The handsome Presenting gelding arrived at West Lockinge Farm in mid-December 2013. I drove Terry into the main yard in my car and then led the horse out of his stable for Terry's approval. He gave him the thumbs up, saying that he particularly liked his head and eye, but that since he was big and immature, he would need time.

My last trip to Connemara with Terry, in July 2013, was heartbreaking. I managed him on my own at the airports with his fold-up wheelchair, but it was not easy. There was a special vehicle to lift him into the aeroplane and the officials were extremely helpful. Many of the airport personnel knew him from previous journeys and loved his humour. It was not straightforward at Ballynahinch Hotel, either, due to the many steps there, but we coped and in certain places the management put down ramps for the wheelchair. Terry did not get out of his chair in the bar area nor did he do so in the dining room, but he had great chats with all his mates. Our great friend and Connemara breeder Padraic Hynes also joined in for some drinks and local gossip. Both he and his wife, Mary, had proved great friends to us during our holidays in Ireland. Mary had for many years worked at the hospital in Clifden, and on one occasion, had helped me deal with Terry when he had suffered a colossal nosebleed during the Clifden Pony Show.

On the Sunday of our four-day visit, we went to the Roundstone Connemara Pony Show and I parked the hired car close to the ring – the organisers saw Terry arrive and gave him a prime vantage point at the bottom of the showground. It was a great spot, away from the hurly-burly, with a lovely view of the mountains behind the ring. We watched all the classes and numerous pony friends flocked round the car – Terry kept the sliding door open and chatted to everybody. It was a sunny day and a very happy one.

We both enjoyed the show and we drove back to the hotel via Dog's Bay, Ballyconneely and the Bog Road, which was always Terry's favourite drive. He never ceased to be fascinated by this road; there are no houses for miles and miles, but it has the most indescribably beautiful scenery – rocks, lakes and bogland covered in wild flowers and purple heather. The backdrop is made up of the 'Twelve Bens' – the most famous mountains in Connemara. The light is never the same across the bog and it can change every hour. On that particular evening it was particularly stunning and we had a magical drive. It was the last time I ever drove Terry along that road and now that he is gone, I cannot bring myself to go down it on my own.

Henry O'Toole clearly remembers Terry's last Sunday in Connemara. 'The Roundstone Pony Show on a beautiful July day was the last occasion on which we spent time with Terry,' he says. 'He was frail, but in high spirits, clearly enjoying the attention shown by all his Connemara friends who came to pay their respects. Hen had parked the car in a place where they had a bird's-eye view of everything, and he was as sharp and humorous as ever. He watched every class and picked his winners, but still found time for a laugh. Even now it's hard to imagine that Terry is gone. We will never forget him.'

On the Monday after the Roundstone Show, Terry had a bad turn. He woke up fine and we had lunch in our favourite restaurant, Mitchells, in Clifden. Terry always got on particularly well with the owner, J. J., and over the years we had some memorable days in there. As usual, Terry ordered a plate of oysters but, for the first time in his life, it seems that he ate one that was 'off'.

Shortly after our visit, while I was driving him along the picturesque Sky Road on the west of the town with its breathtaking views of the Atlantic Ocean, he suddenly felt extremely ill and was violently sick. I managed to get him back to the hotel, but once in bed, he did not want to leave our bedroom for the rest of the day or the evening. He looked very pale and obviously felt horribly ill. He shivered and shook; I stayed with him all the time and ordered my own dinner to be brought to the room.

The next day we were due to fly home. Fortunately Terry improved as the night wore on, although he spent more time in the bathroom than in the bed. I drove him back to Shannon Airport on the Tuesday morning. He was weak, but no longer feeling sick. As always, everybody was extremely helpful in getting him onto the plane and we returned to Heathrow without mishap. It was his last journey on an aeroplane. For the rest of the week at Lockinge, he gradually improved, but mostly stayed in the house and slept. Gradually his appetite returned, together with his strength and determination to keep going. He told me that he never wanted to see another oyster again. I can remember my father telling me that when he, too, ate a bad oyster, he had felt ill for at least a week. Similar to Terry, he too never touched an oyster again.

The weekend after our trip to Ireland, I was due to judge at the Northern Connemara Pony Show at Osbaldeston, in Lancashire, which meant a night away. I did not know what to do. I didn't want to let down the organisers of the show, yet I could not leave Terry at home with nobody to look after him. He insisted on accompanying me. Looking back on that journey, I am amazed that he managed it so well and with such cheerfulness, because he was obviously still feeling rough. He spent most of the show day sitting in the car by the ringside, sipping a small glass of whisky. I had taken some miniatures with me and plenty of water. We returned from the show on Sunday night and on the Monday morning I took him straight to the Manor Hospital in Oxford to see his superb consultant, Roger Chapman, who had been monitoring Terry's health for some years. Terry really liked Roger and always enjoyed their discussions about golf. Roger understood Terry's humour and Terry trusted him.

After various tests, Roger told me that he wanted to keep Terry in hospital because his digestive system was in such a poor way. His gut lining was ulcerated and he was badly dehydrated. I hated leaving him there, but it was the obvious solution and after two or three days, he perked up considerably. Tony, his brother, was fantastic and a regular visitor, but like me, he was worried about the deterioration in Terry's health since those sparkling summer months. Mick Channon also visited Terry in the hospital and he always raised Terry's spirits.

When he was released from The Manor Hospital in August 2013, Terry could not walk or even stand up. He never walked again. I do not know what happened to him during his time there, but something must have triggered a mechanism in his brain that affected his mobility. I often wonder whether maybe he had suffered another little stroke, although I was assured that there were no telltale signs from the tests. How can somebody go into hospital walking and come out six days later, inexplicably unable to move?

From mid-August 2013, my life changed completely. Everyday it was hands-on, looking after Terry. While he had been in hospital, I had further improved the living quarters in the drawing room and he was now quite resigned to sleeping downstairs. Of course, he insisted that I slept beside him in the same bed and would not be parted from me for any length of time. I have always had a horror of sleeping on any ground floor, with windows and doors opening out onto a garden. It would be so easy for an intruder to break in, but I gradually grew more accustomed to it, as it was essential for me to be with Terry throughout the nights. There was little that he could do for himself and he even found it difficult to turn over in bed. He needed constant attention and I was the only person he trusted. I had, in the past, looked after numerous sick horses and ponies, but never before had I cared for such an ill human being. All was to change. I learned something new every day, although many of the tasks I performed were based on common sense.

On most days, I was able to get Terry up and dressed and into his wheelchair. In the mornings, I had several extra helpers, including Vanessa Bowsher, my housekeeper, who has worked for me for twenty-six years and comes in every weekday. She was a wonderful support and knew Terry well. Between us, we lifted him into his chair and wheeled him into the kitchen, where he sat at the table in his usual position beneath the windows overlooking the yard. He would watch all his favourite television programmes, especially *Flog It!*, *Bargain Hunt*, *Put Your Money Where Your Mouth Is* and *Cash In The Attic*. He also loved sports programmes on golf, cricket, snooker, tennis, athletics, racing and Formula One. He enjoyed boxing too, and apparently, in his younger days, he had spent some time with Henry Cooper and his contemporaries.

Dominic Elsworth was a huge help to me when Terry was ill. Apart from riding out on a regular basis, he drove me to several car-mobility centres to look at various wheelchair-accessible vehicles. We eventually hired a small car, and this meant that, once again, I could take Terry out for drives and into Wantage to visit all his friends from The Cellar Bar. I used to park the car on the double-yellow lines close to the entrance to the bar and the regulars would come up the steps with their drinks. They would sit and talk to him in the car. Terry thoroughly enjoyed those visits. On a couple of occasions I took him to Oaksey House in Lambourn to see if anything could be done to improve his movement, but he found the sessions there extremely hard and they worried him because he could not do the exercises set for him by his therapists. After a while, I decided that he was better off staying at home, as it was less stressful.

One night, at the beginning of November, when Terry and I were lying together in the bed in the drawing room, I heard a strange scratching noise on the outer walls. My mind flashed back to the days when hedgehogs had got into our bedroom, but this noise was more persistent. I asked Terry to listen, but he had already heard the same sounds and although I hoped it was only the pitter-patter of mice feet, Terry said to me that he thought it was a rat. It certainly could not have been birds, because they roost at nights and everywhere outside our room was dark.

Gradually the noise became louder and I put my hand out to grip Terry while the scufflings continued. There are several creatures that I really detest, and rats are top of my list. There were no rats in the farmyard – we had not seen one for over four years. How could we be so unlucky as to have one in the house? Maybe it was due to the chicken corn that I regularly put down on the lawn for my hens. A few days later, I discovered that the rats had indeed worked their way through a small hole in the plasterwork on the outside wall, underneath the window. It seemed that they had established a rat-run along the back of the skirting boards but there was absolutely no evidence of them having made an entrance into the house itself.

A number of experts looked at the damage and I begged them for help. Apparently, it would be necessary to poison these rodents before any of the holes could be sealed off. It would have been pointless to concrete over the openings beneath the window because if the live rats were left inside they would then most probably gnaw inwards and end up in our bedroom.

Rat poison was administered, but for the next couple of weeks we continued to endure noises throughout the night. I discovered that if I placed a radio beside the garden door and tuned it in to a talking programme, this would temporarily halt activities. In the past years I had often used a loud radio to stop foxes pestering my chickens in the garden.

However, with the radio full on, our nights became even more disturbed. I would lie awake for hours, imagining plagues of rats. Where was the Pied Piper? I did not relax until they had all been killed. It soon became obvious that the poison had worked because decaying rat bodies began to give off vile odours, which wafted through the vents by the chimney and across the fire grate. The stench spread everywhere. I have smelt dead mice before in a house but the stink of decaying rats was so pungent and disgusting that we could not get it out of our noses. In the end, I placed two scented candles in the drawing room, one on the mantelpiece and one beside the bed.

On 7 November 2013, A. P. McCoy rode his 4,000th winner. Terry was delighted. That evening we were invited by Chanelle McCoy to the celebrations at the Outside Chance Pub near Marlborough. Terry was determined to be there. Carol Titmuss and I looked after him and took him in the mobility car in his wheelchair. He met many friends and received a great welcome. Even though the evening exhausted him, he was immensely happy to have been a part of it. He kept smiling and there are some lovely pictures. It was the last time he ever went out for a celebration, but what a way to end his party days. A. P. was his hero and in Terry's eyes could do no wrong. He worshipped him.

Later in November, Terry Court and Andrew Elliott from Brightwells came to see Terry and me, but the visit upset both of them. After Terry died in January 2014, Andrew wrote to me saying, 'Seeing him so poorly back in November left a strong impression on me and I still cannot imagine how you managed to cope with looking after him when he was in such a helpless way for so long. I was terribly moved after that visit, and seeing the pickle that Terry was in and the love and strength you were demonstrating in caring for him, left me feeling very humble indeed.'

During December, Terry's health deteriorated further. He became weaker and weaker, but he still enjoyed his food and his spirits remained high. He had plenty of visitors and watched racing every day. On one occasion Padraic and Mary Hynes flew over from Connemara to pay him a visit. Fortunately, his mind remained sharp and when watching racing on his television he was as quick as ever in picking up the jockeys' faults.

As the month progressed, I moved him into a single hospital bed with moveable parts so that I could get him propped up into a better position to greet his friends and watch the wildlife through the large window that looked out onto the garden. In particular, my chickens would sit on the windowsill and peck at the glass on the windows for food and the red kites would swoop down onto the lawn, to feast on carcasses that I placed there. Terry loved watching these birds. They have a wingspan of over six feet and they fascinated him.

When the hospital bed arrived, I bought myself a new single bed, so I could continue to sleep beside Terry. I could still hold his hand in the night and talk to him but it was tough going. I was awake for much of the time, as he constantly needed help. In particular he needed to change his position on the mattress. It was not easy to move him, because he was very heavy and sometimes I was not strong enough to ease him over onto his side. Terry also developed horrible ulcers on one of his legs and on the heel of his right foot. These sores added to his misery and pain. I used to do everything I could to make him comfortable, but it was extremely hard. To crown it all, he could only be given certain painkillers, because the really strong ones interacted with his other medication.

Our nights were long and difficult. I dreaded them. They wore me out.

Christmas in 2013 was particularly tough. Terry and I always used to spend Christmas at West Lockinge – ever since the Best Mate days when we had good horses racing on Boxing Day, especially in the King George VI Chase at Kempton. We used to get invited to lunch with Ce and Sam, but always turned down the invitation. I enjoyed cooking the turkey at home with all its trimmings and Terry relished the ladles of bread sauce – one of his favourite foods – plus the Christmas pudding in flames with brandy and the brandy butter.

In 2013 we were never going to enjoy Christmas or spend it like we had in previous years, yet I remember Terry saying to me, 'Whatever happens, I'm going to sit up at the table in the kitchen for my Christmas dinner like I've always done before. I want a proper knife and fork.' Of course, he could not use a knife because of his crippled hands, but I cut everything up for him and he did well to eat most of the food that I gave him.

I became good at feeding him, although he said his brother, Tony, was far better, because I did not always concentrate hard enough and allowed spoonfuls to overflow from his mouth and spill onto his clothes. I remedied this by putting a bib on him at mealtimes, or a towel around his neck.

Terry was surprisingly perky on that Christmas Day. Mike Palmer, who lodges in one of our cottages and sometimes helps in the yard, was around to help me lift him in and out of his chair. I could not have managed without Mike's assistance with the slings that the NHS had provided. These are complicated contraptions, but they took the weight off my back. During the months I cared for Terry, I suffered quite badly from strained muscles and pulled ligaments, due to the many times that I had to turn him over in bed or prop him up on his pillows after he had slipped down the bed. In reality these were not jobs for one person alone and I kept telling Terry that I was not strong enough, but he always insisted that I try my hardest. Indeed, there were times when he was extremely demanding and he used to get quite cross with me if I did not handle him correctly.

While Terry lay in bed and I was elsewhere in the house, garden or stables, I rigged up bells that rang in every room, with three or four different ringtones. He also had a simple mobile telephone, with just one green knob to press if he needed me. I sometimes left him for about ten or twenty minutes, with the telephone positioned on his chest. It gave him confidence and it often rang.

Towards the end of 2013 we managed to find a good local carer, Sue Webb, who came to the farm for a few hours each morning. She had a great sense of humour and was well tuned in to Terry's jokes, which he was still telling until two or three days before he died. Laura, the district nurse, was also very helpful and used to take his blood, while an experienced occupational therapist showed me how to operate the slings.

Prior to employing Sue, I had found some extra outside help from local centres, but Terry would not tolerate most of the carers. There were only two he liked. The rest, he told me in no uncertain terms, to get rid of because they annoyed him and had no sense of humour. I think he was decidedly rude to them. He had expected me to do all the daily chores, but I could not cope on my own. What really annoyed Terry was that the agency workers were not even allowed to give him his pills, even if I had left them ready in specially labelled pots – nor could they cut his fingernails. Health and Safety gone mad.

Still, even without additional carers, I managed and after Christmas, Terry began talking about the next year's plans and how we would get back to Connemara. We envisaged Carol Titmuss coming with us as our extra helper. Terry never thought he was going to die, and he never once spoke about death. He was certainly much weaker than he had ever been before, but he was convinced that he would get better and believed that once the ulcer had healed on his foot, he would be able to stand up and walk again. I had completely healed the ulcer on his leg with homeopathic horse remedies and the one on his heel, though responding more slowly, was progressing in the right direction. All he wanted to do was to be able to take some steps on his own. His optimism was incredible.

At the end of December, when people came to visit Terry, several of them had colds and sore throats. In retrospect, I think he, too, picked up an infection, due to his low resistance and poor immunity. His breathing got more laboured and he became wheezy in his chest. I got nebulizers from the surgery, which helped him, but he mostly stayed in bed. The room was warm and cosy. Mick Channon came to the house on most days. He was brilliant with Terry and kept his spirits high. They would sip little glasses of whisky and reminisce about the past. When discussing the fun they had in their racing and football days, Terry said to Mick, 'The trouble is, there are still plenty out there, but nowadays there is not enough time.'

This is how I got the title for my book.

———

After New Year's Day, which was on a Wednesday, Terry seemed to go downhill and although we had plenty of chats, he was struggling even more with his breathing. He was fine when I puffed the nebulizer into his mouth and he was still able to eat his meals and watch the television, but he did not feel well, and on Friday I had to cancel a visit from A. P. McCoy. This was very unusual, as Terry loved A. P.'s visits, but he told me that he did not feel up to talking to people from outside and preferred to rest and sleep.

His regular doctor, Paul Bryan, was on holiday, which was unfortunate, but that Friday afternoon a locum doctor from Abingdon came to visit. She listened to his chest and prescribed some strong antibiotics, to be started at once. She did suggest that he might be better in a hospital, but Terry flatly refused to leave the farmhouse and I honestly believe that if he'd been driven anywhere in a bumpy ambulance the journey would have killed him. He was too weak to be moved.

As the weekend progressed, he began to improve and became more cheerful. He seemed contented and relaxed, and slept peacefully in between our conversations and watching his favourite television programmes. On the Saturday night, I was greatly heartened by his progress. He drank some nourishing soup and I retired early myself, to get some sleep beside him. During the night he woke on several occasions and I got out of my bed to make him more comfortable. We talked a lot that night and we made our plans for Sunday. He told me that he definitely wanted to get up and go into the kitchen for the day and we agreed to move him in his sling when Sue, the carer, arrived for duty.

On Sunday morning, 5 January 2014, I got up as usual to feed the horses. Terry was sleeping, so I crept out without disturbing him. I spent about thirty minutes in the yard and then returned to our night quarters to check him over. My usual routine was to raise the back of Terry's bed and sit him up, before sponging his face and cleaning his teeth. I would then give him a light breakfast. He loved Weetabix soaked in milk and a cool cup of tea, with plenty of sugar. Sue was due to come in and help me at 9 a.m. Together we would make him comfortable and dress him. I would tend to the bandage on his ulcerated heel.

Yet when I went back into the house I noticed that his breathing had again become noisy. He looked particularly pale and was very quiet. I decided to take his temperature and blood pressure – I had my own machine at home – but all the readings were normal. Thinking he might be a little dehydrated, I gave him a drink of water with electrolytes. He sipped the water and swallowed normally.

I was quietly talking to him and holding his hand when he made a little gurgle, put his head back onto his pillows and closed his eyes. I gave him a little shake and talked to him but there was no response. He was dead. It was as if he had waited for me to come back from the horses to be at his side. I have seen many animals die and I knew that Terry had taken his last breath. It was a weird situation. I felt totally alone. He lay there motionless, but he looked peaceful.

A strange numbness came over me – I continued to sit beside him in a trance. I did not want to leave him. I knew that this was the last time that I would ever see him, but I had to pull myself together and take some action. I remember walking out into the yard and telling two of my Sunday helpers, 'Terry has just died.' They couldn't believe it. There was a long silence, broken only by Nobby, the Chinese gander, loudly honking around the pond. I returned to the house and rang Tony. He was out. I left a message, then telephoned Mick Channon's office, and my sister. Afterwards, shaking with emotion, I pressed the numbers 999 on the kitchen telephone. I tried to explain what had happened. Later in the morning policemen, ambulance men and a doctor came to the farm. I did not cry, because I was in a state of shock. Sue came to the front door at nine a.m.. I remember saying to her, 'We've lost him.' She was distraught.

I was utterly shattered that Sunday morning, but my neighbours and close friends were superb. They comforted me and we talked. I needed to be strong, for Terry's sake. He never liked me to give in to my emotions, even though he would cry regularly himself when moved by a situation. Tony and Mick sat with me for most of the day and dear Elspeth O'Donnell, the local physiotherapist who had so often tended to Terry, made endless cups of tea. She tried to get me to eat something, but I had no appetite. The telephone never stopped ringing and there were plenty of jobs to be done. I had conversations with the press and, even though my head was spinning, I kept myself calm. Ce and Sam visited the farm in the afternoon. They were wonderfully sympathetic and helpful.

That night, I was left totally alone in the house. It was my choice. I did not want anybody to share my grief. It was the first time that I could think about things by myself. In twenty years, I had hardly ever been separated from Terry after dark, except when he had been in hospital or away on a shooting expedition. Now he was no longer around to talk to. I remember slowly climbing the stairs with a heavy heart, tears rolling down my cheeks.

I lay down in our old double bed. I had not slept in it for five months. It was a strange feeling and the bedroom felt empty. There was nobody beside me; no warmth. Terry had been my life. I would now have to live alone and face the future without him.

At daybreak, the cockerel began to crow in the garden. I let out the chickens and they sat on the windowsill beside the drawing room. They peered inwards as if looking for Terry but he was no longer there. The red kite swooped down onto the lawn, but there was no point throwing out any food for him. Terry would not be able to watch him.

On that Monday morning, I gave all the horses their breakfast feeds as normal. I needed to keep busy and animals give great comfort. I was pleased to see my four-legged friends in the stables. I gave my own horse, Red Blazer, a special hug. He was twenty-three years old and had given both Terry and me days to remember on the racecourse. He had even won a race on the day Mum died.

I returned to the house and made myself a cup of tea in the kitchen, then I collected the daily newspapers from the front door and opened them up. I saw Terry's face everywhere. There were some amazing tributes and he was on the front page of the *Racing Post*: big, bold and smiling, having just won the 1967 Cheltenham Gold Cup – 'Terry Biddlecombe – The Last Cavalier'. Inside the paper one of the headlines said, 'He played the game as all games should be played – hard and fair, but above all because he enjoyed it'.

Yes, he enjoyed many of the years in his life and I enjoyed my years with him. I had lost the greatest friend that I ever had. My life would never be the same again. I adored him.

It was a shame that Dr Paul Bryan was not around during Terry's final days, but I have spoken to him many times since. He always enjoyed Terry's humour and we often visited him at the Wantage Health Centre. On those days there was always plenty of banter. 'Terry had a unique personality,' Paul said later. 'Despite his pain, he was always full of devilment. During his last years, he suffered a terrible illness but remained proud and always wanted to be physically strong again – like he had been during his racing days. Amazingly, even with his heart condition, gout, kidney failure, arthritis and later on, ulcerations of his oesophagus, he never complained. He was always cheerful, as well as being open, frank and honest, despite being irreverent. He had obviously had a lot of problems with alcohol in the past, but it was certainly not alcohol that killed him. His liver was in surprisingly good shape. Tragically, however, when he contracted pneumonia at the end of 2013, his body just could not cope any more.'

Tony Biddlecombe still misses Terry as much as I do. 'He was always a wonderful brother,' he says. 'We never had a row and had some great times together. Even when his health was failing, he would talk to me most evenings. He called me, "Boy" and he would finish every conversation by saying, "Night" and abruptly put down the phone. I miss him enormously. Earlier in our lives we were inseparable and shared some great days. He was my best friend. I wish I had been with him when he died.'

Ernest Hemingway once wrote, 'The world breaks everyone and afterwards many are strong at the broken places. But those that will not break, it kills. It kills the very good and the very gentle and the very brave impartially. If you are none of these you can be sure it will kill you too, but there will be no special hurry.'

CHAPTER FIFTEEN

Time for Reflection

When Terry died that cold grey morning in 2014, my world seemed to have come to an end. I had lived for him for twenty years and he had lived for me. In the past we had often discussed what would happen if one of us departed before the other. Terry would say, 'If anything happens to you, I will kill myself. I cannot live without you.' I don't know what he thought I would do if he died first, but fortunately I am surrounded by a great many friends and I never contemplated doing anything stupid.

At first, after Terry's death, I tried to blank out the outside world. I wandered around in a daze, trying to come to terms with what had happened. I often said to myself, 'What have I got left to live for?' and at times I believed that there was very little, as I never had any children and both my parents had died. But then I would think about my sister, Ce, and her constant, loving attention. She had been through so much herself and had survived that horrific stroke in 1995. She is incredibly brave and I needed to be as well.

Mum would have told me to pull myself together. She was a strong lady and I always respected her. Indeed, her words kept flashing up in my mind. She was a philosophical person and had survived numerous tragedies herself, particularly when she had nursed her eldest brother, John, during his illness before he died at her childhood home, Lockinge House, during the war. Then there was Mary, my niece, and my nephews, Arthur and William, all of whom had been supportive during Terry's declining years. I would have to rebuild my life for their sakes. They were the only close blood relations I had left.

Yet it was hard to be normal and unaffected by the events that led up to Terry's death. My staff had always been a great back-up and when Terry died they continued to give me plenty of support. They gave me courage to go on. Then there were my horses and ponies. I could not desert them. They were a big comfort to me and I often felt that I could communicate with them better than I could with human beings. I have always been blessed with the ability to bond with animals – I inherited it from my mother. As a child, if there were problems at school and my exams were imminent, I would saddle up my pony and go off for a ride on the Berkshire Downs and get away from everybody.

A number of people were surprised that I didn't cry at Terry's funeral, nor at his memorial service. When Terry was alive, he often dissolved into tears, but I reacted by doing the exact opposite. There were so many friends around me on both of these sad occasions that I felt it was my duty to be as normal as possible and thank them for their support. I was deeply touched by their respect and love for Terry, also by their kindness.

As for myself, I just felt proud to have been with him for those twenty wonderful years and to have nursed him right up until his end. I owed it to Terry to conduct myself calmly and correctly, even though deep down, it was devilishly hard. I kept telling myself that I must set an example to his children and his relations. Instead of crying, I drove my sorrows down deeper and tried to put them to the back of my mind. I released them later while grieving on my own. Even now, no day ever goes by when I don't think of Terry – morning, noon and night – and I often have tears in my eyes. Never was there a truer saying than, 'Laugh and the world laughs with you; cry and you cry alone.'

I often reread the wonderful letters I received after Terry's death. They are a great comfort, even though they do tend to upset me as well. They were obviously written with great sincerity, using such amazing words. They did, and still do, touch me enormously. I was sent hundreds of letters – even more than when Best Mate won his third Cheltenham Gold Cup – and the postman had to bring them to the door in special boxes – he couldn't carry them any other way. I will keep those letters for ever and I marvel at how beautifully people can write. Some say that with the advent of computers and emails, letter-writing is a dying art but this was certainly not evident when Terry passed. Many of our friends deserve medals for their meaningful words, none more so than Jim Lewis, who memorably said: 'Terry was a good friend with a tremendous sense of humour. People referred to him and Hen as the odd couple, but for me there was nothing odd about them. They were simply in love with each other and enjoyed the victories they shared.' I even received personal handwritten letters from the Queen, the Prince of Wales and the Duchess of Cornwall.

Throughout January 2014, I was kept busy, because there were many plans to be made. I decided upon a small funeral in the neighbouring village of Ardington, followed, at a later date, by a memorial service at Terry's favourite racecourse, Cheltenham. There were so many T. W. Biddlecombe memories wrapped up in that magical turf beneath Cleeve Hill. The funeral was advertised as private and was supposed to be for family members and close friends, but the numbers snowballed. More and more people came out of the woodwork, declaring themselves as special friends – and who was I to say no, when they asked to attend? Terry had thousands of admirers and everybody seemed to be special.

The church was filled to capacity, with loudspeakers outside for those who could not fit in. The lady vicar, Elizabeth Birch, gave a brilliant talk. She had not known Terry but plenty of people had marked her card and she spent many hours at West Lockinge Farm discussing his past. Terry Court gave a moving address – he had, after all, rescued Terry after his return from Australia and had provided him with a job. He had reintroduced him to me at the Malvern Sales in 1993. Without Terry Court,

Terry and I would never have got together. It must have been fate. 'TC', as my Terry called him, was the catalyst for our dream life and twenty years of happiness. Nigel Twiston-Davies, Andrew Elliott and Terry's eldest daughter, Laura, did the three readings. They were all excellent. I sat next to Nigel in the church; he was a great comfort and I remember gripping his arm during the most difficult parts of the service.

On the day after Terry's funeral – Saturday 18 January 2014, I suffered another shattering blow. I had been at a low ebb since the departure of my guests on Friday, but I had wanted to be alone in order to collect my thoughts. It was about 6 p.m. that Saturday and I had taken a stroll around the yard to look at the horses. It was a dark, damp evening, but there were lights shining from the outside walls of the stables and around the duck pond. It was customary every night for a member of staff to drive the farmyard geese into a special shed to protect them from prowling foxes. On that occasion, I could see that they were still swimming on the water and nobody had shut them in, so I plucked a branch off a tree to chase them into their overnight quarters.

It was then that I slipped and fell on the wet paving stones marking the perimeter of the pond. My right leg went into the water and the foot became wedged under an overhanging stone slab. I managed to extricate it, but could not stand up. I remember noticing that my shoe was facing backwards – I presumed I had dislocated my ankle. I crawled along the wet grass beneath the buildings and shouted for help. Fortunately, there were voices to be heard in the yard and some of the staff were still on duty.

Dawn Graham, my secretary and a trained first-aider, was tending to her own horse. She found Terry's wheelchair in the garage and pushed me back to the house. For the first time I was in the chair and not Terry. My trousers were soaking wet and I asked Dawn whether she thought I had broken anything – strangely, I was not in any pain. We pulled up the trouser leg and several bones were visibly protruding. It was then that I realised the severity of the injury.

Not long afterwards, I was lying in the back of an ambulance, en route to the John Radcliffe Hospital – a place I dreaded going, since I had experienced numerous bad days there with Terry and it was there, too, where my mother had died. I had not been on a stretcher since my days in the Pony Club when I concussed myself in the showjumping class at a local gymkhana. It was a strange feeling but I was still able to think straight and my mobile telephone was in my pocket. I made several calls. I was given no painkillers in the ambulance – it was not necessary. I was experiencing very little pain, I just remember a dull ache and that my lower leg was numb.

My saintly neighbour, Janie Roberts, accompanied me in the ambulance. Little did she know that it would be midnight before her husband, Hugh, would be able to fetch her home from the hospital because she would not leave me until I went down to the operating theatre for surgery. I was told that it was an urgent operation and that there was severe danger of infection from the dirty water in the duck pond. Before being wheeled into a special room for my surgery the doctor told me that I might lose my foot. I remember saying to him, 'That's just what I want to hear.' When I came round in the recovery room at 3 a.m., the first thing I did was look down at my leg. To my relief, despite all the dressings, I could still see my toes sticking out at the bottom.

I spent almost a week in hospital. It was a strange experience. There were numerous pins and screws supporting my fractured bones and the open wound had been stitched by an expert plastic surgeon. I had never before been given so many antibiotics and I was attached to an overhead drip for days. The narrow hospital bed was extremely uncomfortable.

How dreadful it must have been for Terry, confined to a similar bed, not only for the last months of his life, but on the many occasions during his jockey days when he had been hospital-bound, recuperating from injuries. There was nothing I could do except lie still and come to terms with my accident. It had been tragic to lose my beloved husband and now I was in a helpless position myself. I could do very little on my own. I could not walk and I could not drive. I was forbidden to put weight on my foot for six weeks.

My friends were incredible and enormously supportive. I had plenty of visitors while I was in the hospital, including my sister and my relations, plus jockeys, trainers and staff. I felt humbled by the attention I received but I also felt extremely sad. I cried a lot at nights and was still suffering from shock. My grief was enormous and there was nobody to hold my hand. On many occasions I seriously questioned my future. Whatever would happen next? How would I be able to remould my life and keep positive? I pined for Terry and for his wonderful smile.

When I returned from hospital in early February, I gradually came to terms with my predicament and my damaged leg. On the days leading up to the memorial for Terry at Cheltenham Racecourse on 17 February 2014, I was fortunately kept extremely busy, not only with plans for that special day, but also with the writing of many letters. The stair lift, which had been removed after Terry's death, was reinstalled and I was able to use it to get myself upstairs each night. In the daytime I sat in the kitchen, but it was strange looking at Terry's empty chair at the end of the table. I had so many memories in the house and they hit me hard. Everything I did, everywhere I went, and everything I saw reminded me of Terry – indeed, I am still easily upset by certain surroundings and there are days when I feel especially sad.

The celebration of Terry's life at Cheltenham was utterly unbelievable. It was incredibly moving and beautifully organised by Edward Gillespie, the former managing director of the racecourse. Everything was arranged to perfection – Edward never does anything by halves. His many years at the helm during the Cheltenham festivals were nothing short of brilliant. No wonder that in December 2014, he was awarded an OBE in the Queen's

New Year Honours list. The memorial service was held in the Panoramic Restaurant, but we did not advertise the occasion; people learned about it through word of mouth. If it had been announced in the newspapers or on the Internet, then I do not think the venue would have coped with the extra numbers. It is not a huge area and has a limited capacity. My wonderful brother-in-law, Sam Vestey, hosted the occasion. He was unable to be there in person due to business commitments abroad, but I made sure everybody knew it was his party. He is such a generous man and had always been especially good to Terry. Edward and I spent many hours planning the day and it went like clockwork.

Channel 4 supplied a carefully composed DVD of Terry's past achievements, with a voiceover by my great friend, Jim McGrath. At the end, he said, 'It was Katharine Hepburn who once famously said, "Obey all the rules and you will miss all the fun." Rest assured, the jockey whom one could easily have mistaken for a matinée idol missed out on nothing in life. In Terry's pomp, when pushing the boundaries on and off the track, we loved him for it. Many saw Hen and Terry as the odd couple, but corny as it seems, they were devoted to one another. Their emotional and dramatic coming together after Best Mate's first Gold Cup win in 2002 was redolent of the final scenes of *The Railway Children*.'

The DVD was shown on several occasions throughout the day on the many TV screens in the restaurant.

There were three speakers and they were all brilliant. Alastair Down was the obvious choice for the main talk. Terry was particularly fond of Alastair and on several occasions the three of us had eaten out in our local pub. Terry was one of Alastair's childhood heroes and I distinctly remember Terry saying to me, 'He's the man I would like to speak at my funeral.'

Alastair did not let me down. His address was superb and produced many damp eyes in the audience. He remembered Terry's riding achievements in the sixties. 'Pain was Terry's constant companion, and every day involved a fifteen-round bruising battle with the scales. But no struggle ever lessened him – he bulldozed through life, fearing no one, always standing up for the underdog, issuing a constant stream of never to be forgotten obscenities and, with that mischievous smile, ever on the look-out for a treble at Ludlow, when as we all know only two of the winning rides that afternoon were booked through Weatherbys.

'He was very simply a hero of my childhood – and please do not ever fall for that cynical old lie that you should never meet your childhood heroes, as there is always that one in a million who has the thumping, shining, life-affirming humanity, humour and sheer heart that makes you understand that among the everyday ebb and flow of life sometimes stride those rare folk that light up a generation. If you want a measure of Terry, the man, then look around this room at the wonderfully diverse cross-section of society here to pay tribute – people who will always miss Terry but would never miss being here for him.

'There are folk from every corner of the land, the young and the old, the great, the good and the happily plain humble, the well-heeled and mildly skint – everyone drawn to the magnet that was Terry, one of jump-racing's beating hearts. Almost every soul in this room, which looks out across a view as sacred to us as any consecrated ground, is here because a flawed, fabulous, foul-mouthed, fantastic man showed us some small kindness or consideration that we have never forgotten. Above all he bestowed upon us the priceless gift of laughter.' (*The Best of Alastair Down*: *Cheltenham et Al*).

Having chosen Alastair for the main address, I believed it would also be appropriate to invite a couple of Terry's jockey contemporaries to give talks. Sadly, some of his greatest friends, such as Dave Dick and Josh Gifford, had already passed away but I knew how much he had thought of David Mould and Bill Smith, so tentatively I asked them if they would contribute. They were stars and told some excellent stories of the old days.

Despite the fact that we hadn't advertised the day, the room was packed. There was an amazing turnout of jockeys, trainers and racing enthusiasts. I will always be grateful to the racecourse for allowing the memorial to be held there. It was a moving occasion.

My own staff and friends from around West Lockinge Farm were transported in two minibuses. For my part, I was still confined to my wheelchair. But fortunately, I was well looked after at Cheltenham by Rachel Geary, who is a good friend and was my driver during my days as a trainer. Rachel chauffeured me to Cheltenham and I was cared for in the confines of the restaurant by Muriel Cadwallader, who had so often been in charge of the

Royal Box in the days when Sam Vestey had been chairman and Terry and I had been invited for lunches. Also in a wheelchair was Mercy Rimell. Terry, having spent many years at Kinnersley with her and Fred, would have laughed to see us side by side on wheels. His relationship with Mercy had always been somewhat volatile. At times he thought the world of her, but on other occasions they fiercely disagreed about the riding of the horses Fred trained. Terry was always annoyed that Mercy accused him of spending too much time with Gay Trip on the outside of the track in the 1972 Grand National. The horse was second to Well To Do, but Mercy told Terry that he had gone further than any other horse in the race and should have won.

Gary Newbon wrote to me after the Cheltenham send-off and said, 'At the celebration of Terry's life, I felt privileged to have been there, and he would have both laughed and cried at the many tributes.' Hector Brown said, 'To his many friends, T. W. B. was a one-off, a real player who felt life had to be enjoyed and packed with as much fun as possible. Whilst sometimes close to the mark, you knew, when you heard that unique cackle of a laugh, that he had sprung yet another surprise on the unsuspecting innocent. At all times he exuded those characteristics that defined his riding career – strength and determination and the will to win, coupled with a never-say-die attitude. Yet everything was wrapped up with a huge sense of fun and a kindly outlook towards the frail and suffering.'

It was a great effort for David Mould to come over from Spain to talk at Terry's Cheltenham memorial, and before he returned home, he brought me a framed quotation that movingly summed up Terry. 'The only life worth living is the adventurous life. Of such a life the dominant characteristic is that it is unafraid. It is unafraid of what other people think. It does not adapt either its pace or its objectives to the pace and objectives of its neighbours. It thinks its own thoughts it reads its own books. It develops its own hobbies, and it is governed by its own conscience. The herd may graze where it pleases or stampede where it pleases. But he who lives the adventurous life will remain unafraid when he finds himself alone.' (Raymond B. Fosdick).

Farewell Terry.

You were the love of my life. I miss you every day and, on many occasions, it is hard to keep going without you. All that I do is in your memory, but I can feel you telling me how to arrange my new life. Anything that I achieve in future years will be due to you. You were everything that I lived for. You were unbelievably special and there will never be anybody remotely like you again.

I have enjoyed writing our story, but it has not been easy. How I wish you could have been around to read it. I think you would have been proud to have been reminded of all that you achieved – and to know that you had such a colossal number of friends and admirers.

When I told Bill Smith that I still find that every day brings me sad moments, he said he could well believe the void left by you will never be refilled – such was your enormous, charismatic personality, but Bill reckoned that you would only have said, 'Fuck it. We can't live in the past. Let's have another drink.'

Such true words.

It is far better to remember the good times in life and rejoice, rather than dwelling on sad memories. I will never forget the wonderful years you and I shared. We had countless happy days together and there was an uncanny chemistry between us. I always believed in you and in return, you believed in me and bestowed your love. Separation is hard and always will be, but I am surrounded by our wonderful friends and beautiful memories. We all miss you and we all loved you, but nobody loved you as much as I did. You will never leave me. Everything I do reminds me of our years together and I see your smiling face every night, beside my bed, before I go to sleep.

You are everywhere. Your spirit will live on for ever.

Acknowledgements

I owe a big thank you to my editor, Rosie de Courcy, for the expert guidance she gave me while I wrote the book. Her attention to detail and her insistence that my story was written in a coherent chronological way were invaluable. She has a gift for the correct use of the English language and although, at times, she put me under extreme pressure, I could not have organised my thoughts without her. She was my mentor and I always listened to her comments. We had many fascinating discussions and some good laughs.

I would also like to thank my agent, Heather Holden-Brown who seemed happy to take me under her wing from day one and without whom I would never have got started. She has been supportive and understanding throughout the 10 months that it has taken me to complete this book. She has been a jewel and I value her sensible advice. A true friend.

Finally, I could not have written my story without the backing of Andrew Longmore. He assisted me with my books on Best Mate and inspired me to get started on my latest venture. He kindly wrote the synopsis for this book which was subsequently handed over to prospective publishers. He too gave me plenty of encouragement and I hope that he approves of the finished article. I have removed most of the exclamation marks because I know he disapproves of them!

Numerous people at Head of Zeus have helped me along the way and their support has touched me. They too deserve a big thank-you. I have enjoyed working with them and I am now more able to understand the complicated issues associated with a successful publishing house.

The many friends who supplied me with anecdotes to include in most of the chapters have been wonderful. I could not have written my book without their co-operation and as a result of their recollections I have learnt plenty – particularly regarding lifestyles in the last century.

Overall, I have enjoyed writing about my years with Terry but it has been a challenge and on occasions extremely hard. There were days when I laughed and days when I cried. But I will always be proud of him and I know that I am extremely lucky ever to have met him. We believed in each other from the very beginning and I whole-heartedly adored him. To me he was special – the love of my life. I will continue to miss him for as long as I live but I instinctively know that he would have been pleased with *Not Enough Time*, and touched by the memories. His life was unique and my world is empty without him.

Index